Investing Japan

Harvard East Asian Monographs 370

Investing Japan

Foreign Capital, Monetary Standards,
and Economic Development, 1859–2011

Simon James Bytheway

Published by the Harvard University Asia Center
Distributed by Harvard University Press
Cambridge (Massachusetts) and London 2014

Printed in the United States of America

The Harvard University Asia Center publishes a monograph series and, in coordination with the Fairbank Center for Chinese Studies, the Korea Institute, the Reischauer Institute of Japanese Studies, and other facilities and institutes, administers research projects designed to further scholarly understanding of China, Japan, Vietnam, Korea, and other Asian countries. The Center also sponsors projects addressing multidisciplinary and regional issues in Asia.

Library of Congress Cataloging-in-Publication Data
Bytheway, Simon James, 1969–
    Investing Japan : foreign capital, monetary standards, and economic development, 1859–2011 / Simon James Bytheway.
        pages cm. — (Harvard East Asian monographs ; 370)
    Includes bibliographical references and index.
    ISBN 978-0-674-41713-7 (hardcover : alk. paper)   1. Investments, Foreign—Japan—History.   2. Monetary policy—Japan—History.   3. Economic development—Japan—History.   4. Japan—Economic policy—1868–   5. Japan—Economic conditions—1868–
I. Title.
    HG5772.B97 2014
    330.952—dc23

2014011099

Index by June Sawyers and the author

♾ Printed on acid-free paper

Last figure below indicates year of this printing

24   23   22   21   20   19   18   17   16   15   14

For my two joys,

Ashley and Hannah

Contents

PART I ANTICIPATING FOREIGN CAPITAL: THE ADOPTION OF THE GOLD STANDARD

PART II FOREIGN CAPITAL AND THE PREWAR JAPANESE ECONOMY

**PART III   FOREIGN CAPITAL AND THE POSTWAR
JAPANESE ECONOMY**

Tables and Figures

Figures

Acknowledgments

I did my postgraduate studies in Japan, and if I had the opportunity to start them all over again, I would surely do things differently, for nothing could take what this work has taken from me. At the very least, I would pick a topic in Japanese economic history that generates more foreign interest and less Japanese aversion. Surprise, surprise: foreign Japanologists—and more broadly, their compatriots—are generally interested in the peculiar and multifarious forms of "Japaneseness" in Japan, while, horror of horrors, Japanese people do not generally appreciate the significance of foreign capital and the depth of the foreign contribution to their daily lives. It may, in fact, go deeper than aversion, as the Japanese went to great and even extraordinary lengths to adopt essentially Western institutions, such as the gold standard and formal alliances, with the hope of finding foreign acceptance, only to later reject them, or to have them repudiated, with extreme prejudice. The non-Japanese role in Japan's modernization, or Westernization, indeed remains fiercely contested and deeply problematic. What was I thinking? How can I honestly explain the form and intent of my research into Japan's economic and financial history? What is the intellectual journey presented here in *Investing Japan*? Who or what must be acknowledged, and to whom do I owe gratitude, thanks, and love?

Right from the outset, I think it is only proper that I acknowledge those journals and publications where my research was first tested, and thank those editors and publishers who gave me a chance to be published and permission to re-present those ideas here. Part 1 of this volume draws on work that was first published under the title "Japan's Adoption of the Gold Standard: Financial and Monetary Reform in the Meiji Period," in *Evolution of the World Economy, Precious Metals, and India*, edited by J. McGuire, P. Bertola, and P. D. Reeves (New Delhi: Oxford University Press, 2001). Part III draws on work that was first published as "Liberalization, Internationalization, and Globalization: Charting the Course of Foreign Investment in the Finance and Commerce of Japan, 1945–2009," in *Japan Forum* 22, no. 3–4 (2010). In formulating a conclusion, some of my findings draw on work found in "The Dynamics of *Wakon Yōsai* (Japanese Spirit, Western Technology): The Paradoxes and Challenges of Financial Policy in an Industrializing Japan, 1854–1939," which I wrote with Michael Schiltz, in *People, Place and Power: Australia and the Asia Pacific*, edited by D. Bennett, J. Earnest, and M. Tanji (Perth: Black Swan Press, 2009). Finally, a special note of thanks to the late Michiya Kuwabara and Fumie Nakamura of Tosui Press in Tokyo for publishing my earlier book, *Nihon keizai to gaikoku shihon* (The Japanese economy and foreign capital), and a word about how that Japanese-language publication relates to *Investing Japan*.

What I have written here is similar to *Nihon keizai to gaikoku shihon* in that both books share the same topic, or basic premise: the foreign contribution to modern Japanese economic development. While my earlier Japanese work analyzes capital loans up to 1931 and shines a light on private foreign investments up until 1939, *Investing Japan* attempts to extend the analysis into the present, ending in 2011 on the eve of the 3/11 Tōhoku earthquake, tsunami, and nuclear disaster. Necessarily the tone of the work has changed, from discussing Japan's failure to acknowledge and honor the contributions of the West to highlighting the growing international multinational presence in Japan, as evidenced by the growth of franchises, subsidiaries, joint ventures, and strategic alliances. To their credit, the publishers of *Nihon keizai to gaikoku shihon* always understood my desire to publish something more ambitious and topical in English, and actively encouraged me to do so.

Personal acknowledgments start with my mother, Irene, and father, Bryan, brother, Ian, and sister, Donna, and all my family and friends in Perth. They have my undying love and gratitude. Some great teachers deserve my thanks, especially Paul Woodley, Marie Holmes, Jennifer Robinson, and Robert Hymus. Without any one of them I fear I would be less than what I am (and might not have made it through adolescence). During my university years, the example and constant advice of my big brother, Ian, was inspirational, and friends such as Amanda and Clive Watkins deserve special thanks for their love and support. At Curtin University I was very fortunate to benefit from a large and talented staff of Japanese language teachers and to become an honors student under professors Peter Reeves and the late John McGuire. For four hardworking years, their courses challenged and changed me, and provided me with a foundation in the discipline of history. As supervisors, they guided me in the innovative use of primary materials and encouraged me to *write* history. Pat Bertola was the overall honors coordinator during my final year, and I still value his encouragement and advice; my intellectual debt to these three men is most profound.

In Japan, thanks are due first to Shuya Maeda, who (with the late Motohashi Uno) encouraged me to study in Tōhoku, not Tokyo. Without his guidance and support, I might well have joined the ranks of frustrated would-be Japanologists. While I was at Tōhoku and Tōhoku Gakuin Universities, Professor Yoshiteru Iwamoto was my supervisor: in fact, he is still supervising me now. He is indefatigible, always writing, a living encyclopedia on all things Japanese, and the most daunting intellect I have ever met. Almost all the Japanese language materials used in the production of *Investing Japan* were read (aloud) by me (to him), under his direct supervision, for his correction, analysis, and critique. In six years of classes that ignored almost all holidays, typhoons, snowstorms, floods, and earthquakes, I would usually arrive to find Iwamoto-sensei somewhat impatiently waiting for me: no wonder we both scored a 100 percent for attendance! He has always found time to review my work, working with whatever I presented on a given day. I consider myself fortunate in so many ways to be a *deshi* (student) of Iwamoto-sensei.

In Tokyo, I wish to thank my colleagues at Nihon University's College of Commerce, especially those in the finance, English, and commercial science departments. On the world stage, I feel fortunate to count Richard J. Smethurst, Mark Metzler, Katalin Ferber, Michael Schiltz, Janet Hunter, and, more lately, a growing number of scholars that includes Steve Bryan, Martha Chaiklin, Steve Ericson, Chester Proshan, and John Sagers, among my mentors and friends. In particular, I want to publically thank Mark Metzler for his generous editorial insights and intelligent suggestions: I have not always taken his advice, but I have always learned from it.

And there are so many more to thank from where I stand now, perched somewhat precariously between Perth, Sendai, and Tokyo: the Roberts family, the Okamoto family, Paul Torrance, Georgette Leah Burns, Alfie Gryg, Richard Ellis, Joseph Chan, Sanae Fujisaki, June Holmes, Harumi Tsugawara, Kazuko Endo, Ichiro Yamamoto, and Peter and Tami McGrath.

In the production of this book, special thanks go to the editorial staff of the Harvard University Asia Center, the incomparable Deborah Del Gais, Julie Ericksen Hagen, and especially the center's director, Bob Graham, who went to the greatest possible lengths to assist me through the final stages of the submission process. Special thanks are also due to Kei Matoi for her splendid artwork on the cover.

Finally, how can I adequately express my feelings toward my wife, Masumi, and my two daughters, Ashley and Hannah, to whom this book is dedicated? Ever since you have known me, I have been writing, or trying to write, this book. For countless nights, weekends, holidays, year after year, in fact, you have shared my biblio-ambitions and have had to negotiate your way through my overriding academic obsessions. As this journey ends I would promise to reform myself, but research and the questions it raises never really end. Thank you for sharing your lives with me, and for your unqualified love.

If I had the opportunity to start my postgraduate studies all over again, all said and done, I might very well research the theme of foreign capital and the Japanese economy. For nothing could give what this work has given to me.

Note to the Reader

In the following work, Japanese names appear in the customary Japanese order: surname first and given name second (except in the acknowledgments and bibliography). All dates are given according to the Gregorian calendar, in day-month-year format, although the Japanese officially used the lunar calendar until 1873. Chinese place names are presented in the contemporary Wade-Giles style, with Pinyin transliteration supplied as needed. Finally, Japan's modern legal system developed sporadically, resulting in legislation denoted as acts, imperial ordinances, and laws. These are best differentiated by their assigned names, numbers, and the dates of their promulgation. Accordingly, the relevant Japanese names, numbers, and dates for all pieces of legislation are included on first citation wherever possible.

Abbreviations

The following abbreviations are used for sources cited in the notes.

Primary sources

BFRB   Benjamin Strong Papers, No. 610.2, Federal Reserve Bank of New York.

BOE   Bank of England Archives, London.

FOJ   Great Britain, Foreign Office. *Japan: Correspondence.* London: Scholarly Resources, 1975. Microfilm.

GBSP   Great Britain, House of Commons. *Sessional Paper.* New York: Readex Microprint, 1967. Microfilm.

JFRB   Japan—Bank of Japan Correspondence, C. 261, Federal Reserve Bank of New York.

JRA   Japan—Miscellaneous, XI/III/681a, Rothschild Archive, London.

NAUK   National Archives (United Kingdom), London.

RCL   Russell C. Leffingwell Papers, MS 1030, Yale University Library.

TWL   Thomas W. Lamont Papers, Box Nos. 185–90, Baker Library, Harvard University.

USSD   U.S. Senate, 61st Congress, 2nd Session (1909–1910), vol. 37, Senate Doc. 586. Washington, DC: Government Printing Office, 1911.

Newspapers

JT   *Japan Times*

TE   *The Economist*

TT   *The Times of London*

Introduction

While Japan is generally known today as the world's largest creditor nation (and has been since the 1980s), very few people realize that this came about only after a long and troubled history of heavy government borrowing from foreign markets. Since the forced opening of the country through the imposition of treaty ports in 1858, and from the earliest days of international commerce, most studies of Japan have emphasized the closed, inward-looking nature of its society and culture. Similarly, in the spheres of trade and economy, historical analyses have highlighted Japan's closure to foreign investment and participation in the economy, and in doing so have implicitly downplayed the importance of foreign investment. Japan, apparently unique among nations, has managed to adopt foreign knowledge and fuse it with a native soul, as the slogan *wakon yōsai* (literally, "Japanese spirit, Western technology") audaciously proclaims.

It follows, then, that the Japanese experience of modernization has been characterized as one of "autonomous" development. Indeed, the dominant narrative is of a large number of Japanese official and nonofficial missions scouring the world to discover new (foreign) science and knowledge and, on returning to Japan's fertile shores, almost immediately putting their practices and ideas to the test and establishing the latest (Western) institutional models in Japan. While the resultant historiography is essentially factual, and has incorporated a token tip of the hat to honored instructors and temporary advisers (*oyatoi gaijin*), it is at heart deeply misleading, problematic, and disingenuous: misleading in that it says little about the individual and collective influence that non-Japanese agents have had on Japan's modernization; problematic in that the processes of technology transfer (with its questions of agency) and industrialization are left largely unaccounted for; and disingenuous in that it ignores long periods of sustained foreign investment in the Japanese economy, an enormous import of capital memorably described as a "golden tide" by British diplomats. Moreover, the flow of foreign capital into Japan did more than support the financial position of the government of the day; ultimately it represented, in its widest sense, the empowerment of a Japanese "vision" for the future. A new, more layered and imbricated conception of Japan's remarkable experience of rapid socioeconomic development is thus needed: one that moves beyond the rhetoric of "Westernization without the Westerner" and explores a long history of international cooperation and shared endeavor.

Investing Japan demonstrates that foreign investment has been a vital and misunderstood aspect of Japan's modern economic development and remains important today. Foreign borrowing was nothing less than the crux of Japan's prewar capital formation: it simultaneously financed domestic industrial development, the conduct of war, and territorial expansion on the Asian continent. Foreign borrowing also financed the provision of infrastructure in Japan's largest cities, the nationalization of railways, the interrelated capital-raising programs of "special banks" and parastatal companies, and the rapid electrification of the Japanese economy. *Investing Japan* investigates the role played by foreign companies in the Japanese experience of modernization, examining them as key agents or necessary components in the processes of industrialization and technology transfer, supplying the economy with a stream of direct foreign investments and joint ventures.

While 1945 is overwhelmingly used as a point of contrast in Japanese historiography, there are important, if underresearched, continuities that *Investing Japan* attempts to clarify. For example, the prewar and postwar roles of the zaibatsu conglomerates and American multinationals receive attention in this regard. Indeed, there is much more to the topic of "foreign capital" than immediately meets the eye. It is a complex, multifaceted subject, intersecting as it does with the histories of formal and informal economic imperialism, diplomacy and war financing, domestic and international financial markets, parastatal and multinational enterprise, and "internationalization" vis-à-vis the emerging global market (globalization).

Research for *Investing Japan* was conducted inside the archives of the Bank of Japan, the Bank of England, N. M. Rothschild and Sons, the

Federal Reserve Bank of New York, the National Archives (of the United Kingdom), and in the libraries of many universities in Japan and around the world. Written over a lengthy twenty-year period, *Investing Japan*'s critical sources of reference are the government publications of Meiji Japan's longtime minister of finance Matsukata Masayoshi (his associates and minions), and the Ministry of Finance–sponsored *Meiji zaiseishi* (Meiji financial history) and *Meiji Taishō zaiseishi* (Meiji Taisho financial history) series. Much of the research incorporates material in microfilm catalogues and newspaper collections, although references have largely been restricted to freely available, English-language materials. Moreover, my research methodology changed as the Internet increasingly provided access to primary-source archives and online secondary sources. Owing to limitations of space and to romanization (or transliteration), the footnotes and bibliography have been largely stripped of Japanese sources (to the point that some might question the author's commitment to Japanese scholarship).[1] Nevertheless, there is a sufficient wealth of research material cited here, indeed in the depth of the English-language sources alone, to encourage new research and further reflection.

Investing Japan is divided into three separate parts and nine chapters. Each chapter stands alone thematically, which entails some chronological cycling, but *Investing Japan* is best read in context and order from acknowledgments to postscript, and historians, especially, will want to incorporate the footnotes and bibliography. Part I, "Anticipating Foreign Capital: The Adoption of the Gold Standard," seeks to contextualize the role of Meiji Japan's financial, monetary, and economic development within the wider framework of nineteenth-century economic history. It elucidates the process, motives, and significance of the gold standard's adoption in Japanese history, a key aim being to show the way in which the adoption of the gold standard facilitated the import of foreign capital. Part II, "Foreign Capital and the Prewar Japanese Economy," starts with a consideration of the close financial ties between Japan and Great Britain during the period of the Anglo-Japanese alliance (1902–1923) to uncover underappreciated aspects of Anglo-Japanese financial cooperation. The wider import and employment of foreign capital in the

---

1. Readers who want more information on the Japanese sources used in the research and writing of *Investing Japan* are encouraged to read my Japanese-language works.

Japanese economy is then investigated in the period from the opening of the treaty ports in 1859 to the last instance of "peaceable" foreign investment in 1939. Taken together, the chapters in Part II argue that the issuance of Japanese government, municipal, and corporate loans on the premier financial markets of London, New York, Paris, and Berlin was a central component in Japan's modern capital formation. In addition, a survey of direct foreign investment in the Japanese economy seeks to uncover those sectors or areas of economic activity that were most affected by the import of foreign capital. Given that the process of technology transfer is integral to the development of Japanese capitalism, and a vital component of postwar revival and economic prosperity, Part II concludes by shedding some light on what is a largely unknown episode in Japan's economic and financial history.

Part III, "Foreign Capital and the Postwar Japanese Economy," moves beyond the prewar frameworks of colonialism and imperialism to examine how the postwar state attempted to reconfigure the role of foreign capital in Japanese capitalism. It starts by noting that the foreign presence in the immediate postwar economy was all but eliminated. The use of foreign currency was restricted, and commercial sovereignty was reasserted across all areas of the economy through the pursuit of protectionist policies. Throughout the 1950s and 1960s, however, the Japanese position was gradually exposed as being untenable; loans were sought from the World Bank, and some sectors of the Japanese economy were liberalized. After considering the subsequent internationalization of the 1980s and 1990s, we turn to an analysis of the scale and significance of the recent upsurge in foreign activity on the Japanese market. Is the growing international multinational presence, as evidenced by the growth of franchises, subsidiaries, joint ventures, strategic alliances, and mergers and acquisitions, really indicative of a profound change in the operations and workings of the Japanese market? Finally, Part III incorporates the findings on all of these questions in considering the effect of the neoliberal "big bang" legal reforms on Japan's finance, markets, and economy— keeping the emergence of new (and combined) threats to the Japanese economy, such as those posed by the present global financial crises, and the earthquake/tsunami/nuclear crises, firmly in mind. Thus, the notion of Japan's autonomous economic development is shown to be one of the last great fallacies of Japanese historiography.

PART I

Anticipating Foreign Capital:
The Adoption of the Gold Standard

CHAPTER I

The Domestic Imperatives
of Monetary Reform, 1868–1890

The monetary system based on gold as the standard measure of value was central to the operation of the world's financial markets from 1873 to 1914, a period that roughly corresponds with the reign of the Emperor Meiji in Japan. Regimes that adopted the gold standard enjoyed certain basic economic advantages: the convertibility of domestic currency and gold at a fixed official rate, freedom for private individuals to import or export gold, and regulations fixing the quantity of currency in circulation in relation to the regime's gold reserves. An international gold-exchange standard came into existence when a group of countries broadly adhered to these principles and agreed to convert their respective national currencies into a specified standard weight in gold. Although the commodity value of gold fluctuated on the world market, the international gold standard determined fixed exchange rates between the participating national currencies to ensure their monetary values remained unchanged. According to the operation of the international gold standard, therefore, international balance-of-payment transactions were settled through the transfer of gold or, rather, through the transfer of equivalent gold-convertible paper currencies.[1]

---

1. Eichengreen, "Editor's Introduction," pp. 1–35; Brown, *New Gold Standard*, pp. 3–4; Crowther, *An Outline of Money*, pp. 311–46; and Gallarotti, "The Scramble for Gold," pp. 1–15.

What was the process by which conditions were established for the adoption of the gold standard in Meiji Japan? In answering this question, we start by examining Japan's economic and financial situation at the commencement of the Meiji period in 1868. Perhaps the first point that should be considered is that the Meiji Restoration itself was very much a consequence of economic turmoil. Primarily due to population growth and harsh, parasitic landlordism, consumption requirements had expanded beyond the means of what was essentially a premodern, exploitative, agrarian society. The production and distribution of the agricultural surplus in the feudal Japanese framework was subject to rural and urban tensions, disturbances, and violent insurrections, which often resulted in a redistribution of political power within the institutions of Japanese feudalism.

Circumstances sharpened the struggle between contending classes as the Tokugawa era drew to a close. Undermined by the slow growth of the commercial economy, which was controlled by an increasingly ambitious and powerful class of merchants and traders, the traditional institutions of the warrior aristocracy lost their relevance. New and revolutionary forces were at work, not the least of which was the imposition of foreign trade on Japan, an imposition that ended Japan's policy of *sakoku*, or isolationism.[2]

Financial and Monetary Legacies from the Edo Period

At the commencement of the Meiji Restoration in 1868, the Meiji regime inherited a monetary system that had remained largely unchanged since its establishment in 1601 by Tokugawa Ieyasu, two years *before* he became shogun. During the period of the Tokugawa *bakufu*, or shogunate, however, the Japanese economy was not generally monetized; trade at markets was conducted on a barter basis, and the stipends paid by the Tokugawa *bakufu* to the daimyo—the feudal lords—were accounted for in quantities of rice, measured in a unit of volume called a *koku* (equal to approximately 180 liters). Nevertheless, in the big commercial centers, such as Osaka, Kyoto, and Edo (now Tokyo), moneylenders and money changers profited from the debasement of coins, arbitrage in various coinages and currencies, and an understanding of the changing relative values of a wide variety gold and silver specie on the internal market.[3]

---

2. Lockwood, *Economic Development of Japan*, pp. 5–6.
3. Matsukata, *Adoption of the Gold Standard*, p. 1, and Shinjo, *History of the Yen*, pp. 4–6.

While the monetary system was deficient in that it catered to only a relatively small part of society, its deterioration was primarily brought about by the debasement of circulatory coins, in both quantity and quality, through successive recoinage operations undertaken by the Tokugawa *bakufu* in times of financial shortfalls. In addition, counterfeit coins among the 270 or so governments of the feudal domains, called *han*, contributed to the deterioration of the monetary system. Most of the governments of these domains also issued inconvertible paper money called *hansatsu*, or notes of the fief, within their respective jurisdictions, in order to meet their financial commitments.[4] *Hansatsu* were often termed *kinsatsu* (gold notes) or *ginsatsu* (silver notes) to suggest that they were directly convertible to gold or silver bullion, yet at best they could be converted to only a nominal amount of gold or silver coinage. In some instances, it was more expedient for the value of the *hansatsu* to be expressed in terms of rice.[5] The currency situation had deteriorated to the extent that in the last days of the Tokugawa *bakufu*, there were some 1,600 varieties of *hansatsu*, often of crude manufacture, in a wide range of designs and shapes.[6]

Japan's monetary system was to deteriorate further when international trade commenced in 1859, as a proximate result of the coercion of Commodore Matthew Perry of the U.S. Navy and the fleet of "black ships" under his command. The previous isolationist policy of *sakoku*, which for 220 years had permitted a limited amount of highly regulated international trade with Dutch and Chinese merchants, had not prepared the Tokugawa *bakufu* for large-scale foreign trade, and the treasuries of the shogun were in a perilous situation.[7] When the export of Japanese gold and silver coins was permitted in 1859, foreign interests exploited the difference between Japan's gold-to-silver parity and the international gold-to-silver parity.[8] For example, in 1859 the gold-to-silver parity for some

---

4. Matsukata, *Adoption of the Gold Standard*, pp. 1–2.

5. Shinjo, *History of the Yen*, pp. 11–12.

6. Matsukata, *Adoption of the Gold Standard*, p. 21.

7. See Toby, *State and Diplomacy*, and Yamaguchi, *Sakoku to kaikoku*. The correspondence of the British Foreign Office of Japan elucidates the currency problems that the Tokugawa *bakufu* confronted. See Tennant to Committee of Privy Council for Trade, 1 December 1866, in Great Britain, Foreign Office, *Japan: Correspondence* (hereafter, FOJ), pp. 2–4, and Copy Translation: Memorandum on the Foreign Relations of Japan Drawn Up by the [Japanese] Foreign Office, 26 June 1869, FOJ, pp. 129–34.

8. See Arbuthnot to Treasury on Japanese Currency, 1862–63, 1863 (513) L.25, in Great Britain, House of Commons, *Sesssional Paper* (hereafter, GBSP), pp. 25–53; Takekoshi, *Economic Aspects*, pp. 317–37.

Japanese specie was equivalent to 5.24 at the mint or 6.36 in the markets. At the same time, in London the corresponding gold-to-silver ratio was steady at 15.19, with little difference between official and market prices.[9] In addition to arbitrage, the trade deficit, internal inflation, mounting demands for Western arms and technological equipment, and the loss of tariff control all served to intensify the outflow of Japan's precious metals.[10] Within the space of two years, the Tokugawa *bakufu* lost the bulk of its gold specie and precious metal reserves. The disordered state of coinage and the ensuing depreciation of the Japanese currency were a pressing concern of the Tokugawa and *han* authorities. Nevertheless, the Tokugawa *bakufu* was unable to ameliorate the problem by the time of its overthrow.[11]

The New Coinage Act: A Gold Standard Yen

Amid the revolutionary wars of the Meiji Restoration, the new imperial regime was quick to introduce coinage reform. In April 1868 it enacted legislation for recoinage and the construction of a government mint.[12] In November 1869, further legislation established a new and distinctive unit of Japanese currency called the yen, theoretically valued at 1.5 grams of gold. In contrast to previous monetary units, the term "yen" did not relate to the concept of weight; rather, it meant a circle, or roundness.[13]

---

9. Profits of arbitrage were often in excess of 200 percent. For the method and calculations, refer to R. Mikami, *Edo no kahei monogatari*, pp. 271–87, and Shinjo, *History of the Yen*, pp. 7–10.

10. See Inkster, *Science and Technology in History*, p. 188.

11. Matsukata, *Adoption of the Gold Standard*, p. 2.

12. See Hanashiro, *Thomas William Kinder*. British diplomats went to great lengths to impress the importance of modern coinage on their Japanese counterparts. Machinery purchased from the British mint in Hong Kong was soon put into operation in Osaka. See Parkes to Hall, 21 April 1871, FOJ; and Parkes to Hall, 29 April 1871, FOJ; and Fox, *Britain and Japan*, pp. 402–4. For reports on the operations of the Japanese Imperial Mint, see First Quarterly Report of the Director of the Imperial Mint of Japan, Confidential, 3 March 1871, FOJ; Royal Mint to Treasury, 19 October 1882, FOJ; Parkes to Foreign Office, 14 December 1882, FOJ; and Trench to Foreign Office, 30 November 1888, FOJ.

13. The term "yen" is most likely derived from the Hong Kong dollar, or yuan, which served as the original model for the Japanese yen. Certainly, the first yen coinage used the same Chinese ideogram as the *yuan*. See Hamashita, "History of the Japanese Silver Yen," p. 323, and R. Mikami, *Edo no kahei monogatari*, pp. 288–98.

The new coin was easily recognized because prior to its manufacture, the only round coins circulating in Japan were copper in color and, without exception, had a square hole in the center. Moreover, the new legislation boldly stated that the metric system would be introduced and that silver would be established as the official standard of value.[14]

The receipt of a memorandum from Ito Hirobumi in early 1871, however, was to be instrumental in the change of coinage policy from a silver standard to gold. Ito, who, in his capacity as the vice minister for finance, was carrying out investigations in the United States of America, stated: "In regard to the question of which metal should be made the standard of value, the opinion of all the economists tends to coincide in regarding gold as the fittest metal for a standard. . . . It will be a wise policy for Japan, therefore, to consider the trend of opinion in Western lands and establish her new system in accordance of the best teachings of modern times."[15] Accepting the argument outlined in Ito's memorandum, the Meiji regime legislated for the adoption of a gold standard with Imperial Ordinance No. 267 of 10 May 1871. The New Coinage Act (Shinka Jōrei), as it came to be known, clearly articulated the importance that the new regime attached to coinage regulation: "Now that trade with foreign countries is daily increasing, the reform of coinage is the most pressing necessity of the hour, and it is indeed the one essential foundation for the prosperity of the country."[16] Thus, with the promulgation of the New Coinage Act in 1871 Japan appeared to have adopted gold as its official monetary standard.[17]

Japan's attempt to introduce gold monometallism in 1871, however, faced a number of formidable obstacles. Envoys from the British government and representatives of the Oriental Bank in Japan pointed to the fact that the silver Mexican dollar was the de facto international currency in East Asia, and that Japan's gold reserves were depleted to the extent that foreign loans were necessary.[18] Furthermore, British merchants

---

14. Matsukata, *Adoption of the Gold Standard*, p. 2.

15. Matsukata, *Adoption of the Gold Standard*, pp. 2–5.

16. Matsukata, *Adoption of the Gold Standard*, p. 6.

17. T. Nakamura, *Matsukata zaisei to shokusan-kogyo*, p. 223.

18. The Oriental Banking Corporation (chartered in 1851) established itself in Yokohama during 1868 and initially handled the external financial transactions of the Meiji regime. In common with the other foreign banks, however, the Oriental Bank was to enjoy only limited success. Its Japanese operations ceased in 1884, after the Meiji

trading in Japan, backed by their consulate, were piling up merchandise on the wharves and refusing to pay customs duties at the market value of Japanese currency, insisting that they be able to pay at the nominal value of debased Japanese currency, as had been the earlier practice.[19] Indeed, protests against Japan's proposed adoption of the gold standard continued, despite Treasury correspondence informing the Foreign Office that Japan's decision to adopt the gold standard was "consistent with sound political economy" and might well be in Britain's future interest.[20] For the British in Japan (as in China, India, and throughout Southeast Asia), the operation of a silver standard was ultimately important to the preservation of the export monopoly that Britain enjoyed throughout its empire and that, in turn, maintained the British gold standard.[21] Under duress, the Meiji regime responded by allowing the silver Mexican dollar to be legal tender in those ports ceded to foreign trade—that is, the treaty ports of Nagasaki, Hakodate, and Kanagawa (Yokohama), which were opened on 1 July 1859, and the ports of Hyogo (now Kobe) and Niigata, which were opened as of 1 January 1868. Thus, with the doors now "opened," the monetary system of Japan could inadvertently become based simultaneously on both gold and silver standards.[22]

A De Facto Bimetallic Standard

As mentioned, the difference between Japan's domestic gold-to-silver ratio and the international gold-to-silver ratio had created a source of

---

regime's international transactions were taken over by the newly established Yokohama Specie Bank. See Baster, *The Imperial Banks*, pp. 258–89; Checkland, *Britain's Encounter with Meiji Japan*, pp. 36–39, 251; and Fox, *Britain and Japan*, pp. 383–84. See also Question of New Currency: Adams to Foreign Office, 6 October 1871, FOJ, pp. 33–45.

19. The contradictory nature of the British position was striking. On the one hand, the British urged the Meiji regime to immediately adopt strenuous currency reform: hence Japan's purchase of British minting equipment from Hong Kong. On the other hand, they constantly fought for the maintenance of the old exchange rates enjoyed by British traders. See Letter of Foreign Representatives with Reference to New Currency Regulations, 15 July 1871, FOJ; Adams to Hall, 18 July 1871, FOJ, pp. 197–203; Japanese Currency: Conversations with Date, Okuma, and Yoshida, 18 July 1871, FOJ, pp. 221–25; and Adams to Sawa and Terashima, Confidential, 18 July 1871, FOJ, pp. 216–17.

20. Law to Hammond, 30 June 1871, FOJ, p. 261.

21. De Cecco, *Money and Empire*, pp. 28–29.

22. Copy Translation: New Regulations of Japanese Mint and Currency Standard, 27 June 1871, FOJ, p. 207.

quick and easy profits for foreign merchants when they first gained access to the Japanese market. Indeed, after the commencement of international trade with Japan in 1859, the trade in currencies and specie quite often eclipsed the trade in goods (see Table 1.1). Although the transfer of domestically produced gold for Mexican silver was most pronounced during the so-called Yokohama Gold Rush of late 1859, the steady flow of gold currency from Japan continued, despite the Meiji regime's introduction of a new monetary system.[23] Moreover, much of the better Japanese silver specie had also disappeared from circulation.[24] In an attempt to stem the outflow, Imperial Ordinance No. 35 of 28 February 1875 replaced the silver yen, which weighed 416 grains, with a new silver trade yen (*bōeki gin*) weighing 420 grains, the same specifications as the Mexican silver dollar. It was hoped that a Japanese equivalent could drive the Mexican dollar from Japan. The extent of the failure, however, was such that by the end of May 1878 Imperial Ordinance No. 12 sanctioned the free use of the Mexican dollar throughout Japan. Thenceforth, the value of a Mexican dollar was theoretically equal to that of both the Japanese silver trade yen and the scarce gold yen coin. Moreover, Imperial Ordinance No. 35 of 26 November 1878 suspended the coining of the silver trade yen and announced the resumption of the minting of the standard yen silver piece. Thus, as of May 1878, the monetary system of Japan had legally changed from one based on a gold standard to one with a bimetallic standard.[25]

The reasoning behind Minister of Finance Okuma Shigenobu's decision to advise the Meiji regime to adopt a bimetallic standard is readily understood. With only a small national output of precious metals, worth between ¥400,000 and ¥500,000 annually, the Japanese economy was unable to cope with the sustained consumption of its gold and silver reserves. The difference between the international and Japanese gold-to-silver parities initially drove the large-scale export of Japanese gold, but as the magnitude of the difference in parities significantly decreased after 1860, the overissue of inconvertible paper money was increasingly

---

23. See R. Mikami, *Edo no kahei Monogatari*, pp. 269–87.

24. Apparently the strong Chinese demand for yen was a result of the practice of splitting the yen, scooping out its silver core and replacing it with a suitable alloy, and then placing the debased silver coin back into circulation. See Mackenzie, *Realms of Silver*, p. 98.

25. Matsukata, *Adoption of the Gold Standard*, pp. 9–15.

Table 1.1. Exports and Imports of Merchandise, Bullion, and Specie, 1868–1923 (units: ¥1,000)

Years (average)	Merchandise		Bullion and specie	
	Exports	Imports	Exports	Imports
1868–1872	15,800	22,611	—	—
1873–1877	22,124	26,585	10,780	2,978
1878–1882	30,267	32,618	9,250	3,396
1883–1887	42,114	32,769	6,616	7,331
1888–1893	77,118	72,466	8,379	12,011
1894–1898	139,200	223,040	35,897	39,116
1899–1903	243,880	270,406	20,593	20,522
1904–1908	377,041	441,879	34,493	27,693
1909–1913	495,683	544,133	22,315	23,199
1914–1916	808,895	628,204	34,098	44,811
1917–1919	1,887,992	1,625,904	53,243	241,573
1920–1923	1,571,608	1,956,925	2,816	136,304

Source: Hamashita, "History of the Japanese Silver Yen," p. 329.

responsible for encouraging the export of Japanese specie overseas (see Tables 1.1 and 1.2).[26]

Printing Paper Currency

The Meiji regime first began to print paper money in response to the need for currency amid the struggle to establish a new centralized state. Desperately short of specie, bullion, and capital, the regime created new kinds of paper money, in addition to the 1,600 or so *hansatsu* already in circulation. Imperial Ordinance No. 316 of 9 June 1868 announced the issue of new *kinsatsu* (gold notes), which became known as "imperial regime notes" (*Dajōkan satsu*), to the value of 48 million *ryō* (the prime monetary unit used in Japan prior to the introduction of the new metricated yen in November 1869). The issue of *Dajōkan satsu* between May 1868 and December 1869 was augmented by the 7.5 million *ryō* in smaller-denomination notes, called "Home Department notes" (*Minbushō satsu*),

---

26. Matsukata, *Adoption of the Gold Standard*, pp. 10–15, 70.

Table 1.2. Gold to Silver Parities in London and Tokyo, 1871–1897 (units: ratio to one part gold)

Year	London Market parity	Japan Market parity	Japan Official parity
1871	15.57	15.55	16.01
1872	15.63	15.55	16.01
1873	15.92	15.55	16.01
1874	16.17	15.48	16.01
1875	16.59	15.85	16.17
1876	17.88	16.82	16.33
1877	17.22	16.43	16.33
1878	17.94	17.03	16.17
1879	18.40	17.87	16.17
1880	18.05	17.22	16.17
1881	18.16	17.58	16.17
1882	18.19	17.40	16.17
1883	18.64	17.82	16.17
1884	18.57	17.79	16.17
1885	19.41	18.66	16.17
1886	20.78	20.15	16.17
1887	21.13	20.96	16.17
1888	21.99	21.49	16.17
1889	22.10	21.22	16.17
1890	19.76	19.47	16.17
1891	20.92	20.42	16.17
1892	23.72	22.78	16.17
1893	26.47	25.97	16.17
1894	32.56	—	16.17
1895	31.61	—	16.17
1896	30.65	—	16.17
1897	34.34	—	16.17

Source: Yamamoto, *Ryō kara en he*, p. 225.
Note: From 1871 to 1875 the legal parity was 100 silver yen to 101 gold yen; after 1875 silver and gold yen were exchanged at parity. From 1875 to 1877 the silver trade yen was Japan's official silver specie.

issued from October 1869.[27] Moreover, in an attempt to balance the deficit in government revenue, the banking arm of the Mitsui Company was exclusively authorized to print "Treasury convertible bills" (*Okurashō dakan shōken*), of which almost ¥7 million were issued by February 1872.[28] The fourth type of note to be issued was designed to defray the costs of the colonial government in Hokkaido. Issued in the first four months of 1872, these "colonial government bills" (*Kaitakushi dakan shōken*) were issued to the face value of ¥2.5 billion.[29] As the amount of fiat paper money increased in quantity and type, the purchasing power of such notes naturally declined.[30]

The formal abolition of the semi-independent domains, the *han*, in July 1871 forced the centralized administration to seize direct control over the tremendous variety of *hansatsu*. The Meiji regime could not allow feudal currency to circulate indefinitely; indeed, it had imposed strenuous political reforms owing to the economic imperative of gaining control of the financial affairs of the feudal lords.[31] Moreover, the regime's own issues of notes were of such poor quality that they were often subject to counterfeiting. By December 1871 the Meiji regime decided to order the manufacture of new and elaborate notes printed in Germany. The regime's paper currency—that is, the *Dajōkan satsu*, *Minbushō satsu*, and, by inference, *Okurashō dakan shōken* and *Kaitakushi dakan shōken* notes—was nominally equivalent to gold and silver specie, but Imperial Ordinance No. 482 of 7 July 1869 legally recognized the growing public price differentials between its paper currency and specie by *discontinuing* convertibility. German-made notes at the nominal value of ¥121 million were then issued, of which ¥22 million replaced the *hansatsu* of the 270 domains, and ¥62 million replaced the above-mentioned notes of the Meiji regime. Thus, the exchange of the new German-made notes for the

---

27. Shinjo, *History of the Yen*, pp. 28–29.

28. Mitsui received "various types of favourable considerations" from the Meiji regime owing to the financial support it had provided to it in order to bring about the "restoration" of 1868. See Mitsui, *History of Mitsui*, pp. 12–13, 15–50. Most controversially, Mitsui's head clerk apparently secured a remittance of 320 thousand *ryō* from the Tokugawa *bakufu*, which was then used by Mitsui to help finance the "restorationist" revolutionaries. See Hirshmeier, *Entrepreneurship in Meiji Japan*, pp. 213–14.

29. Matsukata, *Adoption of the Gold Standard*, p. 20.

30. According to Shinjo, the initial market value of the regime's notes was approximately 40 percent of their nominal face value. See Shinjo, *History of the Yen*, p. 29.

31. See Sakudo, "From Ancient Coins to the High Yen," pp. 151–53.

previously convertible notes of the Meiji regime (between July 1872 and early 1877) meant that Japan's entire paper currency became inconvertible to specie.[32]

Establishing Exchange Companies and National Banks

The new Meiji regime was also confronted by the need to supply capital to burgeoning industries and companies. In 1869 the Official Trade Office (Tsūshōshi) was established to develop Japan's trade and industry. It, in turn, established eight new financial institutions, which had the basic functions of a bank, called "exchange companies" (*kawase kaisha*), in the commercial centers of Tokyo, Yokohama, Osaka, Kyoto, Kobe, Niigata, Tsuruga, and Otsu.[33] These exchange companies manufactured yet another series of notes, convertible only to government notes, which were intended to supply the capital for industry. These new notes, issued by each *kawase kaisha*, were called gold (*kinken*), silver (*ginken*), and copper notes (*senken*). *Kinken* were the most commonly issued notes and represented larger denominations, whereas the *ginken* and *senken* were mostly issued in small denominations (and were largely made redundant by the issue of *Minbushō satsu*, the Home Department notes). *Ginken* and *senken* were virtually the same notes; however, in Tokyo gold had been the standard of value, so silver was used to represent the smaller denominations. In Kyoto and Osaka, silver was formerly the standard of value, so copper was a more appropriate expression for notes of smaller values.[34] The public declined to accept these new notes, however, because of the sizable paper-currency depreciations of the period. In fact, only the exchange company of Yokohama was able to continue business operations, owing to its exclusive privilege of issuing "foreign silver notes" (*yōginken*), which were freely convertible to non-Japanese silver coins.[35]

---

32. Matsukata, *Adoption of the Gold Standard*, pp. 20–24, and Shinjo, *History of the Yen*, p. 29.

33. The use of the word *kaisha* was important in that it introduced the Western concept of a company. The present word for bank, *ginko*, did not exist at that time and is said to have come from a Chinese-English dictionary. See Adams, *History of Modern Japan*, p. 9.

34. See Shibusawa, "The Development of Banking," pp. 488–89.

35. Shinjo, *History of the Yen*, p. 29. It was hoped that the Japanese foreign silver notes would replace foreign bank notes as the main currency of trade in the treaty

Anxious to replace the existing forms of paper currency with sound bank notes, and concerned about the increasing national debt, the Meiji regime attempted to reinvigorate the banking system. On the advice of Ito Hirobumi and after petitions from the Meiji regime's financiers, namely the Mitsui, Ono, and Shimada houses, Minister of Finance Inoue Kaoru decided to introduce a national banking system.[36] Significantly, Yoshida Kiyonari's proposal for a centralized banking system was dismissed outright by Inoue.[37] Imperial Ordinance No. 349 of 15 December 1872 promulgated a National Banking Act based on the American model; this was supported by Imperial Ordinance No. 121 of 30 March 1873, which provided regulations relating to *kinsatsu*-exchange bonds. According to these two ordinances, 60 percent of every national bank's capital was to be held in government *kinsatsu*-exchange bonds, bearing 6 percent interest, from which the bank could issue new bank notes.[38] The remaining 40 percent of the capital was to be used to maintain a specie reserve, which should represent two-thirds of the notes issued, to ensure the convertibility of the new bank notes.[39]

Five national banks (*kokuritsu ginkō*) were established under these conditions. Named according to the numerical sequence in which they received their charters, of these banks the First National Bank was by far the most important. The fiscal agents of the Meiji regime and former financial houses of the Tokugawa *bakufu*, Mitsui and Ono, when threatened with the loss of government transactions, jointly subscribed to form the First National Bank in June 1873.[40] Only the second bank, reorganized from the Yokohama *kawase kaisha*, was able to compete against the lending power of the First National Bank, owing to its issue of notes

---

ports, and remove other forms of Japanese currency from the control of foreign interests. See Shibusawa, "The Development of Banking," p. 489.

36. Inoue Kaoru had very close connections with Mitsui. See Mitsui, *History of Mitsui*, pp. 23–25, and J. G. Roberts, *Mitsui: Three Centuries*, pp. 95–96, 110–28.

37. Shinjo, *History of the Yen*, pp. 29–30. Yoshida was a protégé of Okuma Shigenobu and had studied the Bank of England's financial operations in London. See Checkland, *Britain's Encounter with Meiji Japan*, p. 37.

38. Matsukata, *Adoption of the Gold Standard*, pp. 23–24.

39. Shibusawa, "The Development of Banking," p. 493, and Shinjo, *History of the Yen*, p. 30.

40. Roberts, *Mitsui: Three Centuries*, pp. 98–99, and Shibusawa, "The Development of Banking," p. 495.

convertible into silver trade dollars.[41] What became evident was that the operations of the national banks were hamstrung by the government's convertibility reserve requirements: the banks could not raise loanable funds without significant increases in deposits.[42] The large number of notes in circulation, and the relative scarcity of specie, prevented the regime from realizing its intention of retiring all paper notes in exchange for the new unified bank notes. As soon as new convertible bank notes were issued, they were returned to the banks for conversion into silver. The inability of the national banks to reform the currency situation was such that new bank notes to the value of only ¥2 million were exchanged.[43] Moreover, the financing of the Third National Bank (in Osaka) collapsed before its banking operations even started.[44]

In March 1875, therefore, the four remaining national banks petitioned the government to allow their bank notes to be convertible into (inconvertible) government paper money, rather than convertible into specie. At the same time, the Meiji regime wanted to replace the annual pensions of the samurai, or warrior aristocracy, with a single issue of hereditary pension bonds (*kinroku kōsai*). Thus, in changing the capital requirements for the issue of bank notes, the Meiji regime wanted to strengthen the national banking system, provide funds for Japan's economic development, and assist the dispossessed but still powerful and potentially disruptive aristocracy.[45] Imperial Ordinance No. 106 of 1 August 1876 amended the existing regulations to allow national banks to issue bank notes for up to 80 percent of the paid-in capital, with a reserve of just 20 percent of the capital. Moreover, the reserve could be in any form of currency, thereby creating a situation in which national banks could issue notes without physically holding specie.[46]

---

41. Shinjo, *History of the Yen*, p. 30.

42. Central bureaucracy and prefectural governments provided the bulk of bank deposits: the level of personal savings was insignificant. Pressnell, *Money and Banking in Japan*, p. 7.

43. Matsukata, *Adoption of the Gold Standard*, pp. 23–24.

44. See Adams, *History of Modern Japan*, p. 10, and Shibusawa, "The Development of Banking," p. 495.

45. Shibusawa, "The Development of Banking," pp. 499–501.

46. Matsukata was later critical of the decision to issue the hereditary pension bonds, stating, "It was believed that . . . the economic market would be supplied with the much needed capital in the form of bank notes. It is needless to notice that these

The large issue of ¥174 million in the form of hereditary pension bonds, when combined with the more liberal national banking regulations, provided tremendous opportunities for profit. The response was so enthusiastic that in 1879, after the establishment of the 153rd National Bank in Kyoto, the Meiji regime refused to grant further charters for national banks. In effect, Imperial Ordinance No. 106 of 1 August 1876 had established a banking system at the cost of dramatically increasing the number of inconvertible government paper notes in circulation, which in turn caused ruinous inflation. Conditions were such that peasant uprisings were occurring at an unprecedented rate during the inflationary trauma of the early to mid-Meiji period. In all probability, only the distinct lack of cooperation between the former peasant and samurai classes, compounded by the regionally isolated nature of the uprisings, saved the Meiji regime.[47]

Currency Chaos and the Yokohama Specie Bank

The unification of bank notes and the retirement of the regime's currency notes were further impeded, in 1877, by the samurai rebellion in Kyushu led by Saigo Takamori.[48] The Seinan (Southwestern) Civil War forced the Meiji regime to borrow ¥15 million from the Fifteenth National Bank and to print yet another ¥27 million in currency notes to meet its military expenditures.[49] In addition, the regime's first notes, the *Dajōkan satsu*, had begun to expire in 1880 only to be replaced by new notes, while at the same time the Ministry of Finance had been meeting deficit shortfalls by "reissuing" paper notes officially being held in reserve (purportedly to the amount of approximately ¥20 million annually in the years

---

ideas were based on an erroneous notion that capital and currency were interchangeable terms." See Matsukata, *Adoption of the Gold Standard*, pp. 25–26.

47. See Smith, *Political Change and Industrial Development*, p. 30.

48. See Memorandum by E. W. Satow (on the grounds of dissatisfaction), 10 March 1877, FOJ, which offers valuable insight into the Seinan Civil War.

49. Of course, the Meiji regime could have met the entire costs of the war in Kyushu by printing paper money, raising loans, or increasing taxation. Under the circumstances of war, however, the regime did not risk increasing taxation. Instead, it chose to print extra notes and to shore up support with the former feudal lords by applying for the loan of ¥15 million from their bank, the Fifteenth National Bank. After all, the conflict highlighted the resentment of the declassed samurai aristocracy. See Adams, *History of Modern Japan*, p. 12, and Shibusawa, "Development of Banking," pp. 503–4.

following the outbreak of civil war).[50] While the total value of Japan's paper currency was ¥68 million before the rapid establishment of national banks in 1873, by the end of January 1880 the total amount of inconvertible paper money in circulation approached ¥125 million (see Table 1.3), with approximately ¥34 million in paper money being issued in the form of national bank notes.[51]

As minister of finance, Okuma Shigenobu was largely responsible for the development of financial policy between 1873 and 1880.[52] Okuma recognized the importance of establishing a sound currency system and was sympathetic to the creation of a central bank. Okuma's analysis of Japan's economic situation, however, was that domestic inflation and currency depreciation were the effects of an unfavorable balance of trade. Moreover, Okuma believed that silver's appreciation against domestic paper currency in Japan was brought about by conditions in which imports exceeded exports. Therefore Okuma founded a silver exchange in Yokohama, in February 1879, to lower the paper-currency price of silver by increasing its supply. One year later the Yokohama silver exchange was renamed the Yokohama Specie Bank, when it was supplied with silver from the regime's own specie reserve and become the Meiji regime's financial agent in all of its international financial transactions.[53]

Okuma's failure to understand that inflation and currency depreciation were the cause rather than the effect of an unfavorable balance of trade is highlighted by the poor performance of the Yokohama Specie Bank. In early 1878 the ratio of silver to paper was about 1 to 1.08, and then the increased issue of paper currency changed the ratio in favor of silver, to 1 to 1.21. The financial authorities explained that the depreciation of paper currency was caused by the appreciation of silver, and they began to sell more government silver, through the Yokohama Specie Bank, in an attempt to lower domestic silver prices. Nevertheless, not only was paper money depreciating against silver but silver was also depreciating

---

50. Shinjo, *History of the Yen*, pp. 31–32.

51. Matsukata, *Adoption of the Gold Standard*, p. 27. It was later suggested by Matsukata that the devaluation of paper currency was not entirely due to the overissue of notes. Matsukata asserts that the notes' inability to command credit, as they were inconvertible to specie, was responsible in equal measure for the devaluation of paper currency. See Matsukata, *Adoption of the Gold Standard*, p. 73.

52. Lebra, *Okuma Shigenobu*.

53. Yokohama Specie Bank, *Yokohama shoken ginkoshi*, pp. 10–11, 19, 61–62, 309–14.

Table 1.3. Issuance and Redemption of Paper Currency, 1868–1898 (units: ¥1,000)

Year	Notes issued	Notes redeemed	Notes circulating	Special issue	Total issue
1868	24,037	0	24,037	0	24,037
1869	26,035	0	50,072	0	50,072
1870	5,409	0	55,481	0	55,481
1871	5,772	0	61,253	0	61,253
1872	4,528	0	65,781	3,600	69,381
1873	13,334	853	78,262	11,000	89,262
1874	14,633	1,112	91,783	11,000	102,783
1875	2,443	1,962	92,264	7,788	100,052
1876	510	1,530	91,244	11,824	103,068
1877	514	1	91,757	11,961	103,718
1878	27,000	1,035	117,722	19,618	137,340
1879	2	5,611	112,113	16,118	128,231
1880	0	5,778	106,335	16,528	122,863
1881	0	2,507	103,828	13,000	116,828
1882	0	536	103,292	4,000	107,292
1883	0	7,370	95,922	0	95,922
1884	0	4,619	91,303	0	91,303
1885	0	5,305	85,998	0	85,998
1886	0	20,544	65,454	0	65,454
1887	0	11,986	53,468	0	53,468
1888	0	9,080	44,388	0	44,388
1889	0	5,544	38,844	0	38,844
1890	0	7,918	30,926	0	30,926
1891	0	5,386	25,540	0	25,540
1892	0	7,058	18,482	0	18,482
1893	0	4,421	14,061	0	14,061
1894	0	3,002	11,059	0	11,059
1895	0	2,275	8,784	0	8,784
1896	0	1,753	7,031	0	7,031
1897	0	1,925	5,106	0	5,106
1898	0	2,039	3,067	0	3,067

Source: Shinjo, *History of the Yen*, p. 71.
Note: The amount of paper notes in circulation and the total issue have been recalculated by the author.

against gold, and the Yokohama Specie Bank endured a costly loss. By April 1880 the ratio of silver to paper was 1 to 1.55 (see Figure 1.1); Okuma resigned in 1880.[54] Sano Tsunetake, who succeeded Okuma, conscientiously continued Okuma's policies until his replacement by Matsukata Masayoshi in October 1881.[55]

Matsukata and the Bank of Japan

Upon his appointment, Minister of Finance Matsukata cited the threat of an impending economic crisis to convince the government of the economic and financial benefits of establishing a central bank in Japan. In a memorandum presented on 1 March 1882, Matsukata criticized the system of national banks as a remnant of discredited Tokugawa feudalism.[56] He also successfully petitioned for the establishment of a central bank to be called the Bank of Japan (Nippon Ginkō), which would have the sole right to issue convertible bank notes, regulate currency throughout Japan, discount foreign bills of exchange in order to regulate the circulation of specie and bullion, and provide treasury services. Imperial Ordinance No. 32 of 27 June 1882 established the regulations of the new central bank, and on 10 October of the same year, the Bank of Japan was founded to act as the government's fiscal agent.[57]

---

54. Okuma's resignation was not related to the poor performance of the Yokohama Specie Bank. Rather, Okuma (of Hizen) pressed the Meiji oligarchs, consisting mainly of former Satsuma and Choshu samurai, to introduce representative democracy, and he was compelled to resign his post as a consequence. See Lebra, *Okuma Shigenobu*, pp. 38–54, and Shinjo, *History of the Yen*, p. 39.

55. Matsukata was born in Kagoshima in 1835 and worked as a "samurai of Satsuma" until his promotion to the Ministry of Finance in 1870. In 1875 he traveled to France to study the principles of finance and banking under Leon Say, and he is believed to have studied the establishment of the central banking system in Belgium, and the adoption of the gold standard in Germany. Matsukata's service was entirely domestic, perhaps due to the fact that he spoke no foreign languages and had a marked regional accent that was very difficult for foreign speakers of Japanese to comprehend. See Longford to Campbell, Confidential, 26 April 1902, FOJ, pp. 134–36.

56. Matsukata's comment, "While political feudalism with its particularism and separatism . . . has been happily overthrown, in financial matters we seem to be . . . under a system of feudalism," still resonates in the early twenty-first century, for Japanese finance remains, in many ways, defined by its feudalistic "particularism and separatism." See Matsukata, *Adoption of the Gold Standard*, p. 45, and Nishikawa and Saito, "Economic History of the Restoration Period," pp. 185–86.

57. Matsukata, *Adoption of the Gold Standard*, pp. 43, 67; Shinjo, *History of the Yen*, p. 69; and Yoshino, *En no rekishi*, pp. 59–67.

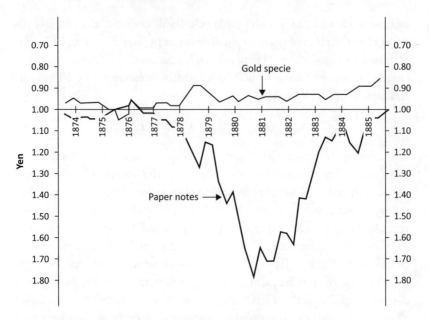

Figure 1.1. Silver Yen in Terms of Gold and Paper Yen, 1874–1885.
Source: Yamamoto, *Ryō kara en he*, p. 229.

To give the Bank of Japan the exclusive right to issue bank notes, Imperial Ordinance No. 14 of 5 May 1883 amended the National Bank Regulations to reduce the existing national bank charters to a period of just twenty years from the date of their establishment. Those national banks that wished to continue to operate under the new conditions were to do so as private commercial or deposit banks, and each new private bank was required to keep a reserve fund for the redemption of notes equal to 25 percent of the amount of the same notes it had issued as a national bank. The legislation also served to reinforce the importance of the Bank of Japan by giving it, as the central bank, sole authority to conduct transactions in which currency was required to be exchanged for silver.[58] Of the 153 national banks in existence between 1873 and 1898, 16 banks disappeared owing to amalgamations, 8 were forced to dissolve, and 7 chose to close their doors. The vast majority, 122 remaining national banks, converted into private banks and changed their names in the

---

58. Yoshino, *Nihon ginkō seido*, pp. 61–83.

manner of the First National Bank, which became the First Bank by dropping the "National" designation.[59]

Unifying Paper Currency

Having established a central bank to redeem inconvertible notes, Matsukata next moved to increase government revenue and thus create a surplus in the national budget by implementing levies on medicines, taxes on brokers of rice and stocks, and revised taxes on sake and tobacco.[60] The government was then able to keep its expenditures constant for three years and provide the Treasury with a surplus of ¥40 million. From the surplus raised by the end of 1885, notes worth more than ¥13.5 million were destroyed and the remaining notes were held in reserve. The government's surplus national budget was also augmented by the increase in Japanese exports, facilitated by the establishment of consulates in Japan's strongest foreign markets and the deflated prices of Japanese exports owing to the depreciation of silver relative to gold.[61]

As a result of Matsukata's deflationary policy, the value of notes in circulation had decreased by ¥88 million in the 1881–1885 period, and the percentage of specie reserve rose from 8 percent to 35 percent in the corresponding four-year period.[62] Thus, to secure Japan's industrial development, Matsukata's bold policy of severe deflation succeeded in providing private enterprise with a sound currency and the government with an adequate source of revenue.[63]

---

59. See Shibusawa, "The Development of Banking," p. 517, and Shinjo, *History of the Yen*, p. 70.

60. Pressnell, *Money and Banking in Japan*, p. 10. It was clear to British consuls in the treaty ports of Japan that confidence in the Japanese currency could be restored only through redemption of paper notes and the promise of convertibility. Until the Japanese currency was on a sound financial basis, it was thought that improvements in trade would be impossible. See Papers from H.M. Representatives and Consuls in Foreign Countries on the Silver Question, 1884–85 (227) LVIII.655, GBSP, p. 776.

61. The surplus was to be divided equally between the purchase of old notes (for the redemption of currency) and the purchase of specie. Specie had to be imported, as the domestic production of gold and silver was, as noted, worth less than ¥500,000 annually. See Matsukata, *Adoption of the Gold Standard*, p. 70.

62. Matsukata, *Adoption of the Gold Standard*, pp. 70, 73–74, and Nakamura, *Matsukata zaisei to shokusan-kogyō*, pp. 229–38. Shinjo, *History of the Yen*, pp. 40–41.

63. Ohkawa and Rosovsky, "A Century of Economic Growth," p. 66. While the importance of the Matsukata deflation is widely acknowledged in economic history

The first steps toward the reintroduction of convertible currency were taken with the promulgation of Imperial Ordinance No. 18 on 26 May 1884, which promised that the Bank of Japan's bank notes would soon be convertible to silver coinage.[64] Imperial Ordinance No. 14 of 6 June 1885 notified the general public that government paper money could be exchanged for silver specie when presented at the Bank of Japan, and that the exchanged notes would subsequently be canceled and withdrawn from circulation.[65] In 1886, 1887, and 1888, paper currency worth more than ¥41 million was redeemed in that fashion (see Table 1.3).[66] By July 1888, the redemption of inconvertible notes was proceeding at such a pace that Matsukata, after studying the methods and processes of the European and American banking systems, petitioned for the government to receive a loan from the Bank of Japan toward the total redemption of inconvertible paper notes.[67] The convertibility of Japanese currency was an important precondition for the adoption of the gold standard and an essential component of Japan's acceptance into the international monetary system. The passage of Imperial Ordinance No. 59 through the Diet—the national legislature—on 1 August 1888, allowing the Meiji regime to lend up to ¥22 million for the purpose of redeeming paper money, was a major step toward the adoption of the gold standard.[68]

The drive to facilitate a complete withdrawal of all inconvertible paper money was intensified with the new legislation of Law No. 24 of 28 March 1890, which established a reserve fund of ¥10 million to sustain the redemption of inconvertible currency. By 1890, Japan's rapid industrial progress was thought by the Ministry of Finance to be responsible for the relative scarcity of paper currency; that being the case, the government was permitted to issue additional convertible Bank of Japan notes

---

today, regrettably the motives and mechanisms of its introduction remain largely unexplored.

64. Matsukata, *Adoption of the Gold Standard*, pp. 71–72.

65. In advancing the legislation, Matsukata was acutely aware of how convertibility would be positively perceived by domestic and international financiers. See Matsukata, *Adoption of the Gold Standard*, pp. 74–75, and Yoshino, *En no rekishi*, p. 195.

66. In June 1888, the inconvertible government paper notes found to be in circulation were valued at ¥49 million. Inconvertible national bank notes worth ¥28 million were also in circulation. See Matsukata, *Adoption of the Gold Standard*, p. 84.

67. Parkes to Treasury, 14 September 1888, FOJ, p. 155. To the very end, Parkes maintained that a foreign (British) loan was necessary.

68. Matsukata, *Adoption of the Gold Standard*, pp. 84–86; Shibusawa, "The Development of Banking," pp. 518–19; and Trench to Treasury, 29 August 1895, FOJ, p. 169.

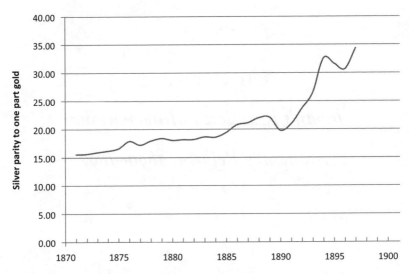

Figure 1.2. Ratio of Silver to Gold in London, 1871–1897.
Source: Yamamoto, *Ryō kara en he*, p. 225.

worth ¥15 million, in accordance with Law No. 34 of 17 May 1890. At the same time, with the reserve fund almost exhausted, Matsukata pressed for the government's loan from the Bank of Japan to be transferred to the reserve fund devoted to the redemption of inconvertible paper money, by changing a clause in the regulations of Imperial Ordinance No. 59 of 1 August 1888. With the change of that clause, the unification of paper currency in Japan was finally accomplished during 1890.[69]

Throughout this process, the notes of the 153 national banks, as well as the various types of government paper currencies, were exchanged for the convertible silver notes of the Bank of Japan. As a result of those exchanges, Japan moved from a nominal gold standard, proclaimed in 1871, to a de facto silver standard. The transfer to the silver standard, made easier after silver's rapid depreciation against gold in 1873, was the cost of creating a stable and unified national currency (see Figure 1.2). Initially unable to arrest the flow of specie from Japan, the Meiji regime had managed to finance itself through the issue of bonds and the establishment of a national and then a central banking system, so that in the 1890s the financial preconditions that would allow Japan to adopt the gold standard had been met.

---

69. Matsukata, *Adoption of the Gold Standard*, pp. 86–88, and Shibusawa, "The Development of Banking," p. 519.

CHAPTER 2

Japan's Reaction to International Monetary Reform, 1890–1897

The Meiji regime managed to establish a unified and stable domestic currency in the second half of the 1880s through a series of laws and legislative acts that ensured the convertability of government notes to silver bullion. Domestic financial and monetary reform also allowed the Meiji regime to enjoy more stable interest rates, while commercial and industrial enterprises began to expand and the volume of Japan's foreign trade began to increase. In the process of reform, however, Japan adopted a de facto silver standard, and as a consequence, the international exchange value of its currency was unstable, owing to the declining value of silver relative to gold (see Figure 2.1). Japan's economic and financial position in the world market was subject to fluctuations in the gold-to-silver ratio on the international financial markets.[1] It is in the context of a worldwide demonetization of silver, which began in the early 1870s, that Japan's transition to a gold standard can be best understood.

International Monetary Reform in the Late Nineteenth Century

Between 1814 and 1870 the gold-to-silver parity was quite steady, at approximately 1 part gold to 15.5 parts silver, and fluctuations in the gold price of silver were generally insignificant. Indeed, the currencies of the United States, China, India, and all the major European states, with the

---

1. Matsukata, *Adoption of the Gold Standard*, p. 145.

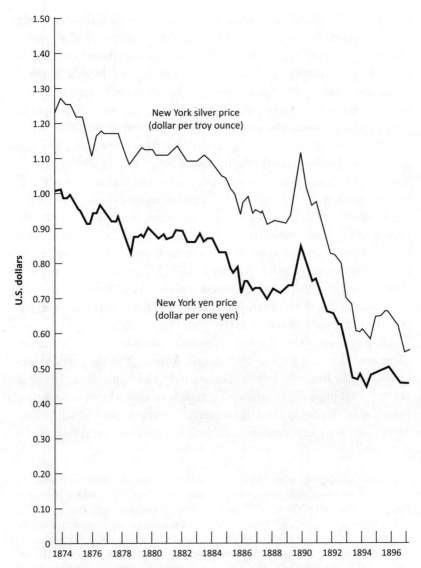

Figure 2.1. Decline of Silver and the Yen Exchange Rate Relative to Gold, 1874–1897.

Source: Umemura and Nakamura, *Matsukata zaisei to shokusan kōgyō seisaku*, p. 222.

exception of England and Portugal, were totally or partially based on a silver standard. The depreciation of the gold price of silver had a number of causes, the most important of which were the significant increases in production at American and Mexican silver mines and the abandonment of the silver standard in favor of the gold by the major European econo-mies.[2] The move by Germany and other European states to adopt the gold standard flooded the world market with silver, forcing the curren-cies of non-European states with silver standards to depreciate. The U.S. government had hoped that the increased production of silver would be absorbed by Asian countries, especially India and China, which would in turn release more gold in the international market.[3] Indeed, the mint-ing of silver trade dollars by the United States from 1873 to 1885, the French silver piaster issued from 1878 to 1925, and the British trade dollar minted from 1895 to 1935 were bold attempts to realize profits on the higher Asian price of silver, counteract silver's depreciation, and extend their respective influences over the economies of Asia.[4] When we use gold as the measure of the standard of value, however, it is clear that from late 1871 the value of silver was in decline (see Figure 2.1).

The precursor of the European economies' abandonment of monetary silver may be traced back to 1865 and the formation of the Latin Mone-tary Union by Belgium, France, Greece, Italy, and Switzerland. For some twenty years prior to the union's formation in 1865, the participant na-tions had been plagued by large arbitrage transactions in which heavier silver coins were exported outside their respective national boundaries

---

2. Although the role of increased silver production should not be overstated, the timing of the production increases clearly played a role in the abandonment of silver by the major economies of the world in the last quarter of the nineteenth century. See De Cecco, *Money and Empire*, pp. 39–61. To the two causes mentioned, one might add the hypothesis that decreased demand for silver in India (probably the world's most signifi-cant consumer of silver, purchasing approximately one-third of the world's supply) also contributed to the decrease in the gold price of silver. See Bagchi, "Substitution be-tween Bills and Silver," p. 1, and Select Committee on Causes of Depreciation of Prices of Silver, and Effects on Exchange between India and England, Rep., Procs., Mins. of Ev., App., Index, 1876 (338) VIII.219, GBSP.

3. See McGuire, "India, Britain, Precious Metals," pp. 23–28.

4. See Hamashita, "Japanese Silver Yen," pp. 322–23, and Correspondence respect-ing Proposals on Currency by Special Envoys from the United States, 1898 (c.8667) CV.601, GBSP, and Correspondence respecting Proposals on Currency by Special En-voys from the United States by the Govt. of India, 1898 (c.8840) LXI.439, GBSP.

only to be replaced by lighter foreign currencies, and thus the member nations, with the exception of France, expressed the desire to adopt the gold standard.[5] It was, however, the creation of a German state in 1871 that undoubtedly led to the depreciation of silver. The new German state faced the same monetary issues that the Japanese state confronted after the Meiji Restoration: namely, the need to establish a stable, uniform currency, and the desire to adopt the gold standard. In contrast to Japan, however, Germany was able to create a uniform currency quickly, and in 1873 it adopted the gold standard. Significantly, the German transfer to the gold standard was in part facilitated by using the F5 billion French indemnity that had been won earlier by Prussia in the Franco-Prussian War of 1870.[6]

After adopting the gold standard, the German government began to purchase fresh gold bullion and to sell large quantities of silver, resulting in the deterioration of the gold price of silver.[7] In 1873 the United States reacted by announcing its intention to cease production of all silver coins, with the exception of its silver trade dollar. Although there were significant increases in domestic silver production, it appeared that the U.S. government was preparing for the adoption of the gold standard. Those European countries with bimetallic standards now confronted the prospect of becoming de facto silver-standard nations through much the same process that pushed Japan onto a silver standard during the same period. As a result, members of the Latin Monetary Union set limits on

---

5. Select Committee on Causes of Depreciation of Prices of Silver, and Effects on Exchange between India and England, Rep., Procs., Mins. of Ev., App., Index, 1876 (338) VIII.219, GBSP, p. 222, and De Cecco, *Money and Empire*, p. 44.

6. McGouldrick, "German Central Bank," pp. 312, 326. The French indemnity was not directly paid in gold; rather it was mostly paid in bonds exchanged for gold in London. See De Cecco, *Money and Empire*, pp. 46–47; Ferguson, *The House of Rothschild*, pp. 205–17; Reti, *Silver and Gold*, pp. 52–53, 58; and Select Committee on Causes of Depreciation of Prices of Silver, and Effects on Exchange between India and England, Rep., Procs., Mins. of Ev., App., Index, 1876 (338) VIII.219, GBSP, p. 343. As a matter of conjecture, to what extent did Japan emulate Prussia's capture of a war indemnity to achieve the adoption of the gold standard? See Droppers, "Monetary Changes in Japan," p. 175.

7. Select Committee on Causes of Depreciation of Prices of Silver, and Effects on Exchange between India and England, Rep., Procs., Mins. of Ev., App., Index, 1876 (338) VIII.219, GBSP, pp. 342–43.

the amount of silver accepted at their mints, and the Netherlands, Denmark, Norway, and Sweden adopted the gold standard in 1873.[8]

Denmark, Norway, and Sweden, in fact, went on to form the Scandinavian Monetary Union in 1875, which then proceeded to release Scandinavian silver coinage on the European market.[9] Also in 1875, the Netherlands ended the free minting of silver and Switzerland ceased its entire production of silver coinage. Belgium, Spain, and Russia followed the actions of the Swiss government in the following year, thereby forcing the American government to abandon the silver trade dollar as legal tender. As a consequence of the European reaction, the average gold-to-silver parity for 1876, as measured in London, was 1 part gold to 17.8 parts silver.[10]

Although the value of silver was clearly declining by 1876, those states that were major producers of silver believed that they could maintain the price of silver by increasing the magnitude of their own silver reserves. Foremost among such silver-producing states was the United States, whose government conceded to the silver lobby by promulgating the Bland-Allison Act in 1878, an act that obliged the U.S. government to purchase a percentage of all the silver mined in the United States. In 1890 the Bland-Allison Act was replaced by the Sherman Act, which further increased the proportion of silver purchased by the U.S. government.[11] The ineffectiveness of such policies, however, was clearly demonstrated by the continuous depreciation of silver relative to gold throughout the period. For 1879 the average gold-to-silver ratio was 1 part gold to 18.4 parts silver, and by 1885 the ratio had moved to 1 part gold to 19.4 parts silver. The process of depreciation intensified to the extent that, on average,

---

8. See Bryan, *Gold Standard at the Turn*, pp. 35–36, and De Cecco, *Money and Empire*, pp. 46–50.

9. Jonung, "The Swedish Experience," pp. 368–70, and Hoare, *The Appreciation of Gold*, pp. 12–32.

10. Matsukata, *Adoption of the Gold Standard*, p. 146. The final remarks in the 1876 Select Committee's report to the House of Commons were that silver's depreciation was due in half to demonetization, in quarter to subsequent depreciation, and in an eighth to increased production of silver. It was thought that the first two reasons would have had no validity, however, if silver production had not increased. See Select Committee on Causes of Depreciation of Prices of Silver, and Effects on Exchange between India and England, Rep., Procs., Mins. of Ev., App., Index, 1876 (338) VIII.219, GBSP.

11. McGuire, "India, Britain, Precious Metals," p. 26. See also De Cecco, *Money and Empire*, pp. 50–51.

1 part gold equalled 20.9 parts silver in 1891, 1 part gold averaged 23.7 parts silver in 1892, and by 1893 the yearly average ratio was 1 part gold to 26.5 parts silver.[12]

Silver's continued depreciation forced the Austro-Hungarian government to adopt the gold standard in 1892, the U.S. government to repeal the Sherman Act in 1893, and the Russian government, which had briefly reinstated the free coinage of silver, to once again stop the minting of silver coins.[13] In the following year, when Persia also stopped minting silver coins and India introduced a 5 percent tariff on all imported silver, fixed the value of the silver rupee, and suspended silver's free coinage, the ratio of gold to silver dropped to 1 part gold to 32.6 parts of silver. In 1895 Chile and South Africa adopted the gold standard, with Costa Rica following suit in 1896. During 1896, silver showed signs of appreciation at the ratio of 1 part gold to 30.7 parts silver, owing to speculation that the silver party would come to power in the U.S. presidential elections, and that the huge Chinese indemnity from the Sino-Japanese War of 1894–1895 would be paid to Japan in silver. In 1897, both sets of suppositions were proved to be false, and the depreciation of silver fell to the century's nadir of 1 part gold to 39.7 parts silver and averaged 1 part gold to 34.2 parts silver for that year. Between 1868 and 1897, then, the yearly average gold-to-silver parity, as measured in London, had decreased from 15.6 to 34.2, with the gold price of silver decreasing to 46 percent of its 1868 value (see Figure 2.1).[14]

Matsukata and Constitutional Government

By 1897 the European nations had revolutionized and transformed their respective monetary systems in a remarkably homogeneous manner that repudiated silver as the measure of the standard of value, in favor of gold.[15] In the midst of the abandonment of silver by the major economies of the

---

12. Matsukata, *Adoption of the Gold Standard*, pp. 146–57.

13. Although the U.S. government repealed the Sherman Act in 1893, it continued to lobby, along with France, for international agreement with regard to the reintroduction of the free minting of silver, particularly in India. See Correspondence respecting Proposals on Currency by Special Envoys from the United States, 1898 (c.8667) CV.601, GBSP, and Correspondence respecting Proposals on Currency by Special Envoys from the United States by the Govt. of India, 1898 (c.8840) LXI.439, GBSP.

14. Matsukata, *Adoption of the Gold Standard*, pp. 146–57, 177, 183–84.

15. De Cecco, *Money and Empire*, pp. 56–57.

world, Japan's political leaders were conducting a volatile experiment with representative government. Throughout the first part of the Meiji era, the Satsuma and Choshu oligarchs of the Meiji Restoration had worked together to maintain their authority and power.[16] The dominion of the "sat-cho" oligopoly, however, was stubbornly contested by other statesmen of the Meiji Restoration who agitated for representative democracy.[17] Finally, in accordance with the Japanese constitution, which was promulgated on 11 February 1889, elections for a National Diet were announced for 1 July 1890.[18]

Matsukata's administration of the Ministry of Finance and his program of financial and monetary revision were to be impaired by his contest for political survival. After the first elections, Matsukata managed to retain the position of minister of finance as a member of the Yamagata government of the first Diet of November 1890, and, indeed, he was prime minister of his own government with the second Diet of May 1891. Matsukata's first term as prime minister lasted just under eight months, as his government refused to yield on policy decisions and declined to consider the views of other parties within the Diet. In desperation, opposition parties united to reject the bills of the Matsukata government, and the Matsukata government retaliated by dissolving the Diet. In marked contrast to the first election, the election that followed was notorious for bribery, intimidation, and strong-arm tactics. Although Matsukata was quick to distance himself from the violence of the elections and relinquished leadership of his government prior to the elections of 1892, he lost his Finance Ministry position on 25 December 1891.[19]

Watanabe and the Currency Commission

Matsukata's replacement as minister of finance, Watanabe Kunitake, was preoccupied by the depreciation of silver relative to gold, and by the un-

---

16. Itagaki, Okuma, and Ukita, "Political Parties in Japan," pp. 152–53.

17. For example, Okuma resigned from the post of minister of finance in 1881 to protest the refusal of his fellow members of the regime to introduce representative democracy. See Lebra, *Okuma Shigenobu*, pp. 38–54.

18. The National Diet was largely based on the operation of the German parliament, as researched by Ito Hirobumi. The number of voters qualified by the constitution for the election was 460,000, out of a population of 42 million. See Itagaki, Okuma, and Ukita, "Political Parties in Japan," p. 164.

19. See Norman, *Japan's Emergence*, pp. 190–94.

certainties the depreciation created. Moreover, Watanabe realized that the operation of Japan's silver standard had to be addressed, as silver's remarkable depreciation had been a topic of intense discussion in all the industrialized economies of the world throughout the time that Japan had been absorbed by the domestic necessities of monetary reform. In a memorandum on 11 September 1893, Watanabe stressed the need to investigate national monetary policy: "The recent fluctuations in the ratio between gold and silver have exerted an extraordinary influence on the economic affairs of the world, and the governments of all countries have been led to pay the greatest attention to the method of averting further calamities from the same source."[20] Thus, under Watanabe's leadership, the Ministry of Finance launched the Currency Commission inquiry into the monetary system of Japan, in October 1893.[21] The three main areas of investigation were: the cause and effect of fluctuations in the price of gold and silver, the influence of such fluctuations on the Japanese economy, and whether such fluctuations demanded revision of the existing monetary system. If, in answer to the third area of investigation, revision was thought necessary, the commission was to recommend what form such revisions might take.[22]

Almost twenty-two months later, on 28 July 1895, the Currency Commission submitted its final report to Minister Watanabe. In regard to the first area of investigation, the commission found that the remarkable decline of silver prices had been caused by the increased production of silver at a time when the demand for silver, for coinage and for works of art, had substantially decreased. Simultaneously, it found that the demand for gold, to be used for coinage, for works of art, and to be hoarded, had substantially increased. It also stated that the amount of silver in existence was quite small when compared with the yearly increases in the supply of silver, and that the rate of increase in the output of gold was less than the rate of increase in the output of silver.[23] In identifying the causes of silver's rapid depreciation, the commission did not evaluate the relative importance of these causes and failed to mention details such as

---

20. Matsukata, *Adoption of the Gold Standard*, p. 158.
21. Yoshino, *En no rekishi*, p. 198.
22. Shinjo, *History of the Yen*, p. 45.
23. Matsukata, *Adoption of the Gold Standard*, pp. 161, 177, 184, and Yoshino, *En no rekishi*, pp. 196–200.

the underlying causes of the decreased demand for silver to be used in coinage.[24]

In regard to the general effect of depreciation and fluctuations in the gold price of silver, the Currency Commission's findings were separated into three categories: the effects on silver countries, the effects on gold countries, and the effects on the economic relations between gold and silver countries. The effects of depreciation and fluctuations in the price of silver on silver countries were found to be both positive and negative. Employment, exports, trade, public revenue, and public expenditure were found to have increased in silver-based economies. Rises in the price of commodities, due to the depreciation of silver, had made agriculture prosperous and reduced the liabilities of debtors and taxpayers who payed in fixed rates. As a consequence of the inflation within silver economies, however, creditors and those who lived on salaries or wages had been disadvantaged. Furthermore, the increasing cost of commodities imported from gold-standard countries had subsequently decreased the volume of imports, while the magnitude and frequency of fluctuations in the gold price of silver had also encouraged the growth of speculative enterprises, which withheld capital from other sectors of the silver economies. Not surprisingly, the commission's findings concerning the effects of silver's rapid depreciation on those countries with a gold standard were essentially the opposite of those it reported for silver-standard countries.[25]

The findings of the commission in regard to the effects of silver's rapid depreciation on the economic relations between gold and silver countries received special attention, as they had important implications for the nature of the economic growth and development of the silver-standard nations. The commission found that economic relations between gold

---

24. Seven years earlier a British Royal Commission, in addition to the Select Committee Inquiry of 1876, had reported to the House of Commons on similar issues. Amid discussion of legislative measures taken by various nations, demonetization, silver's production increases, and the contraction of India's demand for silver, the only point that the full commission could agree on was that the changes in the relative values of gold and silver were despoiled by the actions of the Latin Union in demonetizing silver currencies. See Royal Commission to Inquire into Changes in Relative Values of Precious Metals, First Report, Mins. of Ev., Apps., 1887 (c.5099) XXII.1, GBSP; Royal Commission to Inquire into Changes in Relative Values of Precious Metals, Second Report, Mins. of Ev., Apps., 1888 (c.5248) XLV.1, GBSP.

25. Matsukata, *Adoption of the Gold Standard*, pp. 161–62.

and silver countries had stagnated, and that the number of business transactions between them had decreased. The commission also stated that the amount of capital invested by gold-standard countries in silver-standard countries had decreased significantly as the gold price of silver depreciated.[26] Thus, the silver standard had become an effective hindrance to the economic growth and development of silver-standard countries because it impeded the import of capital from the industrialized, gold-standard countries.[27]

The findings of the second area of investigation that the commission addressed, concerning the effects of silver's depreciation on Japan's economy, were the same as the findings for a silver-standard nation in the first area of investigation. That is, despite increases in the volume of trade and exports, silver's rapid depreciation and remarkable fluctuations had circumscribed Japan's ability to attract foreign capital and negotiate future trade and transactions. In addition, the free coinage of silver at the Japanese Imperial Mint was criticized, as it was found to have encouraged the importation of silver, which in turn was said to have led to the "growth of the habits of luxury."[28] The finding that the policy of free coinage of silver at the Japanese government's own mint had encouraged silver imports into Japan is most probable. Indeed, the same practice was seen elsewhere throughout the world, with the same results. The finding alluding to the "growth of the habits of luxury," however, had a distinctly moralistic tone and is impossible to substantiate. Perhaps the commission was referring to the increasing number of landowners and merchants who had begun to experience some of the luxuries previously enjoyed only by bureaucrats, industrialists, and royalty in the first half of the Meiji period. It must be remembered that before the Matsukata deflation took hold, landowners enjoyed unprecedented profits when silver's

---

26. Matsukata, *Adoption of the Gold Standard*, p. 161, and Yoshino, *En no rekishi*, p. 199.

27. A minority of the British Royal Commission members essentially agreed with the findings of the Japanese government's commission on the question of the effects of silver's depreciation on gold and silver economies. In particular, the difficulties of trade between gold and silver economies and the discouragement of investment by gold-standard economies in silver-standard economies were noted by the Royal Commission. See Royal Commission to Inquire into Changes in Relative Values of Precious Metals, Final Report, Mins. of Ev., App., 1888 (c.5512)(c.5512-1) XLV.285, 455, GBSP.

28. Matsukata, *Adoption of the Gold Standard*, p. 163, and Yoshino, *En no rekishi*, pp. 199–200. See Kato, "Development of the Monetary System," pp. 212–13.

depreciation, and the over-issue of paper currencies, fueled inflation in commodity prices. The price of rice more than doubled while, at the same time, land taxes were fixed and were paid in devalued currency.[29]

The commission's findings concerning the third area of investigation, whether silver's depreciation and subsequent price fluctuations demanded revision of Japan's monetary system, were by far the most controversial. The majority on the Currency Commission were unconvinced of the need to adopt the gold standard. Indeed, the commission stated that "the endless fall of the silver price in the future would be impossible and comparing the effects of the changes of the gold-silver ratio upon the country with those of a gold standard country we judge our advantage to be greater."[30] These views were broadly representative of Shibusawa Eichi, Meiji Japan's leading entrepreneur in business and finance, who forcefully argued that the declining value of the silver-standard yen, relative to the gold-standard currencies of Europe, had allowed Japanese exports to grow. Japan's de facto silver standard, in effect, served as a protective tariff (at a time when Japan was prohibited by "unequal" international treaties from raising tariffs) and encouraged exports. Based on his own commercial experiences, Shibusawa opined that the development of the domestic production of silk (that is, sericulture, filature, spinning, and weaving), paper, and tea were export led and thus very much assisted by the yen's being a silver-based currency. Still, while the majority of the commissioners were content with the de facto silver-standard monetary system, some members were in favor of waiting and watching the developments in the international monetary market, and yet other members proposed to lobby Western countries for the formation of an international bimetallic union, which they hoped Japan would later join.[31]

It appears, however, that the small group of men who were the very core of the Meiji regime were dissatisfied with the commission's reluctance to abandon the silver standard. These men, like Matsukata, who dominated Japan's economic modernization and industrialization in the

---

29. See Ohkawa and Rosovsky, "A Century of Economic Growth," pp. 64–65.

30. Shinjo, *History of the Yen*, p. 76.

31. Matsukata, *Adoption of the Gold Standard*, p. 165, and Yoshino, *En no rekishi*, p. 204. Interestingly, the British Royal Commission was also reticent to make any changes to its own standard. See Royal Commission to Inquire into Changes in Relative Values of Precious Metals, Final Report, Mins. of Ev., App., 1888 (c.5512)(c.5512-1) XLV.285, 455, GBSP, p. 338.

Meiji era, believed that Japan was in essentially the same economic situation as the industrialized nations, with whom the bulk of Japan's trade (some two-thirds, by volume) was conducted (Table 2.1).[32]

Thus, the bureaucrats, financiers, and new industrialists of the Meiji era decided that Japan would best be served by a strong "gold" currency that would increase Japan's ability to import foreign capital and thus find new capital with which to industrialize.[33] Indeed, against the backdrop of huge arms imports from the gold-standard economies to fight China, they realized that the export of primary commodities might decrease, but they strongly believed that Japan should move beyond exporting primary materials to developed economies, to exporting manufactured products to emerging markets in Asia. To facilitate such a transition, they argued for coinage reform and championed the adoption of a gold standard.[34] It appears that as a result of the influence of the gold-standard proponents the membership of the commission was enlarged, so that when the question of whether to revise the monetary system was examined, seven members maintained that there was no need to interfere with the silver standard, while six advocated the adoption of the gold standard and two favored the adoption of a bimetallic standard. Using this count to suit their own purposes, they reasoned that the majority of the commission had recommended changing Japan's monetary system, and that the greater part of that majority had proposed the adoption of the gold standard.[35]

The reasons for advocating the adoption of the gold standard were explained in the final section of the Currency Commission's report, alongside a report from the "minority," which maintained that the silver standard should be continued. The statement of the commission claimed that while Japan had benefited from the changes in the relative values of gold and silver, it was time for Japan to adopt the monetary system of its major trading partners and thus have the ability to compete in terms of

---

32. Matsukata, *Adoption of the Gold Standard*, p. 371.

33. "The Gold Standard in Japan," *TE*, 24 April 1897; "Japanese Trade, Tariffs, and Currency," *TE*, 19 June 1897; De Cecco, *Money and Empire*, pp. 52–61, especially p. 59; and Droppers, "Monetary Changes in Japan," p. 159.

34. Bryan, *Gold Standard at the Turn*, pp. 134–88; Kato, "Development of the Monetary System," p. 215; Matsukata, *Adoption of the Gold Standard*, p. 165.

35. Shinjo, *History of the Yen*, p. 76. For a different reading of events see Bryan, *Gold Standard at the Turn*, pp. 122–23.

Table 2.1. Trade with Gold- and Silver-Standard Countries, 1895–1913 (units: ¥1,000)

Year	Silver-standard countries		Gold-standard countries	
	Exports	Imports	Exports	Imports
1895	37,156	52,109	92,334	75,526
1896	43,704	63,115	66,911	106,749
1897	59,581	95,185	94,101	122,081
1898	75,133	129,479	82,226	144,771
1899	90,682	98,356	114,057	116,262
1900	95,017	92,573	95,419	189,154
1901	111,477	111,309	132,274	139,554
1902	101,269	123,376	147,252	142,569
1903	126,775	169,165	153,026	142,388
1904	134,532	182,539	173,641	178,644
1905	162,754	187,181	148,206	287,610
1906	198,084	165,837	212,181	240,187
1907	191,766	200,096	225,468	275,910
1908	157,401	168,273	205,989	253,459
1909	168,589	176,779	227,699	202,122
1910	186,280	226,058	252,272	218,462
1911	176,917	217,300	248,007	274,815
1912	218,728	260,048	283,002	330,325
1913	275,928	348,055	331,698	342,698

Source: Hamashita, "History of the Japanese Silver Yen," p. 335.

economic growth and progress. In opposition, the minority argued that silver's depreciation and fluctuations in the gold-to-silver ratio had been of great advantage to Japan's economic development, and that Japan should look toward the formation of an international bimetallic union. In accordance with the view of the supposed majority of the commission, preparations were made for the adoption of a gold standard at "some future opportune moment" when Japan commanded the gold reserves to make such a transition possible.[36]

---

36. Matsukata, *Adoption of the Gold Standard*, pp. 165, 184–85.

Negotiating the World's Largest Bank Check

By the time the Currency Commission submitted its proposal to the National Diet in July 1895, Japan had potentially secured a large gold reserve in the form of the Chinese indemnity. The Sino-Japanese War, declared by the governments of China and Japan on 1 August 1894, had ended on 17 April 1895 with the signing of the Treaty of Shimonoseki.[37] Under the terms of the treaty, the Chinese government agreed to pay an indemnity for war expenses of 200 million *kuping taels*.[38] In addition, the Chinese government, in a separate convention, agreed to the annual payment of 500,000 *kuping taels* to defray a quarter of the cost of the Japanese garrison stationed at Wei hai-wei (present-day Weihai), and in the Treaty respecting the Retrocession of the Liao-tung (Mukden) Peninsula, the Chinese government agreed to pay a further 30 million *kuping taels* as compensation for the retrocession of the southern portion of the Liao-tung (Liaodong) Peninsula.[39]

The technicalities of the payment of the indemnity by the Chinese government enabled the Japanese government to adopt the gold standard. The payments specified in the treaties pertaining to the Sino-Japanese War were to be made in *kuping taels*, with the *kuping tael* representing a specific weight (578.84 grains) of pure silver. As the *kuping tael* was not a unit of currency, the type of money in which the indemnity payments were to be made was a matter of negotiation. Despite being without office, Matsukata seized the opportunity, in May 1895, to submit two drafts to Prime Minister Ito Hirobumi concerning the "method and process of payment of the war indemnity." Matsukata proposed that China should pay the war indemnity in London with English pounds, directly

---

37. See Nish, *Japanese Foreign Policy*, pp. 34–40.

38. As specified in Draft No. 2 on the Method and Process and Payment of the War Indemnity, a *kuping tael* represents 579.84 grains (or 37.57 grams). See Matsukata, *Adoption of the Gold Standard*, p. 171.

39. Kajima, *The Diplomacy of Japan*, p. 264, and Matsukata, *Adoption of the Gold Standard*, pp. 166–67. Separate from the various payments, the Japanese were given a free hand in Korea, they were granted the Formosa and Pescadores island groups, and they were provided with the means to secure extensive commercial penetration within China. For full details of the "Treaty of Peace," with the Protocol, the Separate Articles, and Convention to Prolong the Armistice, refer to Kajima, *The Diplomacy of Japan*, pp. 262–67.

convertible to gold, thereby creating the gold reserve necessary for Japan's adoption of the gold standard.[40]

Matsukata suggested, within the text of the drafts, that payment in English currency was of benefit to the Chinese government, as it was known that China intended to raise loans in English or French currency for payment of the indemnity. Furthermore, the price of silver was likely to rise on so large a purchase and it was difficult to raise such a large purchase in the European markets. Moreover, transportation costs would be onerous, bank interest would be lost on the silver in transit, and the transfer of so large an amount of silver bullion from Europe to Asia, in so short a time, was likely to disturb the exchange rates, trade, and the general economic interests of the East Asian nations. Subsequently, on 6 October 1895, after intense negotiations between the governments of China and Japan, the Chinese government agreed with Japan that payment of the indemnity should take place in London using English currency. Thus, the Chinese indemnity amounted to £32.9 million, with a further £4.9 million being paid for the retrocession of the Liao-tung Peninsula and £82 thousand being paid by China to assist the occupation of Wei-hai-wei by Japanese forces.[41] When the first "quarter-payment with ancillaries" was made by the Chinese government, it was the largest bank check ever to be processed, totaling more than £11 million.[42]

The Coinage Law of 1897

The Japanese Treasury now had the necessary gold reserves to facilitate the adoption of the gold standard. Prime Minister Ito, having agreed to the payment of the Chinese indemnity in English pounds, nevertheless opposed the introduction of the gold standard on the same grounds as the seven Currency Commission members who had recommended that the silver standard be maintained. Perhaps Ito was also concerned about the adoption of a gold standard, as the transition to a gold standard would require the use of the Chinese indemnity as specie reserve, rather than to augment government spending. Nevertheless, after March

---

40. Matsukata, *Adoption of the Gold Standard*, pp. 168–71.

41. The figures supplied by Matsukata total £37,918,381. See Matsukata, *Adoption of the Gold Standard*, pp. 168–71.

42. Meiji zaiseishi henshukai, *Meiji zaiseishi*, 2:218–20. The check is often misrepresented as having been for £32 million or £38 million.

1896 Matsukata gradually undermined the credibility of the financial policy under the Ito government and allied himself with Okuma, a then-strident critic of the Ito government's foreign policy. Mounting criticism of the Ito government's handling of financial and foreign policy duly succeeded in forcing Ito to resign in September 1896. The Matsukata-Okuma government was established in the same month, and Matsukata was, for the second time, appointed as both the prime minister and the minister of finance.[43]

Matsukata could now legislate for the adoption of the gold standard, confident that his proposal would be sanctioned by the Diet. On 25 February 1897, he submitted drafts of the Coinage Law (Kaheihō) of 1897, subsidiary coinage laws, and an explanatory memorandum to his cabinet, which accepted his proposals and introduced the drafts of the new coinage laws into the Diet on 1 March 1897. On the first reading of the proposed laws, Matsukata addressed the House of Representatives in a long speech that discussed the history of currency in Japan, the state of domestic and international monetary affairs, and the laws that the Ministry of Finance had brought before the Diet. A twenty-seven member committee, formed by the House of Representatives, then reviewed the bills and reintroduced them into the House with their approval.[44]

Objections were raised to the coinage bills both outside and within the House of Representatives. Foreign interests were quite antagonistic to the proposed adoption of the gold standard, as indeed they had been when the gold standard was first proposed in 1871, and were unable to discern the process and motivations that guided its establishment.[45] On the floor of the parliament, domestic opposition was related to the possibility that discarded Japanese silver coinage would be returned to Japan, where it would disrupt the state's financial system. There were also concerns that Japan, having adopted a gold standard, would be unable to

---

43. Itagaki, Okuma, and Ukita, "Political Parties in Japan," pp. 172–74, and Yoshino, *En no rekishi*, pp. 207–11. Matsukata's second term as prime minister ended on 25 December 1897, in circumstances similar to those of his first dismissal as prime minister in 1891. That is, Matsukata's cabinet, made up with a strong Satsuma contingent, lost the confidence of its allies by refusing to take action on constitutional measures.

44. Matsukata, *Adoption of the Gold Standard*, pp. 174–92.

45. "Japanese Politics and Finance," *The Economist* (hereafter, *TE*), 20 March 1897; "The Japanese Gold Standard," *The Times* (London; hereafter, *TT*), 21 April 1897; and "The Gold Standard in Japan," *TE*, 24 April 1897.

maintain a gold reserve adequate to meet the convertibility obligations of the new standard. Furthermore, many predicted that foreign trade, which had prospered from silver's depreciation, would decrease in such volume as a result of Japan's adopting the gold standard that it would be an unmitigated disaster for the country. Finally, it was also suggested that future depreciation of the gold price of silver might prevent Japan from effectively competing with China, and other silver standard countries, in exporting commodities and goods to gold countries.[46]

Despite objections, Matsukata rigorously defended the proposed adoption of the gold standard in his earlier addresses to the House of Representatives. According to Matsukata, research by foreign consuls revealed that discarded Japanese silver coinage found in China, Hong Kong, Singapore, and Southeast Asia was disfigured and thus posed no threat to Japan's domestic currency.[47] In reality, however, the amount of silver yen found overseas, particularly in Hong Kong and Singapore, was significant and represented a tangible threat to the integrity of the Japanese monetary system. Foreign holdings of Japanese specie were estimated by the Ministry of Finance to be worth ¥10 million, and the Meiji regime had, in fact, asked the British government to make the silver yen legal tender in its Southeast Asian and Hong Kong colonies, in the hope that foreign and Japanese merchants would release silver to be minted in Japan.[48] Similarly, charges that Japan would be unable to maintain a gold standard were curtly dismissed by Matsukata, who simply argued that Japan's geographical position enabled it to readily procure gold from China and Korea, and, if necessary, from Australia or even the gold market in Hong Kong.[49]

In regard to the objections concerning the effects of the adoption of a gold standard on foreign trade, Matsukata argued that the depreciating price of silver was not the decisive factor in increasing Japan's foreign

---

46. Matsukata, *Adoption of the Gold Standard*, pp. 188–90.

47. Matsukata, *Adoption of the Gold Standard*, p. 188.

48. See Ando to Price, 9 September 1878, FOJ; Hennessey to Hicks-Beach, 14 September 1878, *FOJ*; Hennessey to Parkes, 26 September 1878, FOJ; Parkes to Hennessey, 9 October 1878, *FOJ*; Parkes to Hennessey, 11 October 1878, FOJ; Parkes to Hennessey, 24 October 1878, *FOJ*; Terashima to Parkes, 23 October 1878, FOJ; King, *History of the Hongkong and Shanghai Banking Corporation*, pp. 224–29; and Matsukata, *Adoption of the Gold Standard*, pp. 243–307.

49. Matsukata, *Adoption of the Gold Standard*, pp. 188–90, 238–42.

trade; rather, increased exports from Japan were also a result of more effective transport and communications infrastructure and the progress of education. Concerns that silver-standard countries such as China might benefit from the further depreciation of silver were, once again, dismissed by Matsukata, who explained that in Great Britain the Indian Coinage Reform Commission had reported that such suppositions were groundless. Nevertheless, fears that Japan's foreign trade could be placed at a disadvantage by silver's depreciation in relation to gold were far from unfounded. Fortunately for Japan, however, its agricultural products, which for many long years had carried Japan's efforts toward industrialization, did not generally compete with those of the silver-standard nations. For example, Japanese silk competed for the same markets as Italian silk but did not generally interfere with silk production in China or elsewhere in Southeast Asia. Clearly, then, the Meiji government had to consider carefully the merit of staying on a depreciating silver standard, which decreased the price of exports and increased the price of imports, when Japanese trade was predominantly with gold-standard nations (see Table 2.1). Despite the degree of opposition described and some unsuccessful attempts to amend the bills, the proposals brought to the Diet by Matsukata were passed through both houses without amendment, and received imperial sanction from the emperor on 26 March 1897.[50]

The Coinage Law of 1897's reformation of Japan's monetary system finally enabled the adoption of the gold standard, which had first been proposed twenty-six years earlier in the New Coinage Act of 1871. Using as archetypes the National Bank of Belgium's newly drafted regulations and statutes and, to some extent, the Bank of England's banking principles, the Coinage Law of 1897 defined the operational nature of gold circulation, and the "cover system" that linked the amount of bank notes and other currencies in circulation to the state's gold reserves.[51] The Coinage Law of 1897 introduced new gold coins in denominations of ¥5, ¥10, and ¥20. These were not, however, for general use. They were talismans—proud symbols of the gold standard's establishment in Japan. For purposes

---

50. Matsukata, *Adoption of the Gold Standard*, p. 189, and "A Gold Standard for Japan," *TT*, 2 March 1897.

51. The laws regarding the convertibility requirements of Japanese currency, and more generally the laws associated with the introduction of the gold standard, were literally, word by word and article for article, modeled on the operation of the National Bank of Belgium. See Schiltz, "An 'Ideal Bank of Issue,'" pp. 179–96.

of accounting, the gold value of each unit of yen was fixed at 750 milligrams of pure gold, exactly half the gold content of the yen coins minted in 1871.[52] The change in the gold yen's composition (its weight and purity), of course, reflected the corresponding depreciation of the gold price of silver (and hence the silver-standard yen) over the same twenty-six-year period. Nevertheless, the circulation of gold specie would be avoided, despite the absence of *cours force* legislation, because Japan's developing economy could not support a large domestic circulation of gold as exemplified in France or Germany.[53] The Convertible Bank Note Act was passed to maintain the fiduciary issue of convertible banknotes, measured against government bonds, treasury bills, or corporate bonds, at the value of ¥85 million.[54] Subsequently, the Convertible Bank Note Act was revised to allow Bank of Japan's bank notes, which had been convertible to silver since June 1885, to be made convertible to gold.[55] And so, on 1 October 1897, as prescribed by the Coinage Law of 1897, Japan adopted the gold standard.[56]

---

52. "The Japanese Gold Standard Law," *TT*, 31 March 1897; "The Gold Standard in Japan," *TE*, 24 April 1897; Laughlin, "The Gold Standard in Japan," pp. 378–83; and Yoshino, *En no rekishi*, p. 210.

53. *Cours force*, or *corso forzoso*, refers to the institution of legal restrictions on the convertibility of paper currency to gold, in effect forcing the fiduciary issue and circulation of paper currency in place of gold. See De Cecco, *Money and Empire*, pp. 56–57. Moreover, the form and intent of the Bank of England's operation of the gold standard were not always clearly understood. See Keynes, *Indian Currency and Finance*, pp. 15–36.

54. Just two years later, in 1899, the fiduciary issue was increased to ¥120 million. In addition, an "excess issue" regulation, which had been in force since 1871, allowed the minister of finance to increase the amount of paper money in circulation according to the fluctuations of the market. See Laughlin, "The Gold Standard in Japan," pp. 378–83, and Shinjo, *History of the Yen*, pp. 80–83.

55. Yoshino, *En no rekishi*, pp. 214–15. Technically, it may be argued Japan's gold standard was in fact a "gold bullion" standard, that is, in effect a gold standard for financial institutions, as the Bank of Japan guaranteed the convertibility of banknotes with highly expensive monetary gold bullion, rather than gold specie, to restrict the public circulation of gold specie. See Yamasaki, *Honpō kaheiseido kaiseiron*, pp. 1–60, especially pp. 2–11, and Crowther, *An Outline on Money*, pp. 314–15.

56. The gold-standard system would remain in operation until September 1917, when the Japanese government was forced to place an embargo on the export of gold, and yen-denominated bank notes became (not only in reality, but legally) inconvertible to gold. See Shinjo, *History of the Yen*, pp. 83–84.

CHAPTER 3

The Gold Standard and Japan's
Economic Development, 1884–1917

Following the formal adoption of the gold standard in October 1897, Japan enjoyed an unprecedented period of openness toward foreign capital distinguished by rapid economic development. Whereas the role of the depreciating silver standard from 1875 to 1897 in assisting the growth and development of Japan's economy—by increasing the competitiveness of Japanese exports and thus keeping the balance of trade payments in Japan's favor, while at the same time offsetting domestic inflation—is widely noted, the role of the gold standard is often ignored.[1] As the nature of Japanese economic growth and development has changed over time, the gold-standard era came to be perceived as a complex and problematic episode in Japanese economic history. Certainly the adoption of the gold standard by Japan has been strongly criticized since the mid-1920s, and in more recent scholarship it has been seen as a primary cause of economic deflation and depression.[2] Nevertheless we should not lose sight of the fact that the gold standard also operated as a dynamic "engine of development," or powerful developmental factor, as was

---

1. See Allen, *A Short Economic History*, p. 52; Key, *The Long-Term Capital Pattern*, p. 5; Shinjo, *History of the Yen*, p. 94; M. Shinohara, "Economic Development and Foreign Trade," p. 229; K. Takahashi, *Rise and Development*, p. 299; and Yamazawa and Yamamoto, "Trade and Balance of Payments," p. 146.

2. See Ishibashi, "Kin yushutsu kaikin," pp. 539–62, and Metzler, *Lever of Empire*, pp. 115–95.

widely acknowledged during the early twentieth century.[3] An entirely positive view of the gold standard was a mainstay of financial orthodoxy in Japan until the economy began to spin seemingly out of control in the months and years following the Great Kanto earthquake of 1 September 1923.[4] For some, the luster of the gold standard never tarnished until Japan's abandonment of it in 1931, or until the international system of the gold-standard exchange collapsed entirely. Undeniably, however, the long nineteenth-century shine of the gold standard was blackened by its early twentieth-century end. The dynamic, developmental aspect of Japan's establishment of the gold standard has thus been largely neglected in postwar economic historiography, although the work of Takahashi Kamekichi, the prominent, prolific economist and one-time editor of the *Oriental Economist*, is a significant exception.[5]

Recent scholarship has sought to pay attention to issues surrounding the gold standard and thus redress one of the most pressing myopias of postwar Japanese economic historiography. For Metzler, the gold standard is nothing less than the "lever of empire," and its role is of central importance in the works of Smethurst, Schiltz, and a growing number of other scholars.[6] Bryan's compelling treatise on the meaning of the gold standard as seen from Japanese and Argentinean perspectives explores how and why the standard was established and maintained.[7] Arguably, though, while the question of the gold standard in the latter part of the nineteenth century has been dealt with in some detail for other advanced industrialized economies, it has yet to be adequately explained for Japan. In particular, what is the significance of the gold standard in Japan's economic growth and development, and how did its adoption promote Japan's remarkable experience of industrialization in the later Meiji period and beyond? Critically, the link between economic growth and development in the Meiji era and the massive importation of foreign

---

3. See Kindleberger, *The World in Depression*, p. 44.

4. An uncomfortable reminder of the appalling power of natural disasters to damage the economic underpinnings of modern Japanese society.

5. K. Takahashi, *Rise and Development*.

6. Metzler, *Lever of Empire*; Smethurst, *Takahashi Korekiyo, Japan's Keynes*; and Schiltz, *The Money Doctors from Japan*.

7. Bryan, *The Gold Standard at the Turn*, especially chaps. 7 to 9.

capital that resulted from Japan's transition to the gold standard needs to be put into sharper focus.[8]

The Matsukata Deflation and Economic Development in the Mid-Meiji Period

The Japanese economy began to show definite signs of growth and development after Matsukata took hold of monetary policy in the latter half of the 1880s and created a stable and convertible currency through severe economic deflation. That is, during the late 1880s the Japanese economy, using the achievements of the traditional economy as a base, began to expand in both a quantitative sense, as can be demonstrated by increases in gross national product, and in a qualitative sense, as characterized by the movement of labor and capital from agricultural production to industrial production in urban centers.[9] The so-called Matsukata deflation allowed Japan to meet vital preconditions of economic development, providing the Meiji regime with the means to raise adequate finances by creating a stable monetary system on a de facto silver standard, which was conducive to both domestic and international commerce.[10] Moreover, the privatization campaign that accompanied the Matsukata deflation increased government revenue and placed increased amounts of labor and capital in industry, and in doing so supported the development of zaibatsu.[11] Thus, in the period after the Matsukata deflation, the Japanese economy entered into a period of industrialization, or modern economic growth.[12]

---

8. Such a focus presages Part II of *Investing Japan*, "Foreign Capital and the Prewar Japanese Economy."

9. See Ohkawa and Rosovsky, "Capital Formation in Japan," p. 150, and Ito, *The Japanese Economy*, pp. 15–17.

10. Ohkawa and Rosovsky, "A Century of Economic Growth," p. 66.

11. Allen, *A Short Economic History*, p. 42; Ohkawa and Rosovsky, "A Century of Economic Growth," p. 90.

12. See Crawcour, "Industrialization and Technological Change," pp. 391–436, and T. Nakamura, *Economic Growth in Prewar Japan*, pp. 59–69. The concept put forward by S. Kuznets suggests that "modern economic growth" consists of the application of modern technology and scientific thought to agriculture, industry, and transport; a rapid and sustained increase in "real product per capita" combined with high rates of population growth; transformation of the industrial structure; and the presence of international contacts. All of these components must be present, to some extent, for modern economic growth to be said to have occurred. Ohkawa and Rosovsky use Kuznets's

In the 1890s, important events were to accelerate the pace of Japan's economic growth and development. The war against China was one such crucial event. Victory in the Sino-Japanese War provided Japan with a huge indemnity equivalent to almost £38 million, or ¥365 million. Expressed another way, the value of the Chinese indemnity was greater than Japan's total import deficits for the ten years after the commencement of hostilities in the Sino-Japanese War.[13] Under the terms of the Treaty of Shimonoseki, Japan was also provided with new economic opportunities in East Asia, in the form of political dominance in Korea, the cession of the Formosa and Pescadores island groups, a garrison stationed at Wei hai-wei (Weihai) in China's Shantung (Shandong) Province, and unprecedented commercial possibilities inside China.[14]

The adoption of the gold standard in October 1897 was to provide a new and powerful stimulus to the growth and development of the Japanese economy. The transition from a de facto silver standard to a gold standard, as described in the previous two chapters, was largely facilitated by a long program of strenuous domestic monetary reform and the use of the Sino-Japanese War's resultant indemnity as a gold reserve. The relative ease with which the Coinage Law of 1897 passed through both houses of the Diet belied the arduous processes, and consummate politicking, that allowed Japan's monetary, financial, and economic systems to be reformed. That is to say, Japan's successful adoption of the gold standard, and the other reforms required by the Coinage Law of 1897, may be accounted for by a variety of domestic and international factors. In Meiji Japan, for example, gold and silver were rarely found among the populace, and that enabled the Bank of Japan (through the auspices of the Yokohama Specie Bank) to procure adequate reserves of precious metals without having to maintain a large domestic circulation of either gold or silver currency. Moreover, the fact that there was very little direct foreign investment in commerce or industry prior to 1897 simplified the politicking behind Japan's introduction of a gold standard: fervid warnings of a foreign commercial invasion failed to either capture the public's

---

criteria to argue that modern economic growth occurred in Japan during 1886. See Ohkawa and Rosovsky, "A Century of Economic Growth," p. 53.

13. Total import deficits for the decade amounted to ¥352 million. See Baba and Tatemono, "Foreign Trade and Economic Growth," p. 175.

14. Kajima, *The Diplomacy of Japan*, pp. 262–72.

imagination or gain wide traction. Japan's Ministry of Finance was also fortunate that silver's continuous depreciation in value abated during the period of the transition to the gold standard, enabling the sale of silver specie in Hong Kong and Shanghai at a loss of no more than 7 percent of its nominal face value. Furthermore, the Ministry of Finance could also offload extraneous specie on the new Japanese colonies of Formosa, Wei hai-wei, and the nominally independent Korea.[15] The gold standard's adoption and the attendant monetary reform, therefore, were accepted because at a societal level commodity prices and the financial obligations of debtors and creditors remained relatively constant. The successful transition to the gold standard was thus to herald a new era of unprecedented economic growth and development in the Japanese economy.[16]

Currency Stabilization, Trade Recovery, and the Meiji "Modernization" Boom

While the depreciation of Japan's currency under the de facto silver standard made Japanese exports competitive, counterbalanced domestic inflation, and encouraged industrialization, it also effectively prevented Japanese enterprise from utilizing foreign capital, particularly in the form of technology.[17] The extent of the depreciation of the yen under the de facto silver standard can be demonstrated by examining the yen's purchasing power in relation to the U.S. dollar. In 1873, ¥100 purchased, on average, $100.58; during 1885 the same value of yen purchased an average of $84.78; and by 1897, just before Japan adopted the gold standard, Japanese currency had declined to the extent that ¥100 was able to purchase, on average, only $49.31 (see Table 3.1). Moreover, the overall trend of the yen's depreciation on the international markets was often subject to violent fluctuations, which were detrimental to the profits of Japanese manufacturers, and to exporters who had made, or required, long-term commitments. Worse still, fluctuations in the value of Japan's

---

15. Hamashita, "Japanese Silver Yen," pp. 327–38, and Matsukata, *Adoption of the Gold Standard*, pp. 309–41, especially, pp. 333–36.

16. Matsukata, *Adoption of the Gold Standard*, pp. 347–48, 370–71.

17. Allen, *A Short Economic History*, p. 52; Key, *The Long-Term Capital Pattern*, p. 5; Shinjo, *History of the Yen*, p. 94; Shinohara, "Economic Development and Foreign Trade," p. 229; K. Takahashi, *Rise and Development*, p. 299; and Yamazawa and Yamamoto, "Trade and Balance of Payments," p. 146.

Table 3.1. Yen Exchange Values in Dollars and Pounds, 1874–1910 (units: per ¥100)

Year	Pounds/100 yen			Dollars/100 yen		
	High	Low	Average	High	Low	Average
1874	21.3	20.4	20.9	103.0	100.0	101.5
1875	20.6	19.9	20.2	104.5	96.0	100.2
1876	21.1	18.8	19.9	101.5	90.0	95.6
1877	20.8	19.5	20.1	100.0	93.5	96.7
1878	19.5	17.8	18.6	95.0	86.5	90.7
1879	19.4	17.4	18.3	74.5	85.0	89.6
1880	19.4	18.3	18.8	95.3	89.3	92.2
1881	19.0	18.2	19.6	91.3	86.5	89.9
1882	19.1	18.0	18.5	93.0	88.0	90.5
1883	19.0	18.0	18.5	91.5	87.7	89.6
1884	18.7	17.7	18.2	90.7	86.5	88.6
1885	17.9	16.9	17.3	87.0	81.7	84.3
1886	16.9	14.9	15.9	81.7	72.7	77.1
1887	16.7	15.2	15.9	80.3	73.0	76.5
1888	15.8	14.9	15.3	76.3	72.5	74.4
1889	16.2	15.1	15.6	78.8	73.5	76.1
1890	19.2	15.3	17.1	93.0	74.7	83.4
1891	17.4	15.5	16.4	84.7	75.0	79.7
1892	15.5	13.4	14.4	75.0	65.5	70.1
1893	13.8	11.4	12.5	67.0	54.5	60.4
1894	11.5	5.7	8.1	55.0	47.3	55.4
1895	11.2	9.6	10.4	54.5	46.7	50.5
1896	11.1	10.3	10.7	52.0	49.6	50.8
1897	10.6	9.9	10.3	51.5	48.1	49.8
1898	10.2	10.0	10.1	49.6	48.5	49.1
1899	10.3	10.1	10.2	50.0	49.0	49.6
1900	10.1	10.1	10.1	49.5	49.0	49.2
1901	10.2	10.1	10.1	46.6	49.1	49.4
1902	10.3	10.1	10.2	50.0	49.4	49.7
1903	10.3	10.1	10.2	50.9	49.0	49.5
1904	10.1	10.0	10.1	49.3	48.6	48.9

Table 3.1. (continued)

Year	Pounds/100 yen			Dollars/100 yen		
	High	Low	Average	High	Low	Average
1905	10.3	10.1	10.2	49.9	49.1	49.5
1906	10.2	10.1	10.2	49.5	49.3	49.4
1907	10.2	10.2	10.2	49.6	49.3	49.4
1908	10.2	10.2	10.2	49.5	49.3	49.4
1909	10.2	10.2	10.2	49.6	49.4	49.5
1910	10.2	10.1	10.1	49.6	49.3	49.4

Source: T. Nakamura, *Economic Growth in Prewar Japan*, p. 33.

currency on the international financial markets encouraged capital to be invested in speculation, rather than in enterprises that would directly contribute to Japan's economic growth and development.[18]

Japan's adoption of the gold standard was also a powerful stimulus to economic development in the later part of the Meiji era, in the sense that it permitted a large-scale importation of Western technology and capital. Japanese and Western merchants, traders, manufacturers, and industrialists could now invest with confidence and undertake longer-term projects with the assurance that exchange rates would not change. An unnamed "Eastern financial agent" residing in London once remarked that he had never been able to borrow money on behalf of his government "so cheaply" as when his government introduced the gold standard. Tellingly, "the effect was as immediate as that of *touching the button in ringing an electric bell. No sooner did the news of the adoption* reach the lending money market than the drop in rates took place."[19]

Likewise, foreign capital was encouraged by the conclusion of Japan's monetary experiments with various paper monies, bimetallism, and deflationary policies, which had previously deterred investment.[20] Matsukata was quick to trumpet that it was not until the gold standard was adopted that the Japanese government was able to borrow (in June 1899) at 4 percent. Previous loans, also raised in London, were made at rates of

18. Masuda, "The Foreign Trade of Japan," p. 628, and M. Takahashi, *Modern Japanese Economy*, pp. 299–303. Also see Bryan, *Gold Standard at the Turn*, pp. 124–30.

19. Hsu, "The Need and Method of Immediate Reforms," p. 228, emphasis added.

20. Lockwood, *Economic Development of Japan*, p. 322, and Masuda, "The Foreign Trade of Japan," pp. 628–29.

at 9, 7, and 5 percent. The new differences in interest rates presented the tantalizing proposition that earlier high-interest, domestic government debts could be refinanced, or converted into low-interest foreign loans, thus saving the government millions of yen in debt repayments.[21] Through the lens of the gold standard, the foreign investor saw a "strengthened state" of Japanese credit.[22] As Matsukata also commented in 1899:

> Since now that the capitalists of the gold standard countries have become assured that they will no longer be in constant danger of suffering unexpected losses from investments made in this country [Japan], on account of the fluctuations in the price of silver, they seem to show a growing tendency to make such investments. . . . This tendency, if encouraged, will doubtless bring about a closer connection between this country and the central money markets of the world.[23]

Japan had now assimilated with the capitalist world market, and the importance of the gold standard, in allowing foreign capital to be utilized, was paramount.

Certainly the Sino-Japanese War yielded the Chinese indemnity, increased Japan's prestige, and encouraged investment and industrialization. What is most significant, however, is that, of all the purposes to which such a large indemnity could have been put, the Chinese indemnity was used to adopt the gold standard, in order that it might have the greatest impact on Japan's economic growth and development.[24] Indeed, the period after the adoption of the gold standard was dominated by a postwar investment boom that allowed new technologies to penetrate both the public and private sectors of the Japanese economy. Mindful of the tensions that had been created in East Asia by the Sino-Japanese War and by the "Triple Intervention" of France, Germany, and Russia in the settlement of the conflict, the Meiji government decided to embark on a policy of rapid development, especially in those areas related to national defense. The government's modernization program now accommodated the spheres of the military, both army and navy; transport, particularly railway construction and shipbuilding; heavy industry, most notably the founding of the government-owned Yawata

---

21. See Part II, "Foreign Capital and the Prewar Japanese Economy."
22. Hsu, "The Need and Method of Immediate Reforms," p. 228.
23. Matsukata, *Adoption of the Gold Standard*, p. 348.
24. K. Takahashi, *Rise and Development*, p. 300.

Steel Works; education, primarily the development of the Imperial universities (*teidai*); and, finally, the establishment of parastatal financial institutions, the so-called special banks (*tokushu ginkō*).[25] The high level of state-led investment continued through to the end of the Meiji era, further driven later by the exigencies of the Russo-Japanese War.[26]

Japan's new openness to foreign capital after the 1897 adoption of the gold standard did more than just promote economic growth and development; it also eased deficit problems with Japan's international balance of payments. Although the significance of the continuity that the gold-standard exchange provided to Japan's international monetary relations cannot be readily measured, it *was* important.[27] As the Meiji regime's policy slogan of *Shokusan kogyō*, or Increase Production—Promote Industry, was replaced by the partisan slogan *Fukoku kyōhei*, Enrich the Country—Strengthen the Military, increasing amounts of foreign capital were being invested in Japan's military juggernaut. Yet even during the Russo-Japanese War, when most of the increased inflow of foreign capital was used to wage war, a substantial portion was also used to advance the industrialization of Japan's economy.[28] For example, the Yawata Steel Works' operations were expanded to match the growth of other heavy industrial sectors, exemplified by the contemporary expansion

---

25. In addition to the Bank of Japan and the Yokohama Specie Bank, seven parastatal "special" banks were established in the latter part of the Meiji period. Radiating out from the main Japanese island of Honshu to Hokkaido and then on to Taiwan and Korea, these were: the Agricultural Bank of Japan, the Hypothec Bank of Japan, the Industrial Bank of Japan, the Hokkaido Colonial Bank, the Bank of Taiwan, the Industrial Promotion Bank of Chosen, and the Bank of Chosen, formerly the Bank of Korea. See Allen, *A Short Economic History*, pp. 47–55; Pressnell, *Money and Banking in Japan*, pp. 15–19; Sarasas, *Money and Banking*, pp. 234–78; Shibusawa, "The Development of Banking," pp. 527–29; and Shinjo, *History of the Yen*, pp. 92–93.

26. Allen, *A Short Economic History*, p. 43; Baba and Tatemono, "Foreign Trade and Economic Growth," p. 175; Pressnell, *Money and Banking in Japan*, pp. 15–19; Shinohara, "Economic Development and Foreign Trade," p. 229; and K. Takahashi, *Rise and Development*, pp. 297–99.

27. Shinohara, "Economic Development and Foreign Trade," p. 229, and Suzuki, *Japanese Government Loan Issues*, pp. 65–66, 165–74, 180.

28. K. Takahashi, *Rise and Development*, pp. 302–3. Of course, the tremendous importation of foreign capital, often connected with military expenditures, which doubled for each of the last three decades of the Meiji era, would eventually cause problems of its own. See Boulding and Gleason, "War as an Investment," pp. 240–61, especially pp. 250, 257; Emi, *Government Fiscal Activity*, pp. 140–41.

Table 3.2. Foreign Trade during the Meiji Era, 1868–1911
(units: ¥1,000)

Year	Exports	Imports	Balance
1868	15,553	10,693	4,860
1869	12,909	20,784	−7,875
1870	14,543	33,742	−19,199
1871	17,696	21,917	−4,221
1872	17,026	26,175	−9,149
1873	21,635	28,107	−6,472
1874	19,317	23,462	−4,145
		24,487	−5,170
1875	18,611	29,976	−11,365
		31,899	−13,288
1876	27,712	23,965	3,747
		26,544	1,168
1877	23,349	27,421	−4,072
		29,979	−6,630
1878	25,988	32,875	−6,887
		37,722	−11,734
1879	28,176	32,953	−4,777
		38,015	−9,839
1880	28,395	36,627	−8,232
		42,246	−13,851
1881	31,059	31,191	−132
		35,767	−4,708
1882	37,722	29,447	8,275
		33,354	4,368
1883	36,268	28,445	7,823
		32,449	3,819
1884	33,871	29,673	4,198
		33,617	254
1885	37,147	29,357	7,790
		33,499	3,648
1886	48,876	32,168	16,708
		37,264	11,612

Table 3.2. (*continued*)

Year	Exports	Imports	Balance
1887	52,408	44,304	8,104
		53,153	−745
1888	65,706	65,455	251
1889	70,061	66,104	3,957
1890	56,604	81,729	−25,125
1891	79,527	62,927	16,600
1892	71,103	91,326	−20,223
1893	89,713	88,257	1,456
1894	113,246	117,482	−4,236
1895	136,112	129,261	6,851
1896	117,843	171,694	−53,851
1897	163,135	219,301	−56,166
1898	165,754	277,508	−111,754
1899	229,497	243,332	−13,835
1900	220,134	326,929	−106,795
1901	274,807	295,044	−20,237
1902	285,094	300,938	−15,844
1903	315,238	332,404	−17,166
1904	342,078	384,391	−42,313
1905	345,738	500,029	−154,291
1906	454,103	465,107	−11,004
1907	463,363	515,286	−51,923
1908	408,302	464,279	−55,977
1909	443,672	416,257	27,415
1910	495,029	508,379	−13,350
1911	485,458	572,021	−86,563

Source: Shinjo, *History of the Yen*, p. 89, and Yamamoto, *Ryō kara en he*, p. 228.

Note: Two sets of figures are given for the years 1874 through 1887, when Japan had a de facto silver standard (upper amount: unadjusted in gold terms; lower: adjusted for disparities in gold and silver yen exchange values).

The balances, showing either a trade surplus or deficit, have been recalculated by the author.

in shipbuilding and railway construction. Unlike the development of light industry that characterized the late 1870s and the 1880s, the industrial revolution from 1890 onward was distinguished by the expansion and development of heavy industry. The cumulative value of these contributions to growth is expressed in the remarkable increase in international trade that Japan experienced, in part, on the basis of the adoption of the gold standard (see Table 3.2).[29]

Clearly the role played by the Matsukata deflation in promoting economic growth and development in the late 1880s was significant. Again, during the 1890s the effect of the Sino-Japanese War and the resultant indemnity (which enabled Japan to adopt the gold standard) were important new factors. After Japan achieved victory in the war against China and adopted the gold standard, there was a new incentive, an international prestige to investing in Japan that attracted unprecedented amounts of foreign and domestic capital to productive investments, rather than speculative ones. The subsequent large-scale importation of capital in the form of modern technologies, through comprehensive modernization programs, inspired confidence in Japan's use of foreign and domestic capital, and facilitated its alliance with the most powerful creditor nation of the period. When the individual effects of these events are combined, a new explanation of the powerful forces that drove industrialization in the late-Meiji era emerges, and in each of these key determinants of economic growth and development in the Meiji period, the presence of a gold standard was an important component. That is, at a critical moment in its history, distinguished by rapid economic growth and development, Japan made extensive use of borrowed foreign capital that it would have been unable to attract or utilize without having adopted the gold standard.

---

29. Lockwood, *Economic Development of Japan*, p. 268, and Shinjo, *History of the Yen*, pp. 95–96.

PART II

Foreign Capital and the
Prewar Japanese Economy

CHAPTER 4

British Capital and the
Japanese Economy, 1897–1923

Official relations between Great Britain and Japan began on 12 August 1858, when the HMS *Furious* passed by Kanagawa, ignoring established *bakufu* protocol, and sailed directly into Edo Bay, anchoring within full view of the shogun's castle. On board the *Furious* was Lord Elgin, who had been entrusted with the mission of establishing diplomatic relations between Great Britain and Japan. Initially, negotiations stalled, owing to Elgin's steadfast refusal to proceed to Kanagawa; by 26 August, however, both parties had come to terms and the Treaty of Edo and Regulations for Trade was signed. Just as suddenly as it had come, the *Furious* then departed with promises of future diplomatic and economic cooperation. Elgin was well satisfied by his achievement, for within the space of just two weeks he had secured a trade treaty for the British government, while the conclusion of similar treaties by the governments of the United States and Russia had taken more than five years to realize.[1]

Such were the unlikely beginnings of modern Anglo-Japanese relations—a relationship that would cycle over the course of the following century from one of friendship and alliance to one of antagonism and war. Within the context of diplomatic and political considerations, this chapter will examine the role of British capital in the development

---

1. Beasley, *Great Britain and the Opening of Japan*, pp. 168–93. See Crow, *He Opened the Door*; Dickins and Lane-Poole, *Sir Harry Parkes*, pp. 20–21; and Lensen, *Russia's Japan Expedition*.

of the Japanese economy, most specifically from the time of the formation of the Anglo-Japanese alliance in 1897 until the official end of the alliance in 1923. The significance of the financial elements intricately involved in the formation of the alliance will be discussed, with an emphasis on loans being floated in London for the imperial Japanese government, and the subsequent use of those loans by the Japanese state to develop its national economy. Finally, we will consider questions relating to the wider consequences of Japanese-government borrowing in order to provide a clearer understanding of the Anglo-Japanese alliance and the corresponding financial relationship it engendered.

On the Relationship between Commerce and Finance

With the opening of Japan's treaty ports in 1 July 1859 came an influx of foreign merchants and firms, mostly British, all eager to trade and to profit from Japan's recently initiated cultural, economic, and political transformation.[2] At that time, payments for all international purchases and trade transactions were made through the exchange of precious metals, in the form of bullion and specie, or in the transfer of bills of exchange or banknotes, often directly convertible to silver or gold. Initially, significant disparities between the Japanese and international currency-exchange systems provided Japanese administrators with their most immediate problems and foreign merchants with profits so lucrative that foreign trade in Japan was referred to as the "Yokohama Gold Rush."[3]

Despite the early imbalances, international trade rapidly expanded to become an important component of the new Meiji economy. Indeed, by the 1890s a structure had emerged wherein the bulk of Japan's trade was

---

2. The treaty ports of Nagasaki, Hakodate, and Kanagawa (Yokohama) were opened on 1 July 1859, and the remaining ports of Hyogo (now Kobe) and Niigata were opened as of 1 January 1868. See Checkland, *Britain's Encounter with Meiji Japan*, pp. 20–24. Borton, *Japan's Modern Century*, p. 222, and Dickins and Lane-Poole, *Sir Harry Parkes*, pp. 29–30.

3. See Arbuthnot to Treasury on Japanese Currency, 1862–63, 1863 (513) L.25, GBSP, pp. 25–53; Murphy, "Neither Out Far Nor In Deep," pp. 236–48; Takekoshi, *Economic Aspects*, pp. 317–37; and Yamamoto, *Ryō kara en he*, pp. 59, 69–70. Mikami, *Edo no kahei monogatari*, pp. 269–87, and Shinjo, *History of the Yen*, pp. 7–10. Also see S. J. Bytheway and M. Chaiklin, "Reconsidering the Yokohama Gold Rush of 1859," forthcoming.

directed toward the British Empire (Great Britain and its colonies and dominions), the United States (which after 1898 included Hawaii and the Philippines), and China. Generally, Japan enjoyed a favorable balance of trade with the United States, which received the greater portion of Japan's exports, but Japan accumulated a considerable trade deficit against the British Empire, as Japan's imports were largely from British India, Great Britain, and the other British dominions.[4] Accordingly, revision of the terms of trade, as stipulated in the early treaties, was the focus of intense diplomatic activity by the Japanese government, which felt humiliated and restrained by the imposition of the West's "unequal treaties." Eventually Japan's sustained diplomatic effort was rewarded when, in 1894, the British government acceded to Japanese requests. Under the terms of the Anglo-Japanese Commercial Treaty, signed on 16 July 1894, Britain agreed to relinquish its extraterritoriality privileges relating to the treaty ports in 1899, and to renegotiate a new ad valorem import tariff.[5] Using the treaty with the British as the model, the Japanese government was then able to revise its treaties with other foreign powers. Thus, as of 1 July 1899 Japan had put an end to forty years of treaty ports and extraterritoriality privileges as defined by the so-called unequal treaties and, in doing so it had won an important psychological victory and reasserted its economic independence.[6]

After the Sino-Japanese War of 1894–1895, it was clear to all that Japan was no longer threatened by the economic colonialism of the foreign powers. Through victory in the war with China, Japan had won unprecedented international recognition, prestige, and political influence. The events surrounding the Triple Intervention of France, Germany, and Russia

---

4. Spalding, *Eastern Exchange Currency and Finance*, pp. 153–62. For example, in 1914 Great Britain (including its colonies and dominions), the United States (including Hawaii and the Philippines), and China dominated 78% of Japan's foreign trade. The total value of Japan's trade with Great Britain, with its colonies and dominions, was valued at £40 million, with imports amounting to £28 million pounds and exports £12 million. Trade with the United States was equal to £32 million, with imports at £10 million and exports at £22 million. China's trade with Japan was worth £23 million, with imports at £6 million and exports at £17 million. See also Lowe, *Britain in the Far East*, pp. 4–5; Nish, *The Anglo-Japanese Alliance*, pp. 8–9; and Warner, *Anglo-Japanese Financial Relations*, p. 66.

5. Japan's customs autonomy was not restored until 1911.

6. Checkland, *Britain's Encounter with Meiji Japan*, pp. 13–14, and Nish, *The Anglo-Japanese Alliance*, pp. 10–11.

at the conclusion of the Sino-Japanese War, however, made it clear that Japan could not act in East Asia while diplomatically isolated.[7] Furthermore, by transferring the payment of the Chinese indemnity, derived from negotiations after the Sino-Japanese War, to London where the indemnity was paid in British pounds (as discussed in Chapter 2), the Japanese government was able to secure increased British cooperation in economic, financial, military, and political dealings.

Diplomacy, Financial Relations, and Military Alliance

The role of diplomacy in developing the growing nexus between Anglo-Japanese financial relations and military alliances requires careful consideration. To what extent did diplomacy foster the financial links between Great Britain and Japan in the late nineteenth and early twentieth centuries? How did those financial links relate to, or influence, the establishment of the Anglo-Japanese alliance? In addressing the first part of the question, we must acknowledge that Great Britain's foreign policy in East Asia, right from the very start, revolved around the interests of commerce and trade, and that those interests were later expanded to include finance.[8] Britain's first ambassador to Japan, Sir Rutherford Alcock, made this clear in the 1860s: "Commerce is with us, in Siam, China, and Japan all equally (for with Cochin-China we have no relations yet) the one sole object."[9] In Victorian England, notions of free trade in East Asia—that is, the expansion of non-Asian trade in China, Cochin-China, Japan, and Siam—was pursued as only right and proper, and any distinction between the political and economic was often blurred. As Sir Harry Parkes, Britain's second ambassador to Japan, candidly told a parliamentary committee on a brief return home, "I do not myself recognize any very defined line between our political and our commercial interests; the two are so intimately woven together, that one often leads to the other."[10] However clear the implications of the ambassador's statement may be, the intricate web of links between diplomatic relations and economic interests is much harder to unravel in the ebb and flow of history.

---

7. See Nish, *Japanese Foreign Policy*, pp. 34–40.

8. Platt, *Finance, Trade, and Politics*, pp. 262–67.

9. Alcock, *The Capital of the Tycoon*, p. 352.

10. Minutes of evidence, *Report of the Select Committee on the Diplomatic Services*, GBSP 1872 (314) VII, Q.1135, quoted in Platt, *Finance, Trade, and Politics*, pp. 267–68.

British foreign policy firmly maintained a long tradition of not favoring any one particular British interest over another, thus avoiding conflicts of interest in which the Foreign Office could be perceived as being aligned with a particular interest, as well as suspicions about its own financial impartiality. According to the rhetoric of nonintervention, consular officers might act unofficially, but individual interests were denied exclusive government backing, and diplomatic support was provided only to the extent that it could further the greater aims of British trade and finance.[11] By the 1890s, however, increasing commercial competition threatened Britain's economic presence in East Asia, and the old standards of laissez-faire diplomacy could not be maintained.[12] Clearly it was more effective for the Foreign Office to promote a specific financial group than to give diplomatic support to a diverse collection of British interests. Moreover, the other treaty powers, with much smaller existing interests in East Asia than Great Britain, had fewer scruples about putting their full diplomatic support behind their respective financial groups, as exemplified by the operations of the Banque de l'Indochine of France, the Russo-Chinese Bank of Russia, and the Deutsche Asiatische Bank of Germany. In effect, this left British banks as the only sources of large-scale foreign finance operating in East Asia that had no formal government connection or control.[13] From a British perspective, therefore, economic colonialism in China, succinctly described by Overlach as "conquest by railroad and bank," dictated that Foreign Office diplomacy had to work closely with British finance, especially during the period from 1897 to 1914.[14]

Indeed, the years spanning the late nineteenth and early twentieth centuries were to form a remarkable period in British foreign policy that was, according to the historians Cain and Hopkins, characterized by the "increasingly overt convergence of politics and finance."[15] What had

---

11. Lythe, "Financial Capital of the World," pp. 31–53.

12. Gone were the days when Britain monopolized something like 80% of China's foreign trade. See Platt, *Finance, Trade, and Politics*, pp. 270–74.

13. Platt, *Finance, Trade, and Politics*, pp. 276–94, and Pollard, *Britain's Prime and Britain's Decline*, p. 106. There was, however, undoubtedly a strong informal relationship between the Hongkong Shanghai Bank and the British government. See Dayer, *Bankers and Diplomats in China*.

14. Overlach, *Foreign Financial Control in China*, p. ii. Platt, *Finance, Trade, and Politics*, pp. 294–303. See McLean, "The Foreign Office," pp. 303–21.

15. Cain and Hopkins, *British Imperialism*, pp. 432–46.

changed within British imperialism and the emerging world economy to effect such an important transformation in foreign policy, particularly as it related to East Asia? Put simply, London's hegemonic position in world finance, founded on the "holy trinity" of free trade, balanced budgets, and the Bank of England's operation of the international gold standard, was destabilized by internal weakness and challenged by external competition.[16] This, in turn, had important implications for the operation of British imperialism and its position in East Asia. The first signs of London's financial weakness were exposed during the Baring Crisis of 1890, in which the British government and the Bank of England were forced to rescue the great merchant banking house of Barings from financial collapse.[17] The crisis confirmed what Walter Bagehot had pointed out seventeen years earlier, in 1873: the Bank of England's ratio of reserves to bank deposits was dangerously small, and thus its domestic and international operation of the gold standard were endangered by a scarcity of the gold reserves used to counter the huge liabilities that the gold standard had to support.[18] Moreover, the Bank of England's "entirely private" borrowing Council of India funds to "adjust" the bank rate, and the British monetary authorities' subtle use of Indian monetary reserves to reinforce their own finances, were signs of additional weakness.[19]

Any notion that London might be losing its preeminence in financial matters, however, would be dismissed as incredible until after the outbreak of the Boer War in southern Africa in October 1899.[20] War against

---

16. Friedberg, *The Weary Titan*, pp. 21–279. The entire notion of Britain's "financial hegemony" is being revised. See Gallarotti, *International Monetary Regime*, pp. 86–140.

17. See Alley, "Gold, Sterling and the Witwatersrand," pp. 103–7; Clapman, *The Bank of England*, pp. 326–53; Hawtrey, *A Century of Bank Rate*, pp. 105–10; Kindleberger, *A Financial History*, 1st ed., p. 92; Saw, *The Bank of England*, pp. 71–73; and Zeigler, *The Sixth Great Power*, pp. 229–66.

18. Bagehot, *Lombard Street*, p. 17. Alley, "Gold, Sterling and the Witwatersrand," pp. 103–7.

19. Gallarotti, *International Monetary Regime*, p. 121, and Sayers, *The Bank of England*, pp. 39–41. For a detailed discussion of financial and monetary relations between Great Britain and India, see McGuire, "India, Britain, Precious Metals," pp. 179–98. See also Balachandran, "The Gold Exchange Standard," pp. 201–7.

20. Davis and Huttenback, *Mammon and Empire*, p. 38. "Europe may well have been the world's banker, but Britain was the majority stockholder in that enterprise." Britain accounted for 75% of all international movements of capital, as opposed to finance, in 1900, and although this share declined thereafter, it was still over 40% in 1913.

the Transvaal and the Orange Free State forced the British government to raise quick capital as army expenditures increased from £21 million in 1898–1899 to £92 million in 1900–1901 and £94 million in 1901–1902.[21] Usually funds would be generated through the issue of consols, dated or irredeemable stock that was repayable over five to ten years. The condition of the London financial market was tight, however, requiring high-interest issues, and the government was reluctant to increase permanent debt in the form of consols.[22] Moreover, as London's supply of gold from South Africa's Witwatersrand had all but ceased, it became imperative that the British Treasury locate an alternate source of gold to bolster its reserves.[23] For the first time since the Seven Years' War of 1756–1763, the British government was forced to raise funds in New York. The chancellor of the exchequer, Sir Michael Hicks Beach, turned to J. P. Morgan and the New York financial market to raise a large part of the National War Loan of 1900, worth £30 million, and for three of the four subsequent Boer War loans. In all, New York banking houses took an unprecedented amount of freshly minted bonds from the British government's exchequer (worth some $128 million).[24] While the capital transfers of the Boer War were, in retrospect, symbolic of a transfer of financial power from Lombard Street to Wall Street, we must remember that London was to remain the world's premier insurer and rentier for many years to come, as illustrated by the details surrounding Japanese government loans on the London financial market.[25]

The Chinese Indemnity and the Anglo-Japanese Alliance

In considering Japan's economic history, wider diplomatic and financial contexts should be kept in mind, particularly as they relate to the financial relationships and military alliances of the period from 1897 to 1923. As mentioned, during the last decade of the nineteenth century Japan had renegotiated the "unequal" treaties it had conceded by force in the

---

For example, estimates of the British share of total foreign investment in the United States are 80% for 1880, 72% for 1900, and 59% for 1913.

21. Friedberg, *The Weary Titan*, pp. 99–128, especially p. 106.

22. Burk, "Money and Power," pp. 359–69.

23. Alley, "Gold, Sterling and the Witwatersrand," pp. 107–14.

24. Burk, *Morgan Grenfell*, pp. 111–23; Burk, "Money and Power," pp. 359–60; and Carosso, *The Morgans*, pp. 510–13.

25. Bartlett, *Britain Pre-eminent*, p. 2.

late 1850s. Japan had also won a war against China and received an enormous indemnity worth almost £38 million. Significantly, according to Matsukata Masayoshi's directions, the Japanese government proposed that the Chinese government refrain from releasing its silver and instead pay the war indemnity in London with English pounds, which were directly convertible to gold. In this way, Matsukata employed the indemnity to facilitate Japan's adoption of a gold standard, thereby integrating Japan with the world's largest financial markets, and the emerging world economy. These events had important implications for Japan's economic growth and development, and collectively they transformed the nature of the relations between Great Britain and Japan.

Intimate financial cooperation at the very highest levels, through the auspices of the Yokohama Specie Bank, the Bank of Japan, and the Bank of England, was of great mutual benefit in the era of the classical gold standard, when all international balance-of-payments transactions between member states were ultimately settled by transfers of sterling bills, gold, or banknotes convertible to gold.[26] Following Japan's adoption of the gold standard, financial cooperation with Britain increased, Japan's credit rating on the London money market was raised, and increasing amounts of foreign capital were invested in Japan, most of which originated in London.[27] Japan was, in short, being accepted by Britain as a capable power, and thus, in time, Japan was considered a potential ally, especially as Britain had been internationally isolated by the conduct of the Boer War and was concerned about the situation in the Far East, where Japan might negotiate an agreement with Russia.[28] Financial considerations also favored an alliance, as Japan could relieve Britain of its

---

26. Many countries held accounts at the Bank of England in the prewar period: the British Empire (with the exception of Canada, Newfoundland, and South Africa), Sweden, Norway, Denmark, Finland, Estonia, Spain, Portugal, Greece, Turkey, Iran, and Siam (Thailand). By 1930 the central banks of more than seventeen nations deposited and held funds at the Bank of England. These accounts were not necessarily active, but served as important conduits for international financial cooperation. See Clapman, *The Bank of England*, p. 421, and Stern, *United States in International Banking*, p. 30.

27. Cain and Hopkins, *British Imperialism*, p. 434.

28. Bartlett, *British Foreign Policy*, pp. 7–10; Bartlett, *Defence and Diplomacy*, pp. 96–131; Beloff, *Britain's Liberal Empire*, pp. 100–103; Chamberlain, *Pax Britannica*, pp. 162–70; Checkland, *Britain's Encounter with Meiji Japan*, pp. 14–16; Monger, *The End of Isolation*, pp. 46–93; and the standard work on the Anglo-Japanese alliance, Nish, *The Anglo-Japanese Alliance*, pp. 99–229.

self-appointed role as "policeman" in East Asia and reduce Britain's naval expenditure at a critical time for London's finances.[29]

The Japanese government had also shown that it was prepared to cooperate with British financial authorities in administering the Chinese indemnity, which had been deposited at the Bank of England to serve the dual functions of an exchange fund and a specie reserve.[30] Owing to Japanese initiative, the bilateral indemnity payment of £38 million from Peking to Tokyo was deposited in a tailor-made Bank of England account, and in a triangular arrangement, London's financial authorities would presumably supply China with £38 million in loans to complete a masterful exercise in credit creation.[31] The importance of the Japanese deposit, equivalent to 36 percent of the British government's total expenditure in 1895–1896, can best be explained in relation to the Bank of England's operation of the gold standard at that time.[32] Given the tolerances within which the bank operated, often referred to as the thin "film" or "wedge" of gold, the value of gold bullion and coin reserved in

---

29. Not only was the "financial hub of the world" becoming reliant on capital from New York's financial market, but also the Royal Navy was desperately trying to match French and Russian naval power in East Asian waters, and after 1904 it was in an arms race with the Imperial Navy of Germany. See Monger, *The End of Isolation*, pp. 8–14, and Steeds, "Anglo-Japanese Relations," p. 201.

30. Britain's financiers were thus to benefit from both China's borrowing of the indemnity and Japan's depositing of the same indemnity in the Bank of Japan's account at the Bank of England. See Cain and Hopkins, *British Imperialism*, p. 434. The exchange fund held at the Bank of England, which doubled as a specie reserve and was thus a key component of the gold standard in Japan, also shaped the "day-to-day" operations of Japanese finance in the era of the classical gold standard. These arrangements indicate, to some extent, just how tenuous Japan's gold standard was. Certainly the maintenance of the combined exchange fund and specie reserve was to be a source of considerable anxiety for the Japanese Ministry of Finance until the gold standard was abandoned on 12 September 1917. Fujise, "Kokusai kinhonisei to sekai shijō," pp. 1–28; Suzuki, *Japanese Government Loan Issues*, pp. 165–74; Tamaki, *Japanese Banking*, p. 93; Yamasaki, *Honpō kaheiseido kaiseiron*, pp. 1–60; and Yamazawa and Yamamoto, "Trade and Balance of Payments," p. 145.

31. As it turned out, things did not initially progress as expected. Foreign Office intervention, however, did secure London's participation in the two £16 million loans of 1896 and 1898. When we consider that China had also raised £6.6 million from London in 1894, we once again arrive at the total of £38 million. See Kann, *The Currencies of China*, p. 79; Platt, *Finance, Trade, and Politics*, p. 281; and Pollard, *Britain's Prime and Britain's Decline*, p. 106.

32. Monger, *The End of Isolation*, p. 8.

the Issue Department of the Bank of England fell below £40 million in the latter part of 1896 (see Table 4.1).[33] Indeed, the Bank of England's reserve had fallen to £32 million on 9 September, just below £26 million on 21 October, and, despite consolidation during 1897, it had dived to £18.4 million during April 1898. At the onset of the Boer War, in late November 1899, the Bank of England's gold reserves stood at just £19.3 million.[34] Thus, the Japanese government's "reputably huge" London balances could go a long way toward easing the Bank of England's ratio of deposits to liabilities and maintaining the effectiveness of bank rate, providing they stayed at the Bank of England.

The Bank of England's acceptance of large-scale reserve funds, such as Japan's, caused great concern within London's financial community.[35] As early as 18 December 1896, bank governor Albert E. Sandeman wrote to Chancellor of the Exchequer E. W. Hamilton:

> I write to ask if you would, if possible, obtain for us some precise information as to the intentions of the Japanese Government in connexion with the large amount which they have at the present moment on deposit with us.
>
> This matter concerns the Bank to some extent, but, in a far larger degree, the *commerce of the country.*
>
> . . . On taking charge of this large amount of money belonging to Japan in the Autumn of 1895 we made no special stipulations, presuming that the nature of the operation was a temporary one, but numerous transactions have since taken place, and lately the Japanese Government have withdrawn a certain amount in gold for export. It has been done in a very discreet manner,[36] but, should these withdrawals assume large

---

33. On the slim tolerances within which the bank operated, see, for example, Clapman cited in Sayers, *The Bank of England*, pp. 9–10. Clapman, *The Bank of England*, p. 365.

34. Hawtrey, *A Century of Bank Rate*, pp. 112–22.

35. See Carosso, *The Morgans*, pp. 422–23; Gallarotti, *International Monetary Regime*, p. 134; Suzuki, *Japanese Government Loan Issues*, p. 173; and Warner, *Anglo-Japanese Financial Relations*, p. 65.

36. London's concern was so great that direct transport of gold from Great Britain to Japan was strictly avoided by Japan. According to Wakatsuki Reijiro, gold transactions between Great Britain to Japan were masked by an agreement whereby Japan would import gold from Australia, with London transporting gold to Australia at a later date. See Bytheway, "Nichigokan no kinboeki," pp. 41–53, and Wakatsuki Reijiro, *Meiji/Taisho/Showa sekaihishi*, pp. 121–24.

proportions, and become generally known, they might easily create alarm at a time like the present when, from various causes,—some known better to you than to us,—both the markets for stocks and funds are in a very sensitive condition.

Further large amounts may be expected, and it becomes a question whether it is prudent for this Bank in the public interest to again receive moneys which, *unless some arrangement can be come to with the depositors,* seriously imperil the money market.[37]

Table 4.1. Bank of England Gold Reserves and Bank Rates, 1894–1914 (units: £1,000)

Year and financial quarter	Gold reserves on the day	Increase for quarter	Gold imports for quarter	Average monthly bank rate for quarter (%)
1894 / Mar. 7	22,893	5,996	8,496	2.00
June 6	28,889	2,005	5,447	2.00
Sept. 5	30,894	−5,155	−3,261	2.00
Dec. 5	25,739	3,177	1,663	2.00
1895 / Mar. 6	28,916	−1,180	1,435	2.00
June 5	27,736	4,120	5,211	2.00
Sept. 4	31,856	3,468	4,064	2.00
Dec. 4	35,324	5,059	3,152	2.00
1896 / Mar. 4	40,383	−2,107	1,996	2.00
June 3	38,276	−4,954	1,706	2.00
Sept. 2	33,322	−7,097	−10,318	3.31
Dec. 2	26,225	3,530	780	3.62
1897 / Mar. 3	29,755	−4,509	2,153	2.58
June 2	25,246	−677	586	2.00
Sept. 1	24,569	−2,735	−3,295	2.65
Dec. 1	21,834	1,772	−663	3.00
1898 / Mar. 2	23,606	2,440	8,387	3.58
June 1	26,046	−2,255	−361	2.64
Sept. 7	23,791	−2,922	545	3.54

(continued)

---

37. "Governor to Chancellor of the Exchequer," 18 December 1896, Secretary's Letter Book, G23/87, pp. 167–69, Bank of England Archives, London (hereafter, BOE); emphasis added.

Table 4.1. (*continued*)

Year and financial quarter	Gold reserves on the day	Increase for quarter	Gold imports for quarter	Average monthly bank rate for quarter (%)
Dec. 7	20,869	2,893	−586	3.58
1899 / Mar. 1	23,762	−4,231	2,018	3.00
June 7	19,531	4,816	8,570	3.31
Sept. 6	24,347	−5,395	−808	4.64
Dec. 6	18,952	4,944	5,025	4.88
1900 / Mar. 7	23,896	−3,486	1,074	3.92
June 6	20,410	3,351	4,500	3.58
Sept. 5	23,761	−4,236	−1,679	4.00
Dec. 5	19,525	5,902	2,157	4.46
1901 / Mar. 6	25,427	−740	4,266	4.00
June 5	24,687	2,146	3,166	3.04
Sept. 4	26,833	−3,187	−2,493	3.38
Dec. 4	23,646	2,650	−191	3.62
1902 / Mar. 5	26,296	−1,492	3,448	3.00
June 4	24,804	1,009	4,216	3.00
Sept. 3	25,813	−4,431	−2,217	3.69
Dec. 3	21,382	3,790	1,720	4.00
1903 / Mar. 4	25,172	−948	3,836	3.92
June 3	24,224	218	691	3.08
Sept. 2	24,442	−3,345	−4,248	4.00
Dec. 2	21,097	4,454	−981	4.00
1904 / Mar. 2	25,551	−2,961	1,629	3.50
June 1	22,590	4,918	4,017	3.00
Sept. 7	27,508	−5,042	−5,422	3.00
Dec. 7	22,466	7,386	4,375	3.00
1905 / Mar. 1	29,852	−2,525	3,725	2.54
June 7	27,327	−2,632	957	2.50
Sept. 6	24,695	−1,526	978	3.77
Dec. 6	23,169	4,653	4,030	4.00
1906 / Mar. 7	27,822	−4,797	−1,835	3.85
June 6	23,025	4,342	6,706	3.58
Sept. 5	27,367	−4,425	−6,858	5.10
Dec. 5	22,942	3,467	2,205	5.46

Table 4.1. (continued)

Year and financial quarter	Gold reserves on the day	Increase for quarter	Gold imports for quarter	Average monthly bank rate for quarter (%)
1907 / Mar. 6	26,409	−2,228	4,825	4.46
June 5	24,181	2,968	2,485	4.12
Sept. 4	27,149	−5,240	−5,075	5.36
Dec. 4	21,909	7,609	3,059	5.31
1908 / Mar. 4	29,518	−2,032	3,006	3.04
June 3	27,486	−185	−2,911	2.50
Sept. 2	27,301	−3,215	−4,711	2.50
Dec. 2	24,086	3,519	92	2.77
1909 / Mar. 3	27,605	−1,441	6,222	2.65
June 2	26,164	2,764	3,350	2.50
Sept. 1	28,928	−3,152	−3,735	3.81
Dec. 1	25,776	360	−495	3.88
1910 / Mar. 2	26,136	4,381	9,594	3.85
June 1	30,517	−829	1,207	3.04
Sept. 7	29,688	−3,803	−3,135	4.27
Dec. 7	25,885	3,196	1,025	4.21
1911 / Mar. 1	29,081	−114	6,195	3.04
June 7	28,967	1,184	5,107	3.00
Sept. 6	30,151	−3,393	−3,398	3.85
Dec. 6	26,758	2,517	−46	3.85
1912 / Mar. 6	29,275	776	4,687	3.35
June 5	30,051	1,317	4,528	3.08
Sept. 4	31,368	−5,106	−2,646	4.54
Dec. 4	26,262	1,552	−1,061	5.00
1913 / Mar. 5	27,814	−403	7,329	4.73
June 4	27,411	4,826	9,548	4.50
Sept. 3	32,237	−5,953	−5,978	4.85
Dec. 3	26,284	5,454	5,333	4.08
1914 / Mar. 4	31,738	−6,290	576	3.00
June 3	25,448	5,487	15,075	4.13
Sept. 2	30,935	—	—	—

Source: Hawtrey, *A Century of Bank Rate*, pp. 297–300.

The governor clearly expresses the predicament faced by the bank, the need of the Bank of England for "precise information" on any withdrawals in gold for export, and the imperative of coming to "some arrangement." Rather than destabilizing Britain's finances, however, the Bank of England came to employ the Japanese government's account to defend the position of sterling as the leading currency of international finance.[38] In this way, administrative details intricately connected with the operations of international finance and the gold standard encouraged a close financial relationship between Britain and Japan, and seem likely to have played a significant part in the formation of the Anglo-Japanese alliance, signed on 30 January 1902.

Anglo-Japanese Finance and Anglo-Japanese Alliance

In discussing the monetary background and financial nature of the Anglo-Japanese alliance, we must acknowledge that the alliance was, first and foremost, one of military expedience. The alliance was officially consummated on 30 January 1902 with a short, six-article treaty relating to strategic concerns in East Asia. The alliance was renegotiated and formally extended on two occasions, 12 August 1905 and 13 July 1911, and was not officially terminated until the signing of the Four Powers Pact on 25 July 1923, which followed the Washington Naval Disarmament Conference of 1921–1922.[39] Careful reading of both British and Japanese diplomatic papers uncovers no explicit mention of any economic or financial agreements, secret or otherwise, within any of the articles of the three Anglo-Japanese treaties.[40] While it is clear that political consid-

---

38. See Alley, "Gold, Sterling and the Witwatersrand," pp. 116–19; Clapman, *The Bank of England*, p. 383; Hawtrey, *A Century of Bank Rate*, p. 112; and Sayers, *The Bank of England*, pp. 28–47.

39. The benefits derived from the alliance by the Japanese government were significant, including political dominance in Korea, increased opportunities to interfere with Northern China, increased international status, and access to British finance. Perhaps most importantly, in sliding in under the canopy edges of the British Empire's umbrella, Japan took a necessary step to prevent a repeat of the Triple Intervention by France, Germany, and Russia that had so tarnished the 1895 victory over China. Cain and Hopkins, *British Imperialism*, p. 438; Checkland, *Britain's Encounter with Meiji Japan*, p. 16; Murashima, "The Opening of the Twentieth Century," pp. 159–96; Nish, *The Anglo-Japanese Alliance*, pp. 216–18; and Steeds, pp. 197–223.

40. See Foreign Office Folios, 1901–2, FO.46/563; 1903–5, FO.46/672; 1905, FO.46/673; 1905–6, FO.371/85; 1911–12, FO.371/1137; 1911–12, FO.371/1140; 1915, FO.371/2384; and 1915, FO.371/2388, FOJ.

erations predominated in the formation of the treaty, the financial dimensions of the Anglo-Japanese alliance were suggested by the visits to London in 1902 of the Shibusawa and Matsukata missions, which were specifically organized to attract the city's capitalists to invest in Japan.[41] Furthermore, the British government's own Foreign Office and Treasury intervened in the supply of financial capital to Japan, and the establishment of the Anglo-Japanese Bank in 1906, straight after the Russo-Japanese War, suggested that the alliance did indeed have some financial dimensions.[42]

The role played by the Foreign Office in the extension of loans to the Japanese government is difficult to substantiate and thus requires clarification. After the signing of the Anglo-Japanese alliance in January 1902, Japan's financial authorities were eager to capitalize on closer diplomatic relations, or more succinctly, on the prestige of being Great Britain's ally. By October 1902, the Industrial Bank of Japan and the Hongkong and Shanghai Bank had been appointed by the Japanese government to raise ¥50 million through the resale of domestic bonds, and these two issuing banks approached Baring Brothers, the London Rothschilds, and Ernest Cassel, a distinguished merchant banker, to join them in raising subscriptions. Previous to this, Lord Rothschild had already inquired of the Foreign Office's position in regard to the Japanese government loans. The reply, dated 22 September 1902, from Undersecretary of State for Foreign Affairs Francis Bertie (that is, the most senior unelected department head) provides a most revealing insight into the thoughts of the British government: "[Marquess Lansdowne (the Foreign Secretary)] authorizes me to say that His Majesty's Government regard it as a matter of political importance that Japan should be able to raise in this country,

---

41. See "Count Matsugata's Visit to England," *TT*, 29 April 1902, and "Japan's Chief Man of Business Arrives," *New York Times*, 14 June 1902.

42. Treasury to Foreign Office, 1 October 1902, FO.46/560, FOJ, p. 357, and Nish, *The Anglo-Japanese Alliance*, pp. 253–56. The role of the Foreign Office in securing British capital for loan to Japan is, indeed, a startling example of the "increasingly overt convergence of politics and finance" that defined British foreign policy in the late nineteenth century. See Cain and Hopkins, *British Imperialism*, pp. 432–46. See also Warner, *Anglo-Japanese Financial Relations*, p. 70. Despite some high-level support from the financial circles of London and Tokyo, the Anglo-Japanese Bank failed to attract business and establish itself in Japan. It changed its name to the Commercial Bank of London in 1913, and ceased operations after the commencement of hostilities in the First World War. See Baster, *The International Banks*, p. 176, and Hunter, "Bankers, Investors and Risk," pp. 176–98.

rather than elsewhere, the money which she requires."[43] The British government clearly wished for its ally to receive all the financial support it required. In Bertie's letter, however, he quickly qualifies his statement by reaffirming the Foreign Office's traditional position of nonintervention toward private transactions, as if to indicate that the whole affair was out of Foreign Office hands. Whatever the case, the undersecretary of state's reply was enough to convince Rothschild—and Baring Brothers, who were also provided with a copy of the letter—to take part in the business.[44]

In a letter to the Treasury, Bertie seems to contravene the nonintervention policy that he quoted to Lord Rothschild, when he asks the Treasury to persuade the Bank of England to inscribe the bonds on their books. Inscription from the Bank of England would imply that the loan was an official affair of state and provide a tremendous "stamp of approval" stimulus to investors. A punctilious reply from Treasury to the undersecretary of state, dated 11 October 1902, confirms Foreign Office assistance, and intervention, in ensuring the success of the Japanese government loan: "With further reference to Sir F. Bertie's letter . . . I am directed by the Lords Commissioners of His Majesty's Treasury to request you to inform the Marquess of Lansdowne [the foreign secretary] that They have received an intimation that the authorities of the Bank of England have complied with Their Lordship's request that the new Japanese Loan [of October 1902] might be inscribed in the Books of the Bank."[45] The Bank of England agreed to the Foreign Office's favor, through the intercession of the Treasury, and inscribed the bonds for a total of almost ¥6 million.[46] With such high-level support, fruit of the Anglo-Japanese alliance, the Japanese government was for the first time able to secure cooperation from Britain's leading financiers and merchant

---

43. "F. Bertie for Lord Lansdowne to Messrs.' N. M. Rothschild & Sons," Confidential, 22 September 1902, Japan—Miscellaneous, XI/III/681a, Rothschild Archive, London (hereafter, JRA).

44. Warner, *Anglo-Japanese Financial Relations*, p. 48, and Suzuki, *Japanese Government Loan Issues*, p. 76.

45. Treasury to Foreign Office, 1 October 1902, FO.46/560, FOJ, p. 357.

46. "Deputy Secretary to F. Mowatt," 8 October 1902, Letter Book No. 25, G23/70, BOE, pp. 262–63. The Bank of England, the Treasury, and the City were often said to act in concord, to cooperate in a financial triangle. See Green, "Influence of the City," pp. 193–218.

banks.[47] In this way, the first "inscribed" loan set an important precedent for Japan's financial operations, and the Japanese government came to expect financial assistance from its ally. The British government, while reluctant to guarantee Japanese loans, acceded to Japan's increasing use of the London financial market to raise international capital.[48] That Japan enjoyed Britain's financial support while, at the same time, the Russian government was effectively shut out of the London financial market is of great significance, particularly in the context of Japan's coming war with Russia (see Tables 5.1, 6.1, and 6.2 in Chapters 5 and 6).[49]

It is pertinent to point out that the episode quoted above is not recounted to assert a crude or deterministic notion of diplomacy controlled by capital, whereby the Sino-Japanese and Boer Wars were fought simply over access to gold and the Anglo-Japanese alliance was formed by Tokyo to import capital, and by London to bolster its gold reserves. Nevertheless, what becomes clear is that many seemingly unrelated events of the period from around 1890 to 1910 cannot be fully understood without an appreciation of their financial and monetary backgrounds. It is tempting to dismiss the events surrounding the Japanese government loan of 1902 as an aberration or an exceptional moment in British imperialism, and to succumb to the mantra of the British government's consistent institutional denials of financial interference. The Bank of England, as early as 1855, however, publicly guaranteed state loans to Turkey for £5 million. The same service was provided to Egypt in 1885, for £9 million, and to Greece in 1898, for £7 million.[50] Pollard also notes that there were signs of "semi-official" steering of the Bank of England by the Foreign

---

47. In a letter of thanks to the Marquess of Lansdowne, Hayashi commented, "The success of the recent sale of the Japanese bonds was no doubt greatly due to the announcement that the Bank was prepared for its inscription." See Hayashi to Lansdowne, 16 October 1902, FO.46/558, FOJ, and Nish, *The Anglo-Japanese Alliance*, p. 254.

48. Nish, *The Anglo-Japanese Alliance*, pp. 253–56; Pollard, *Britain's Prime and Britain's Decline*, p. 106; and Suzuki, *Japanese Government Loan Issues*, pp. 75–88.

49. Russia was not able to float loans on the London market until 1907 and 1909, after an Anglo-Russian entente had been reached. See Ferguson, *The House of Rothschild*, p. 406. Throughout 1905 and the early part of 1906, however, the Russian government tried, unsuccessfully, to enlist the help of the Morgan house in floating a large loan on the New York market. J. P. Morgan's withdrawal from negotiations with the Russian government lead to charges of "treachery" but was apparently based "purely on business considerations." See Carosso, *The Morgans*, pp. 516–22.

50. Suzuki, *Japanese Government Loan Issues*, p. 87.

Office, and Pollard cites the example of the Russian government, which had trouble raising capital in London until strained political relations were smoothed over in 1907, *after* its war with Japan. Moreover the British government "clearly" intervened in the cases of the Imperial Bank of Persia in 1889, the Peking Group (Hongkong and Shanghai Bank and Deutsche Asiatische Bank) loans to China in 1896–1898, and the National Bank of Turkey in 1909.[51]

Bank of Japan Lending to the Bank of England

In the context of financial cooperation engendered by the Anglo-Japanese alliance, an extraordinary relationship developed between the Bank of England and the Bank of Japan. In particular, the Bank of Japan played a role in maintaining the Bank of England's bank rate, and in reinforcing the international position of the pound sterling. Traditionally the Bank of England had three main duties: to maintain an income for its stockholders, to cater to the financial needs of the government of the day, and to protect the operation of the gold standard by maintaining the convertibility of its bank notes, or pound sterling, to gold. After the Baring Crisis of 1890, the Bank of England was put under increasing pressure to protect the sterling's gold convertibility, as this duty was, in fact, a statuary requirement. Rather than purchasing and hoarding more gold, the Bank of England compensated for its slender gold reserve through the monetary instruments of its gold devices and the bank rate.[52]

The "gold devices" is an oblique term that refers to the operations of the Bank of England in the London gold market, wherein it would purchase gold at prices above its fixed statutory level, or sometimes increase the selling price of foreign specie, or even refuse to sell gold bars, so as to "widen the gold points."[53] The importance of gold devices resided in their ability to provide the Bank of England with control over the inter-

---

51. McLean, "The Foreign Office," pp. 303–21. While not officially guaranteed by the Bank of England, the Peking Group's loans to China were inscribed on the bank's books. See Suzuki, *Japanese Government Loan Issues*, p. 79. Pollard, *Britain's Prime and Britain's Decline*, p. 106.

52. Alley, "Gold, Sterling and the Witwatersrand," pp. 116–17, and Sayers, *The Bank of England*, p. 8. The Bank of England replaced the bank rate with the term "minimum lending rate" in October 1972.

53. For a discussion of the significance of gold points and the distance between them—that is, "The possible range, between the terms on which one currency can be

national movements of gold; therefore, internal and external challenges often forced the bank to resort to using them. Buying bullion or specie at high prices, or providing gold importers with interest-free loans may seem ineffectual, but when accompanied by a rise in the bank rate, their cumulative effect was usually decisive, especially after 1903, when the Bank of England could once again rely on regular weekly shipments of unrefined gold from South Africa.[54]

Bank rate had traditionally been the primary weapon used by the Bank of England to protect its gold reserves and, hence, the operation of the British gold standard. A rise in the bank rate entailed an increase in the rate at which the Bank of England discounted loans to other banks. This, in turn, led the banks to pass the higher interest rates on to their customers, which reduced the outflow of sterling funds, attracted funds from other financial markets, and thus eased the pressure against British reserves and increased the strength of the pound. By the early part of the twentieth century, however, the Bank of England was hesitant to rely solely on the institution of bank rate, owing to the tendency of high interest rates to depress the domestic economy.[55]

Indeed, throughout the height of gold's reign from 1874 to 1913, the bank rate was raised above 5 percent on only eight occasions, and it rarely stayed there for more than a month. Pressure against the Bank of England's gold reserves forced the prolonged use of a high-interest bank rate on only two occasions, from October 1906 to February 1907 and from October 1907 to mid-January in 1908. These periods of high interest rates profoundly affected the movement of capital, Britain's international balance of trade, and thus, the world's financial markets.[56] In the period between late 1906 and 1908 when London reasserted its financial standing, Amsterdam, Berlin, and New York fell into deep financial panic. In particular, New York was "thrown back on to her own immense but

---

exchanged for another and the terms on which the exchange can be reversed at a later date"—see Keynes, "The Significance of the Gold Points," pp. 131–39.

54. Sayers, *The Bank of England*, pp. 47–53.

55. Alley, "Gold, Sterling and the Witwatersrand," pp. 116–19; Collins, *Money and Banking*, pp. 178–88; Gallarotti, *International Monetary Regime*, p. 137; Hawtrey, *A Century of Bank Rate*, p. 1–39; Roberts, "The Bank of England and the City," pp. 159–60; and Sayers, *Central Banking after Bagehot*, pp. 1–19.

56. Cairncross, "The Bank of England," p. 59, and Hawtrey, *A Century of Bank Rate*, pp. 115–18.

strained resources" and forced to endure a series of humiliating bank runs and bankruptcies.[57] Ordinarily, though, the Bank of England preferred to employ the gold devices to avoid causing domestic and international disruption, and when this became ineffective, it collaborated with other sources of funds, most notably the Council of India and the Bank of Japan.[58]

The Council of India funds were tapped from 1890 to 1899, usually for moderate amounts of £1 million or sometimes £2 million. What the Bank of England required was an obliging source of quick capital that could be discreetly employed to enforce higher-interest bank rates and tighten the market. The timing and finesse of these operations were more important than the actual amounts involved. Obviously the desire for secrecy, to minimize market knowledge of the artificial withdrawal of funds from the market in reaction to the higher bank rate (the "induction of tightness," in the Bank of England's jargon), was paramount. Publicity surrounding the Council of India funds, however, had the potential to compromise bank operations in the market and forced the Bank of England to seek out new sources of short-term funds. It approached the Bank of Japan in the autumn of 1905, and a close relationship developed over the next ten or so years. Almost immediately the Bank of England borrowed funds, in amounts ranging from £0.5 to £2 million, on at least ten occasions between 14 December 1905 and 2 April 1906, renewing or extending the loans on at least four occasions (see Table 4.2).[59] In the financially turbulent period of 1906–1907 the bank borrowed large sums in the latter part of 1906 and took loans for £1 million from 3 to 12 January 1907, £0.5 million on 21 January, and £1.5 million from 9 to 28 February. A smaller amount was also borrowed in August of the same year. Heavy borrowing of various sums resumed from late August to mid-September, but with the crisis in New York's financial market peaking, the bank rate was thought to be sufficiently "tight" to require fur-

---

57. Clapman, *The Bank of England*, pp. 389–94.

58. Cairncross, "The Bank of England," p. 59, and Sayers, *The Bank of England*, pp. 39–43. The inability of the Bank of England to enforce its own bank rate on the market without outside assistance can be seen as startling evidence of the bank's weakness. See Gallarotti, *International Monetary Regime*, p. 121.

59. Histories of the Bank—Prof. R. S. Sayers Research Papers by B/E Staff, 11.20, M124.21, BOE, pp. 1–2, and Histories of the Bank—Prof. R.S. Sayers Research Papers by B/E Staff, 21–24, M124.21, BOE, pp. 1–2.

Table 4.2. Bank of England Short-term Borrowing from the Bank of Japan, 1905–1906

No.	Date borrowed	A Rate (% per annum)	B Period (days)	C Amount borrowed from BOJ (k£)	D Total amount borrowed (k£)	E Percent of total borrowed (C/D)	Remarks
1	14 Dec. 1905	2.875	15	500	4,000	13	
2	28 Dec. 1905	3.625	60	1,500	10,100	15	£1.1 million renewed for 13 days at 4.125%, then £0.5 million renewed for 59 days at 3.625%.
3	11 Jan. 1906	3.000	21	1,600	4,900	33	
4	16 Jan. 1906	3.750	59	1,000	9,650	10	
5	18 Jan. 1906	3.750	29	1,200	10,850	11	£1 million renewed for 25 days at 3.75%, then £0.6 million renewed for 60 days at 3.25%.
6	16 Feb. 1906	2.500	18	1,200	7,950	15	
7	26 Feb. 1906	2.500	18	2,000	2,600	77	
8	1 Mar. 1906	2.500	18	1,000	1,600	63	
9	16 Mar. 1906	2.500	18	1,000	1,600	63	
10	2 Apr. 1906	2.500	18	600	600	100	

Source: Histories of the Bank—Prof. R. S. Sayers Research Papers by B/E Staff, 21–24, M124.21, ADM33/11, 23A, pp.1–2, Bank of England Archives, London.
Note: BOJ = Bank of Japan.

ther borrowing. It must be remembered that a number of other British banks were initially involved in lending operations to the Bank of England, and that financial cooperation between Britain and France, often negotiated through the services of the Rothschilds, was a vital component of the bank's operations prior to the First World War; nevertheless, the Bank of Japan emerged as the Bank of England's preeminent lender.[60] In all, in the period between December 1905 and September 1907 the Bank of Japan would provide loans to the Bank of England on at least eighteen separate occasions, totaling at least £18 million. Although time has obscured many of the transactional details, the information we have available is enough to conclude that during the period of the Anglo-Japanese alliance, the central banks of Britain and Japan were involved in a confidential and intimate relationship wherein the Bank of Japan did much more than just help enforce the bank rate: it supported the Bank of England in asserting the international standing of its currency, the pound sterling.[61]

Diplomacy, the New East, and the Ending of the Alliance

As the medieval poet and Buddhist monk Yoshida Kenko observed in the fourteenth century, in all things it is the beginning and the end that people find themselves most interested in.[62] And so we turn to the events of the Washington Conference and the subsequent ratification of the Four Powers Pact by all parties on 25 July 1923, whereby the Anglo-Japanese alliance officially came to an end.[63] Studies of diplomatic correspondence have led to notions of the alliance being in decline after its third renewal in 1911, but we should consider that, as Nish warned in a classic piece of understatement, "Diplomatic exchanges have a way of masking true feelings."[64] Beyond the diplomatic records, there is a great deal of documentary evidence showing that support for the alliance was on a very

---

60. See Sayers, *The Bank of England*, p. 41.

61. Sayers, *The Bank of England*, pp. 39–41.

62. Keene, *Essays in Idleness*, p. 115.

63. The United States of America was reluctant to sign the treaty, owing to the possibility of French amendments. The Americans were, however, obliged to follow the Anglo-Japanese ratification on 5 August 1922, and they ratified the treaty twelve days later on 17 August 1922. France, dissatisfied with the terms of the treaty, reluctantly became a signatory on 25 July 1923. See Nish, *Alliance in Decline*, pp. 386–87.

64. Nish, *Alliance in Decline*, p. 387.

firm footing at the highest levels of government until at least the end of 1921.[65]

An interesting example of the level of support that the Anglo-Japanese alliance enjoyed is the publication *The New East*, a bilingual monthly review founded by R. W. Robertson Scott in June 1917 with the apparent aim of improving Anglo-Japanese relations. In the first issue, Japan's prime minister, Count Terauchi Masaaki; British War Council member (and postwar secretary of state for foreign affairs) Lord Curzon; the foreign minister, Viscount Motono Ichiro; and the Japanese ambassador in London, Marquis Inoue Kaoru, all provided contributions concerning the future of the Anglo-Japanese alliance and emphasized the desirability of its extension.[66] Furthermore, Prince Arthur of Connaught and the president of the House of Peers and last shogun's successor as head of the Tokugawa house, Prince Tokugawa Iesato, provided the *New East* review with a "royal" seal of approval.[67] Prince Arthur could well have been speaking for all the contributors when he expressed hope in the future of Anglo-Japanese relations: "The bonds of friendship which unite the British Empire and the Empire of Japan have been tested by the strain of War, and I cannot doubt that this friendship will continue to be a valuable agent in preserving the peace and promoting prosperity of the world."[68] Clearly the question that concerned British and Japanese statesmen when they considered their respective postwar scenarios was not should the alliance continue but, rather, *how* should the alliance continue? Indeed, as late as 22 January 1919 the Japanese prime minister Hara Kei insisted in parliament that the strength of the alliance was beyond question and stated, "It goes without saying that the Anglo-Japanese alliance stands firm."[69] Ultimately, however, the fact that maintenance of the Anglo-Japanese alliance required a publicity campaign akin to that presented in *The New East* attests to a growing lack of public support for the alliance.

---

65. See Lowe, *Great Britain and Japan*, for a detailed study of the Anglo-Japanese alliance after its third extension.

66. Terauchi, "Will of Heaven," p. 18; Curzon, "Thoughts, Wishes and Hopes," pp. 19–20; Motono, "Made to Last," pp. 20–22; Inouye, "Attitude of Germany," p. 22.

67. H.R.H. Prince Arthur, "A Message," p. 1. Tokugawa, "A Reminiscence of London," pp. 28–29.

68. H.R.H. Prince Arthur, "A Message," p. 1.

69. Murashima, "The Opening of the Twentieth Century," p. 187.

At the time of the 1921 Imperial Conference in London, a periodic gathering of the prime ministers of Australia, Canada, Great Britain, New Zealand, South Africa, and representatives of the government of India that met in London from 20 June to 2 August, the British Empire faced a critical convergence of decisions and events. The question of how it should maintain its security around the globe, most particularly as it related to the issues of military shipbuilding and naval disarmament, was of paramount strategic importance. At the very heart of these issues lay the decision to reject or renew the Anglo-Japanese alliance, made all the more urgent by the fact that the alliance was due to expire on 13 July 1921, ten years after its third ratification.[70]

From the outset, Foreign Minister Lord Curzon opined that to "throw away" the alliance would be to lose "an asset of very considerable value on an international scale and from the widest point of view." Arthur James Balfour, in his role as chairman of the Standing Committee of Defense, supported Curzon by presenting the compelling military situation: Great Britain could not defend its empire against a hostile Japan, and plainly stated that "it is, from a strategic point of view, of very great importance that the Japanese alliance should be maintained."[71] Prime Minister William Morris Hughes of Australia, enjoying the full support of New Zealand's prime minister, William Ferguson Massey, argued that Japan had, with great loyalty, stood by Great Britain throughout the First World War and had every reason to expect the alliance to continue. Hughes also seemed to strike a chord with the participants, especially with British prime minister David Lloyd George, when he suggested that failure to honor twenty years of friendship would go against the codes of gentlemanly conduct, and would ultimately be dangerous to the empire. As Hughes pointed out, the preeminent truth of the age was that the safety of commerce and trade, the very lifeline and prosperity of the British Empire, was secured by naval power:

> Look at this map and ask yourselves what would have happened to that great splash of red right down from India through Australia down to New Zealand, but for the Anglo-Japanese Treaty. How much of these great rich territories and portions of our Empire would have escaped had

---

70. See Article VI of the third Anglo-Japanese Treaty (of 1911), and Nish, *Alliance in Decline*, pp. 351–53.

71. Louis, *British Strategy in the Far East*, pp. 52–62.

Japan been neutral? How much if she had been our enemy? It is certain that the naval power of the Empire could not have saved India and Australia and still been strong enough to hold Germany bottled up in the narrow seas.[72]

In short, Hughes felt that failure to renew the alliance threatened the very existence of not only Australia but also of the British Empire itself. He was thus unequivocally "for the renewal of this Treaty, and . . . against delay."[73]

Significantly, the prime minister of Canada, Arthur Meighen, was the only participant at the Imperial Conference to argue forcefully against the continuation of the Anglo-Japanese alliance, and his confrontation with the Australian prime minister dominated and defined the conference's proceedings. In Meighen's own words, his views were "worlds away" from those of Hughes. The Canadian prime minister, in contrast to Hughes, faced a very different geopolitical reality, and looked toward a new era of "internationalist" diplomacy defined by the League of Nations and the United States of America with hope and optimism. Meighen rejected the old system of bilateral alliances, which in his view had disastrously contributed to the causes of instability and war while purporting to maintain security in the Pacific. The Greater Japanese Empire (Dai-Nippon Teikoku) had come to represent militant imperialism, and Japan's place as Britain's ally had been jeopardized by its aggressive policy toward British interests on the Asian mainland, as exemplified by the Twenty-One Demands it unilaterally made of China in 1915. For Meighen, the United States was Britain's natural ally; and it was increasingly willing to cooperate with the empire. Thus, only close Anglo-American relations could provide a basis for any future world order. To what extent Meighen's arguments influenced the other participants is largely unknown; nevertheless, we can be certain that his objections were what prevented the renewal of the Anglo-Japanese alliance by the Imperial Conference in 1921. The Canadian prime minister's views prevailed, and the question

---

72. Louis, *British Strategy in the Far East*, p. 69.

73. Louis, *British Strategy in the Far East*, pp. 62–70. O'Brien's work acknowledges that the 1921 Imperial Conference was the "turning point" in the debate about the alliance's future, but raises questions for Japanologists about its discussion of how the term "alliance" was "commonly understood." See O'Brien, "End of the Anglo-Japanese Alliance," pp. 267–84.

of the alliance was instead deferred to the Washington Conference, which was in turn resolved by the signing of the Four Powers Pact that formally replaced the Anglo-Japanese alliance on 25 July 1923.[74] Debate about Hughes's analysis of the circumstances facing the British Empire and the merits of continuing the alliance, however, remains one of history's many great unanswered questions.

From the inauspicious beginnings of Anglo-Japanese relations to the revision of Japan's unequal treaties, the development of important financial links, and the formation of a twenty-year Anglo-Japanese alliance, British capital played a key role in the development of the Japanese economy. It was within the diplomatic and political contexts of the Anglo-Japanese alliance that Japan's import of foreign capital occurred, especially from around the time of Japan's adoption of the gold standard in 1897 until the official end of the alliance in 1923. Significant financial elements intricately involved in the formation of the alliance included, in particular, massive financing of Japanese government bond issues through the London financial market.

Regrettably, the Anglo-Japanese alliance, for all its achievements, implications, and significance, seems to have been passed over in Western literature, or at best explained away, without thought to the extraordinary financial relations that helped produce it, and were produced by it.[75] In an attempt to answer broader questions relating to the contribution and consequences of Japanese government borrowing, we have moved toward a new understanding of the Anglo-Japanese alliance and the remarkable financial cooperation it engendered, which in turn had important implications for the operation of British imperialism, and a most profound effect on the modernization of Japan.

---

74. See Nish, "Echoes of Alliance," pp. 255–78.

75. Consider the vast amount of literature concerned with the respective British and Japanese economies and the formal imperialism of the period, and how little of that material comments on Anglo-Japanese financial relations. Indeed, the entire operation of informal empire, and the veritable *Pax Britannica* in East Asia, requires further clarification.

CHAPTER 5

Imperial Japanese
Government Loans, 1870–1930

What do we mean by foreign capital? Where does it come from, why is it important, and how does it relate to Japan's economic development? In *Investing Japan*, "foreign" simply signifies all things that are not Japanese, according to the dichotic (Japanese) model, and the term "capital" is taken from the Scottish contribution to eighteenth-century classical political economy that defined capital as the accumulated wealth of an individual, company, or community that is used as a fund for the creation of new forms of production: that is, wealth in any form used to help in producing more wealth.[1] In the Japanese experience of economic development, capital came from nations that were at an advanced stage in their own economic development and were looking to invest capital outside their own economy through the great financial-capital markets of Europe and North America—that is, London, Paris, Amsterdam, Berlin, Zurich, and New York. It is much more difficult to assess *why* foreign capital is important or, critically, to explain how it relates to Japan. The following investigation of these questions posits that the investment of capital can be seen, at its simplest, as a prime determinant of economic growth and development in the Japanese economy, and as

---

1. See Hont and Ignatieff, *Wealth and Virtue*.

crucial to the processes of technological transfer, technical change, and industrial revolution in Japan.[2]

How significant was the import of foreign capital, in the case of Japan? Certainly there is no shortage of politicians, commentators, and scholars who assert that Japan's economic development occurred without "significantly relying on foreign capital inflow," while only a few economic and financial historians stand by proclamations of its importance.[3] Yet at issue is one of the most important questions confronting students of Japanese economic history today: where and how were the funds needed for industrialization procured? Recent scholarship provides examples of how, in the 1880s, private funds from wealthy merchants, the nobility, and prefectural and local government officials were used to finance the establishment of many railway and textile companies.[4] Indeed, the mechanics of domestic investment and capital formation between 1858 and 1897 promises to become a major area of research, and yet an emphasis on the role of the state in funding enterprise remains valid, particularly during the 1870s and after the Sino-Japanese War. State capital, rather than private capital, played the principal role in developing an economic infrastructure in Japan, and in its colonies of Taiwan, Karafuto, Korea, Nanyo, and Manchuria, and the import of foreign capital made a significant contribution to the state's finances in the period between 1897 and 1931. Although the Japanese government had largely withdrawn from direct investment in manufacturing and state-owned enterprises through the policies of the Matsukata deflation in the 1880s, state investment remained important in the domestic economy, whether through the operation of enterprises like steel foundries, railroads, and telegraph and telephone lines, or through the management of its network of parastatal "national policy" (*kokusaku gaisha*) corporations and special financial organs (*tokushu ginkō*).[5] Much of the debate surrounding these opposing explanations of Japan's capital formation can

---

2. See Rymes, *On Concepts of Capital*, and J. Schumpeter, *The Theory of Economic Development*.

3. While it is perhaps unfair to single out any one author, the quote is from my distinguished colleague J. Teranishi, "Japan: Development and Structural Change," p. 99.

4. See N. Nakamura, "Industrialization and Provincial Vitality," pp. 187–205.

5. See Crawcour, "Industrialization and Technological Change," pp. 391–436, and T. Nakamura, *Economic Growth in Prewar Japan*, pp. 59–69.

be reconciled when the timing and magnitude of public and private financing are considered in their wider historical contexts. Central to the study presented here is the conviction that the import of foreign capital played a vital role in Japan's economic growth and development, particularly after Japan's adoption of the gold standard in 1897.

The Meiji Regime and Foreign Capital

In the context of East Asia, particularly during the latter half of the nineteenth century, colonialism was a pressing threat and dictated the Tokugawa *bakufu*'s attitudes toward diplomatic relations, international trade, and foreign capital.[6] At the beginning of the Meiji Restoration, the new regime also realized that, in many cases, foreign capital served as the advance guard of colonialism, or at least economic colonialism, and decided that Japan should progress through autonomous development and reject the import of capital from foreign powers, particularly after the distasteful initial experience of negotiating British loans. In April 1870, railway construction from Yokohama to Tokyo (Shinbashi) was financed through the issuance of the 9 Percent Japan Customs Loan, which had been sold on the London financial market by J. Henry Schroder and Company to the value of £1 million (see Table 5.1).[7] In fact, the loan was negotiated with the former British diplomat Horatio Nelson Lay, who charged the new Japanese government 12 percent interest, paid bondholders a 9 percent return, and took a full 3 percent for his own peculiar efforts.

When the Japanese authorities became aware of the details of the plan, however, they cancelled their agreement with Lay (who was in their employ as a special foreign adviser), renegotiated the loan's repayment on better terms through the Oriental Bank, and learned an important lesson in nineteenth-century international finance. Still, they could not renege on the terms of the loan itself.[8] Almost three years later, in January 1873, the 7 Percent Japanese Sterling Loan for £2.4 million was issued on

---

6. See Totman, *Early Modern Japan*, pp. 482–546.

7. Matsukata, "Teikoku zaisei," p. 234; Meiji zaiseishi henshukai, *Meiji zaiseishi*, 8:163, 9:125; Ōkurashō, *Meiji Taishō zaiseishi*, pp. 12–22; and Ouchi and Tsuchiya, *Meiji zenki zaisei*, 10:3–50.

8. See Tatewaki, *Zainichi gaikoku ginkōshi*, pp. 271–302; Checkland, *Britain's Encounter with Meiji Japan*, p. 38; Fox, *Britain and Japan*, pp. 387–93; and Nish, *The Story of Japan*, pp. 93–94.

the London financial market through the services of the Oriental Bank to assist with the commutation of samurai pensions.[9] There was general dissatisfaction within the Meiji regime as to the high interest rate on these two loans, and no further foreign loans were sought until after the adoption of the gold standard had been promulgated in 1897. Thus, the autonomous nature of Japan's capital formation was established as a significant feature of economic development in the post-restoration period.[10]

The 1894–1895 war against China made the continuance of autonomous capital formation untenable. Victory in the conflict might well have increased Japan's international (military) standing, but only at the cost of seriously imperiling Japan's limited financial reserves. Confronted by the need to push ahead with its national program of modernization, and urgently needing to defray the costs of war in China, the Japanese government was now prepared to reconsider its policies in regard to the import and use of foreign capital. Perhaps of greater importance, domestic and international entrepreneurs, financiers, industrialists, and manufacturers were prepared to invest, and the Meiji oligarchs were ready to accommodate their change in attitude. Following the Sino-Japanese War there was a tremendous increase in the number of public and private enterprises that required capital investments beyond the scale of those available in Japan, and many enterprises were forced to postpone or shelve projects. Not surprisingly, there was a growing call for the use of foreign capital and foreign entrepreneurs by Japanese business magnates and politicians. From an economic perspective, the conditions necessary for Japan's assimilation into the capitalist world market were gradually being realized. It was only after the adoption of the gold standard, however, that subsequent Meiji governments felt confident that they could attract and use foreign capital on their own terms, and so reverse the previous policy of autonomous development.[11]

---

9. Tatewaki, *Zainichi gaikoku ginkōshi*, pp. 303–18. See Macpherson, *The Economic Development of Japan*, p. 34; Matsukata, "Teikoku zaisei," p. 234; Meiji zaiseishi, *Meiji zaiseishi*, 8:164–74, 9:126–28; Ōkurashō, *Meiji Taishō zaiseishi*, pp. 23–33; and Ouchi and Tsuchiya, *Meiji zenki zaisei*, pp. 10:51–246.

10. M. Takahashi, *Japan's Modern Economy*, p. 183.

11. See "The Gold Standard in Japan," *TE*, 24 April 1897; Shibusawa, "The Development of Banking," p. 524; and M. Takahashi, *Japan's Modern Economy*, p. 300.

Table 5.1. Japanese Government Loan, Bond, and Note Issues, 1870–1930

Loan no.	Issue date	Issue market	Name of loan	Interest (% per annum)	Maturity (years)	Issue amount in k¥	Issue amount in k£ [kF] {k$}	Purpose of issue	Issuer
1	Apr. 1870	London	9% Japan Customs Loan	9.00	13	4,880	1,000	railway construction	J. Henry Schroeder and Co.
2	Jan. 1873	London	7% Japanese Sterling Loan	7.00	25	11,712	2,400	samurai pension scheme	Oriental Bank
3	June 1897	London	5% Military Loan	5.00	55	43,000	4,389	military expenditures	Capital and Counties Bank; Chartered Bank of India, Australia, and China; Hongkong and Shanghai Bank; Yokohama Specie Bank
4	June 1899	London	4% Sterling Loan (First Series)	4.00	55	97,630	10,000	railways; steelworks; telegraph and telephone networks	London Group
5	Oct. 1902	London	5% Domestic Bonds (Resale)	5.00	55	50,000	5,104	railways; steelworks; telegraph and telephone networks; military expenditures	London Group, Baring Bros. and Co.

(continued)

Table 5.1. (continued)

Loan no.	Issue date	Issue market	Name of loan	Interest (% per annum)	Maturity (years)	Issue amount in k¥	Issue amount in k£ [kF] {k$}	Purpose of issue	Issuer
6	May 1904	London, New York	6% Sterling Loan (First Series)	6.00	7	97,630	10,000	military expenditures	London Group; Kuhn, Loeb and Co.; National City Bank; National Bank of Commerce
7	Nov. 1904	London, New York	6% Sterling Loan (Second Series)	6.00	7	117,156	12,000	military expenditures	London Group; Kuhn, Loeb and Co.; National City Bank; National Bank of Commerce
8	Mar. 1905	London, New York	4.5% Sterling Loan (First Series)	4.50	20	292,890	30,000	military expenditures	London Group; Kuhn, Loeb and Co.; National City Bank; National Bank of Commerce
9	July 1905	London, New York, Berlin	4.5% Sterling Loan (Second Series)	4.50	20	292,890	30,000	military expenditures; refinancing high-interest domestic bonds	London Group; Kuhn, Loeb and Co.; National City Bank; National Bank of Commerce; M. M. Warburg and Co.

10	Nov. 1905	London, New York, Berlin, Paris	4% Sterling Loan (Second Series)	4.00	25	244,075	25,000	refinancing high-interest domestic bonds	London Group; N. M. Rothschild; Kuhn, Loeb and Co.; National City Bank; National Bank of Commerce; M. M. Warburg and Co.; Deutsche Asiatische Bank; Rothschild Frères
11	Mar. 1907	London, Paris	5% Sterling Loan (First Series)	5.00	40	224,550	23,000	refinancing 6% Sterling Bonds (First and Second Series)	London Group; N. M. Rothschild; Rothschild Frères
12	May 1910	Paris	4% Franc Loan (First Series)	4.00	60	174,150	17,813 [450,000]	refinancing high-interest domestic bonds	Rothschild Frères
13	May 1910	London	4% Sterling Loan (Third Series)	4.00	60	107,393	11,000	refinancing high-interest domestic bonds	London Group
14	Mar. 1913	London	Sterling Railway Bonds (First Series)	5.50	1	14,644	1,500	railway nationalization	London Group; Panmure Gordon, Hill and Co. (private placement)

(continued)

Table 5.1 (continued)

Loan no.	Issue date	Issue market	Name of loan	Interest (% per annum)	Maturity (years)	Issue amount in k¥	Issue amount in k£ [k£] {k$}	Purpose of issue	Issuer
15	Mar. 1913	London	Sterling Railway Notes (First Series)	5.00	2	14,644	1,500	railway nationalization	London Group; Panmure Gordon, Hill and Co. (private placement)
16	Apr. 1913	Paris	French Treasury Bonds	5.00	10	77,400	7,916 [200,000]	railway nationalization	Rothschild Frères
17	Feb. 1914	London	Sterling Railway Bonds (Second Series)	4.75	1	24,307	2,500	refinancing Sterling Railway Bonds (First Series)	London Group; Panmure Gordon, Hill and Co. (private placement)
18	Feb. 1915	London	Sterling Railway Bonds (Third Series)	5.75	1	29,289	3,000	refinancing Sterling Railway Bonds (Second Series)	London Group; Panmure Gordon, Hill and Co. (private placement)
19	Feb. 1924	New York, Amsterdam	6.5% Dollar Loan	6.50	30	300,900	30,823 {150,000}	refinancing 4.5% Sterling Bonds (First and Second Series); earthquake reconstruction	J. P. Morgan; Kuhn, Loeb and Co.; National City Bank; First National Bank of Commerce; Hope and Co.

No.	Date	Location	Loan					Purpose	Syndicate
20	Feb. 1924	London	6% Sterling Loan	6.00	35	244,075	25,000	refinancing 4.5% Sterling Bonds; earthquake reconstruction	Westminster Bank; Hongkong and Shanghai Bank; Yokohama Specie Bank; Baring Bros. and Co.; Morgan Grenfell; N. M. Rothschild; J. Henry Schroeder and Co.
21	May 1930	New York	5.5% Dollar Loan	5.50	35	142,426	14,588 {70,000}	refinancing 4% Sterling Loan of Nov. 1905 (Second Series)	J. P. Morgan; Kuhn, Loeb and Co.; National City Bank; First National Bank of Commerce; Hope and Co.; Yokohama Specie Bank
22	May 1930	London	5.5% Sterling Loan	5.50	35	122,037	12,500	refinancing 4% Sterling Loan of Nov. 1905 (Second Series)	Westminster Bank; Hongkong and Shanghai Bank; Yokohama Specie Bank; Baring Bros. and Co.; Morgan Grenfell; N. M. Rothschild; J. Henry Schroeder and Co.

Source: Bytheway, *Nihon keizai to gaikoku shihon*, pp. 106–7.

Note: In this and the following tables, the London Group refers to the syndicate consisting of the Yokohama Specie Bank, Parr's Bank, and Hongkong and Shanghai Bank.

Government Loans from the Gold Standard to the War with Russia

In examining the circumstances surrounding the issuance of Japanese government loans, bonds, and notes, we must consider the wider influences that facilitated Japan's remarkable import of foreign capital. In this regard, the financial upheavals associated with Japan's adoption of the gold standard, the formation and abrogation of the Anglo-Japanese alliance, the outbreak and conclusion of the First World War, the Great Kanto earthquake, and the march of Japanese imperialism in East Asia all played important roles.

The Japanese government's announcement of its plans to adopt—or, in point of fact, reestablish—a gold standard as of 1 October 1897 provided foreign capital with an unprecedented investment opportunity. Before the transition was officially enacted, an Anglo-Japanese investment syndicate was formed, on 1 June 1897, among the Capital and Counties Bank; the Chartered Bank of India, Australia, and China; the Hongkong and Shanghai Bank; and the Yokohama Specie Bank, with S. Samuel and Company acting as its chief negotiator and Panmure Gordon, Hill and Company acting as the main stockbroker and underwriter. The Japanese government employed the syndicate to raise a loan to effect the conversion of short-term, high-interest domestic bonds, issued during the time of the Sino-Japanese War, to long-term, lower-interest foreign bonds, thus reducing its overall debt burden. Accordingly, in June 1897 the 5 Percent Military Loan was floated on the London financial market to the value of ¥43 million, with a very long fifty-five-year maturity (see Table 5.1).[12] Although the loan's issue (or flotation, in financial terms) was successful in that it was oversubscribed by six times, it had been almost twenty-five years since Japan's last foreign loan, and the lack of Japanese experience in negotiations and borrowing (raising) foreign capital expressed itself in a number of ways. Critically, the government's characterization of its debt conversion as a "military" loan was misguided and undermined the credibility of the whole operation, as it led many investors to speculate that Japan was in fact preparing for a new war. Significantly, the Japanese government never made the same faux pas again: future loans would be directed toward productive enterprises, it

---

12. Nomura, *Nihon kinyū shihon*, pp. 215–17; Suzuki, *Japanese Government Loan Issues*, pp. 66–69; and Tamaki, *Japanese Banking*, pp. 95–96.

would claim, regardless of whether they were actually to be used for military purposes or not. Unsurprisingly, concerns were raised back in Tokyo that Japan had not secured the loan on the best possible terms: greater direct, on-the-spot involvement in future loan negotiations was thought necessary.[13]

Before embarking on further loan negotiations, therefore, Minister of Finance Inoue Kaoru dispatched the deputy-governor of the Yokohama Specie Bank, Takahashi Korekiyo, to Europe and America on 11 February 1898 to research the issuance of foreign loans and the proclivities of the world's premier financial markets. Something of a polymath, Takahashi was an interesting choice for the assignment, as he had started his career in banking as a young employee-cum-servant at the Yokohama branch of the Chartered Mercantile Bank of London, India and China. Naturally enough, on his arrival in London Takahashi turned to his former Yokohama manager, Alexander Allan Shand, for guidance. Now a submanager at Parr's Bank, the didactic Shand was more than happy to introduce Takahashi to members of London's financial community and to tutor him in the peculiar business of issuing loans in London.[14]

As a result of the efforts of Takahashi and Shand, Parr's Bank and the Yokohama Specie Bank established a loan syndicate along with the Chartered Mercantile Bank, the Hongkong and Shanghai Bank, and Panmure Gordon, Hill and Company, with the latter performing the role of the stockbroker and underwriter. The core of the syndicate would, in short time, become known as the London Group, and would subsequently monopolize the issuance of Japanese government loans, municipal loans, and, to a lesser extent, corporate loans (see Table 5.1, and Tables 6.1 and 6.2 in Chapter 6).[15] In June 1899 the newly formed London Group issued, on behalf of the Japanese government, the First 4 Percent

---

13. Kamiyama, *Meiji keizai seisakushi*, pp. 183–84.

14. K. Takahashi, *Takahashi Korekiyo jiden*, pp. 547–78, and Smethurst, *Takahashi Korekiyo, Japan's Keynes*, pp. 130–33.

15. While the makeup of what was loosely referred to as the London Group changed over time, its key members were essentially the Yokohama Specie Bank, as the international financial agent of the Japanese government; Parr's Bank, as the representative of the financial institutions of London; and the Hongkong and Shanghai Bank, as a representative of English financial institutions in East Asia. See Kamiyama, *Meiji keizai seisakushi*, pp. 185–86, and Warner, *Anglo-Japanese Financial Relations*, pp. 50–51.

Sterling Loan for £10 million (with a long, fifty-five-year maturity).[16] The loan was raised to support national finances and was related to the Japanese government's infrastructure policies, which aimed to use foreign capital to modernize key sectors of the Japanese economy. The main beneficiaries of the capital expenditure were associated with the construction and improvement of national railways, particularly in Hokkaido, the establishment of steelworks at Yawata, and the expansion of the government's telegraph and telephone services.[17] The First 4 Percent Sterling Loan, however, was not seen as a particularly attractive investment in the context of the "tight," unresponsive 1899 London market. Even though it had the support of reputable English banks, doubts were expressed about the size of the loan, its terms, and the stability of Japan's finances. As a result of these concerns, only 10 percent of the issue was subscribed on the open market, forcing the Japanese government and the Bank of Japan to discreetly purchase 45 percent of the issue, thus leaving the syndicate members and its main underwriter, Panmure Gordon, Hill and Company, to dutifully subscribe to the remaining 45 percent.[18]

Meanwhile the Japanese government continued to suffer the consequences of running a trade deficit, which, along with overspending, exacerbated the chronic problem of revenue shortfalls. The most obvious solution for a government still burdened with the cost of waging war against China and desperate to establish and expand national infrastructure, was, once again, to resort to the borrowing of foreign capital. After signing the first Anglo-Japanese alliance on 30 January 1902, Japan had new diplomatic grounds for expecting financial success on the London financial market, and indeed it would benefit from the intervention of the British government (as discussed in the Chapter 4).[19] By October 1902, the Hongkong and Shanghai Bank, Yokohama Specie Bank, and

16. Suzuki, *Japanese Government Loan Issues*, pp. 69–74.

17. Matsukata, "Teikoku zaisei," p. 235; Ōkurashō, *Meiji Taishō zaiseishi*, pp. 34–49; and Spalding, *Eastern Exchange*, pp. 174–75.

18. Suzuki, *Japanese Government Loan Issues*, pp. 69–74.

19. Treasury to Foreign Office, 1 October 1902, FO.46/560, National Archives (United Kingdom), London (hereafter, NAUK), p. 357, and Nish, *The Story of Japan*, pp. 253–56. See also Cain and Hopkins, *British Imperialism*, pp. 432–46; Kamiyama, *Meiji keizai seisakushi*, pp. 194–95; and Suzuki, *Japanese Government Loan Issues*, pp. 75–82, 84–88.

Baring Brothers had formed their own subscription and underwriting syndicate (with the ubiquitous Panmure Gordon, Hill and Company acting as the stockbroker), and the "resale" of Japan's 5 Percent Domestic Bonds, worth ¥50 million (with a fifty-five-year maturity), was carried out on the London financial market.[20] With the participation of the Bank of England, Lord Rothschild, and Baring Brothers, the release of the 5 Percent Domestic Bonds was a great success and a source of encouragement to the Japanese government. Japan's ability to attract foreign capital had clearly progressed since the time of the adoption of the gold standard in 1897; nevertheless, foreign capitalists, entrepreneurs, and investors were increasingly restrained in their actions by the mounting tension between Japan and Russia in the Far East.[21]

Government Loans from the Russo-Japanese War to the First World War

Following the signing of the Anglo-Japanese alliance, Japan was confident that it could challenge Russian forces in East Asia. The significance of Japan's adoption of the gold standard, and the import of large-scale foreign capital that it promised to engender, were to be tested during the ensuing Russo-Japanese War of 1904–1905. How would Japan be able to impress the great powers and achieve a meaningful victory over Russian forces in war when its own capital markets and government revenues were known to be incapable of financing the onerous costs of waging war?

The transfer of balances to London by the belligerent governments to pay for armaments, coal, and stores may be seen as the first salvo in the Russo-Japanese War.[22] Japan's financial campaign started in earnest on 8 February 1904, when the new minister of finance, Sone Arasuke, desperate to buttress his country's finances, dispatched Takahashi Korekiyo to London. Takahashi's instructions were essentially to issue a loan worth £10 million, in a repeat performance of his earlier efforts in negotiating the First 4 Percent Sterling Loan of June 1899. The syndicate led by Takahashi's Yokohama Specie Bank and Shand's own Parr's Bank

---

20. Matsukata, "Teikoku zaisei," p. 235, and Ōkurashō, *Meiji Taishō zaiseishi*, pp. 424–28.
21. M. Takahashi, *Japan's Modern Economy*, p. 302.
22. Sayers, *Bank of England Operations*, p. 124.

maintained the trust of the Hongkong and Shanghai Bank, but the Chartered Mercantile Bank declined to take part in the loan, fearing a repeat of the First 4 Percent Sterling Loan's lukewarm response. With only one bank in the syndicate being a major "City" bank, the syndicate members feared that the London financial market would be unable to supply the syndicate with the necessary capital, so Shand, through the introduction of Baring Brothers, contacted Jacob H. Schiff, a powerful Jewish businessman and philanthropist and a senior partner in the banking firm Kuhn, Loeb and Company of New York.[23] Owing to Schiff's convictions about funding the fight against anti-Semitic, tsarist Russia, and to the behind-the-scenes pushes of the financier Ernest "Windsor" Cassel and Baring Brothers, Kuhn, Loeb and Company joined with two other American banks, the National City Bank and the National Bank of Commerce, to form an financial syndicate, sometimes referred to as the New York Group, to issue loans on the New York market.[24]

In May 1904 the new transatlantic financial syndicates simultaneously released the First 6 Percent Sterling Loan, for £10 million, in the financial markets of London and New York. The market's response to the loan was enthusiastic in New York, where the issue was oversubscribed fivefold, and even more so in London, where the loan was over-

---

23. Schiff's long interest in Japanese finance traces all the way back to his participation in the 7 Percent Japanese Sterling Loan of 1873. Takahashi claimed that Schiff, as president of the American Jewish Association, was eager to support Japan, as tsarist Russia's long history of anti-Semitic persecution had made him righteously indignant. K. Takahashi, *Takahashi Korekiyo jiden*, pp. 682–86. Schiff's own correspondence (with Rothschild) confirms Takahashi's claim. See Adler and Schiff, *Jacob H. Schiff*, p. 120.

24. Barings, wary of upsetting the Russian government, was unwilling to be directly connected with Japanese government loans. Rather, the bank offered Schiff a £5 million share of the loan, charged 0.5% commission on introduction (£25,000), and underwrote a £300,000 share of the loan. In the following negotiations for further capital, Baring Brothers anonymously negotiated participation with Kuhn, Loeb, the Warburgs in Hamburg, and with Rothschilds in London, emerging with a total profit of £110,000. At no time was the imperial Russian government aware of, or alerted to, these transactions. See Zeigler, *The Sixth Great Power*, pp. 311–12. See also Smethurst, *Takahashi Korekiyo, Japan's Keynes*, pp. 149–57; Suzuki, *Japanese Government Loan Issues*, pp. 93–104; K. Takahashi, *Takahashi Korekiyo jiden*, pp. 682–93; and Tamaki, *Japanese Banking*, p. 96. The New York group was active in financing East Asian loans, and would later work alongside J. P. Morgan in China. See Overlach, *Foreign Financial Control in China*, pp. 228–32.

subscribed to thirty-three times its stated amount.[25] The Japanese government, needing to bolster its gold reserves and anticipating even greater costs in continuing its war with Russia, was greatly encouraged by the popularity of the issue and felt confident it could achieve more favorable terms with subsequent loans. A significant disparity between the London and New York quotation prices of the First 6 Percent Sterling Loan, however, frustrated the hopes of Japan's financial authorities. Fears of rising international interest rates, along with a fickle market, forced the Japanese government to accept essentially the same terms for a Second 6 Percent Sterling Loan in November 1904. Issued simultaneously in both London and New York, for a higher figure of £12 million, the loan's high 6 percent interest rate again generated tremendous investor interest. It was oversubscribed in excess of thirteen times in London and one-and-a-half times in New York, with additional subscriptions worth more than £100,000 being raised through M. M. Warburg and Company in Hamburg for the New York issue. In the context of the undecided Russo-Japanese War, the invaluable financial support provided by these loans was no doubt a product of the Anglo-Japanese alliance and the fact that the foreign specie reserve for Japan's gold standard was held in pounds sterling and safely deposited in London.[26]

Even as the Russo-Japanese War was drawing to a close, the Japanese government required the continued import of foreign capital to defray its military costs, particularly in relation to the purchase of armaments from Britain, and to support its external gold reserves. Moreover, the Japanese Ministry of Finance was also eager to use the inflow of foreign capital to finance the redemption of its own short-term, high-interest domestic bond issuances with long-term, low-interest foreign loans. Accordingly, the previously established London Group and Takahashi Korekiyo were once again pressed into service. In March 1905 the First 4.5 Percent Sterling Loan was issued, for £30 million.[27]

Just four months later, in July 1905, the Second 4.5 Percent Sterling Loan was issued on identical terms and for the same amount. Both of

---

25. Kamiyama, *Meiji keizai seisakushi*, p. 208.

26. Matsukata, "Teikoku zaisei," p. 235; Ōkurashō, *Meiji Taishō zaiseishi*, pp. 50–115; Shinjo, *History of the Yen*, p. 95; Suzuki, *Japanese Government Loan Issues*, pp. 100–110; and Tamaki, *Japanese Banking*, p. 96.

27. Smethurst, *Takahashi Korekiyo, Japan's Keynes*, pp. 170–81.

these loans (in effect, Japan's third and fourth Russo-Japanese War loans) were simultaneously floated on the financial markets of London and New York, and in July the second loan was also offered on the Berlin market for the first time. German financiers, especially Speyer Brothers, had been pressing the syndicate members in New York for inclusion in the Japanese government bond business since the issue of the First 6 Percent Sterling Loan in May 1904. Schiff of Kuhn, Loeb and Company had previously allowed Speyer's competitor, M. M. Warburg of Hamburg, to take a subsidiary part in the loan, but by July 1905 the pressure was such that German overtures could not be dismissed, and a German syndicate led by M. M. Warburg and the Deutsche Asiatische Bank issued one-third of the loan on the Berlin financial market.[28] The Japanese government very much welcomed the increasing German participation, from both a diplomatic and a financial viewpoint, as they felt it would enable them to secure future loans at better terms.[29]

After the conclusion of the Russo-Japanese War and the signing of the Treaty of Portsmouth on 5 September 1905, Japan's Ministry of Finance continued to demand more foreign capital. In November the London Group joined forces with N. M. Rothschild and Sons of London and their cousins, M. M. de Rothschild Frères in Paris, to form a syndicate capable of simultaneously issuing the new Japanese government loan in the world's four great financial markets: London, New York, Paris, and Berlin. The Second 4 Percent Sterling Loan, as it was called, was issued for £25 million, and it allowed the Japanese government to redeem (meet the repayment of) its own high-interest, short-term domestic "exchequer" bonds, and to raise a further ¥280 million in new, lower-interest, domestic bond issues.[30] The Japanese government, pleased by the low-interest terms of the November 1905 issue, once again negotiated with the Rothschilds of London and Paris to join with the London Group in financing the accelerated redemption of the Anglo-American First and

---

28. Chernow, *The Warburgs*, p. 110; Kamiyama, *Meiji keizai seisakushi*, pp. 210–11; and Suzuki, *Japanese Government Loan Issues*, pp. 114–17.

29. Ōkurashō, *Meiji Taishō zaiseishi*, pp. 115–83, and K. Takahashi, *Takahashi Korekiyo jiden*, pp. 707–18.

30. Ōkurashō, *Meiji Taishō zaiseishi*, pp. 183–229. The negotiations associated with the Paris issue were complex and difficult. See K. Takahashi, *Takahashi Korekiyo jiden*, pp. 726–40, 769–93; and Suzuki, *Japanese Government Loan Issues*, pp. 117–27. Shinjo, *History of the Yen*, p. 95.

Second 6 Percent Sterling Loans of May and November 1904. In place of the first and second of Japan's wartime loans, in March 1907 the new Anglo-French 5 Percent Sterling Loan was issued on the financial markets of both London and Paris at the nominal value of £23 million (with a long maturity of forty years).[31]

The Japanese government's difficulties in servicing its debt obligations would persist until the First World War, when the economic and financial upheavals associated with the war provided Japan with adequate funds in the form of a trade surplus. Constantly aware of the desirability of securing competitive sources of finance and arranging loans on the best of possible terms, the Japanese government's financial authorities were eager to continue to reduce the nation's debts by refinancing through so-called conversion loans, and they began to examine alternate financial markets outside of London.[32] With financial panic, associated with the Bank of England's high bank rates from late 1906 to early 1908, destabilizing the financial markets of Amsterdam, Berlin, and New York (see Chapter 4), Paris was the only financial market left that was capable of challenging London. Fortunately for Japan, the French financial authorities were eager to be involved in new business with their Japanese counterparts.[33]

Following the signing of both the Franco-Japanese Agreement and the Russo-Japanese Convention in 1907, French financiers were released from previous diplomatic constraints and enjoyed a good working relationship with Japan. Mitsui Bank was particularly active on the Paris financial market, and organized a French loan for the Kanegafuchi Cotton Spinning Company in 1908, and two loans for the city of Kyoto in 1909 and 1912 to facilitate road construction, waterworks, and an electric tramway (see Chapter 6). Moreover, M. M. de Rothschild Frères had successfully organized a large syndicate of eminent French banks to cater to Japanese government borrowing, and through the efforts of such financiers, the First 4 Percent Franc Loan for F450 million was floated on the Paris market in May 1910 (with a long, sixty-year maturity). This was the first foreign loan to the Japanese government that was not denominated in

---

31. Ōkurashō, *Meiji Taishō zaiseishi*, pp. 229–70; Spalding, *Eastern Exchange*, pp. 174–75; and Suzuki, *Japanese Government Loan Issues*, pp. 129–45.

32. MacDonald to Grey, Confidential, 14 February 1912, FO.371/1388, FOJ.

33. Suzuki, *Japanese Government Loan Issues*, pp. 139–45.

pounds sterling. It should be noted, however, that the use of the Paris financial market to raise loans did not represent a major Japanese departure from the London market. In reality, the French loan was floated only after careful consultation with London's financiers, where the Third 4 Percent Sterling Loan for £11 million was also arranged, with an equivalent interest rate and maturity.[34]

While the First 4 Percent Franc Loan was applied to financing debts associated with the railway nationalization program, the Third 4 Percent Sterling Loan was raised exclusively to effect the conversion and redemption of the Japanese government's domestic 5 Percent War Bonds of 1895–1896 totaling some ¥43 million, and 5 Percent Bonds of 1901–1902 totaling some ¥50 million. For the first time since 1899, however, the issue of the loan was undersubscribed by 23 percent on the London financial market, owing to large British purchases of the First French 4 Percent Franc Loan, the financial market's subdued reaction to the death of King Edward VII, and the low-interest terms of the British loan itself.[35]

Three years later, on 19 April 1913, a further loan of 5 Percent French Treasury Bonds totaling ₣200 million was exclusively issued on the Paris financial market to assist the Japanese government with ongoing debts incurred through nationalization of the railways.[36] Then, as the final note to the French financial interlude, cooperation between financiers in France and Japan led to the establishment of the Banque Franco-Japonaise on 3 July 1913. Pointedly, it aimed to encourage and develop trade between the two countries by replacing the need to use British financial intermediaries with its own services. Apparently, of the ¥10 million raised in start-up capital, Japan's leading private and parastatal banks optimistically invested ¥4 million, with the Industrial Bank of Japan contributing ¥2 million, and with the Yokohama Specie Bank, the Dai-Ichi Bank, the Mitsui Bank, and the Mitsubishi Bank contributing ¥500,000 each. The coming of war in Europe, however, ensured that the Banque

---

34. Ōkurashō, *Meiji Taishō zaiseishi*, pp. 270–305.

35. Kamiyama, *Meiji keizai seisakushi*, pp. 216–18; Ōkurashō, *Meiji Taishō zaiseishi*, pp. 270–305; and Suzuki, *Japanese Government Loan Issues*, pp. 139–45.

36. Ōkurashō, *Meiji Taishō zaiseishi*, pp. 315–38. For historical background and analysis, see Ericson, *The Sound of the Whistle*, pp. 377–88.

Franco-Japonaise experienced a difficult (interrupted) start, and it never fully realized its founders' hopes.[37]

The final episode in the story of Japanese government loan issues on the London financial market before the First World War was a series of short-term railway loans from 1913 to 1916. The Japanese government, still struggling to meet the financial obligations associated with the nationalization of the railways despite the large French loans already mentioned, was obliged to raise new loans in London to restructure the repayment of its short-term debts. Two confidential loans, to be filled exclusively by private investors ("placements," in financial jargon), were initially raised on 13 March 1913 for the First Sterling 5.5 Percent Railway Bonds, and the First Sterling 5 Percent Railway Notes, each to the value of £1.5 million.[38] It soon became clear, however, that the Japanese government could not restructure its railway nationalization debts within the space of a year, and a further one-year loan, filled exclusively by private placements, was raised on 16 February 1914: the Second Sterling (4.75 Percent) Railway Bonds for another £2.5 million.[39] By the time of the outbreak of the First World War six months later, in August 1914, the Japanese government was still unable to solve what it was calling its "repayment problems," despite a confusing array of short-term railway loans. That is, the Japanese government was unable, or perhaps unwilling, to release the appropriate sum in pounds sterling needed to effect the redemption of its own sterling railway bonds. Under the new tightened wartime circumstances, Britain's financial authorities were eager to put an end to Japan's outstanding short-term loans, while for its part, the Japanese government seemed anxious to maintain its good standing and repay foreign loans. On 16 February and 13 March 1915, a composite one-year loan divided into two separate issues and worth £3 million was issued under conditions identical to the two previous loans, except the interest rate of the Third Sterling Railway Bonds had risen to the higher rate (5.75 percent). Thus, the repayment of the Third Sterling (5.75 Percent) Railway Bonds in 1916 put an end to what was supposed to be a single year's debts, and offered a telling insight into the tenuous

---

37. Hara, "Nichi-fuginkō no keieishi," pp. 139–92, especially pp. 139–51; Horie, *Gaishi yunyū*, p. 115; and Suzuki, *Japanese Government Loan Issues*, pp. 159–60.

38. Ōkurashō, *Meiji Taishō zaiseishi*, pp. 305–14.

39. Ōkurashō, *Meiji Taishō zaiseishi*, pp. 339–44.

nature of the Japanese government's finances on the eve of the First World War.[40]

Government Bonds from the Great Kanto
Earthquake to the Manchurian Incident

As Europe attempted to come to terms with the consequences of modern warfare—the unprecedented and incomprehensible scale of its death and destruction—the Japanese government could reflect on its own situation with a sense of calm. Of all the combatants in the First World War, Japan alone emerged almost unscathed. Indeed, during the war Japan (with its policy of substitute production) had enjoyed surging exports and enviable economic growth, and had been able, as never before, to strengthen its economic position in Asia. Although the state of the government and special bank finances had markedly deteriorated after the dizzy highs of the war years, owing, in no small way, to imprudent and unprincipled lending, Japan had at least avoided the financial costs of war-related reconstruction.[41] Then, in an instant, on 1 September 1923, the Kanto region was struck by a powerful, large-magnitude earthquake that, with the ensuing fires, devastated most of Yokohama and much of Tokyo. The two cities, both impoverished by the disaster and facing massive reconstruction costs, had no choice but to turn to the national government for financial assistance.

The Japanese government lacked the financial reserves to cope with a disaster of those proportions and almost immediately reached out to its international creditors. Given the government's twenty-seven-year history of using, and indeed relying on, the London market to finance its deficits and outlays, and the long association of the London Group with the Japanese government loans, London was the logical place for the Japanese government to start looking for assistance. With reconstruction

---

40. Ōkurashō, *Meiji Taishō zaiseishi*, pp. 344–53.

41. Substitute production (*dai tai seisan*) refers to the policy of replacing Western-made goods with Japanese-made substitutes, by specifically targeting production to those items of European industry most affected by the First World War. It was particularly successful in East, South, and Southeast Asia. See Boulding and Gleason, "War as an Investment," pp. 240–61, especially pp. 250, 257; and Emi, *Government Fiscal Activity*, pp. 140–41.

costs from the earthquake damage estimated at £140 million, or $700 million, and with the purchases of foreign materials and supplies being estimated at just under half of that total, the Japanese government began negotiating to borrow approximately £60 million, or $300 million, from London and New York. Borrowing of that magnitude had not been attempted since the heady days of the Russo-Japanese War, when £60 million had been raised with the first and second series of the 4.5 Percent Sterling Loans in March and July 1905. In fact, it was no coincidence that the Japanese government was negotiating for a loan similar to the 4.5 Percent Sterling Loans, for it was toward the redemption of those two loans that the new loan was primarily directed, with the discussion of funds for earthquake relief being little more than an expedient to elicit international sympathy and support for Japan in its fiscal difficulties, and impending insolvency.[42]

As with the First and Second 4.5 Percent Sterling Loans and the 4 Percent Sterling Loan of November 1905, the Yokohama Specie Bank, the Hongkong and Shanghai Bank, and the stockbrokers Panmure Gordon, Hill and Company of the London Group would need transatlantic cooperation and all the connections that only London's financiers could provide. The fourth core member of the London Group, Parr's Bank, had merged with the London, County, and Westminster Bank during 1918, and was renamed the Westminster Bank as of 1923. Fortunately for the old London Group members, the Westminster Bank continued to perform the role, formerly played by Parr's Bank, of the syndicate's clearing bank in London, and agreed to the formation of a larger syndicate. Accordingly, the syndicate was soon joined by three of London's great merchant banks, N. M. Rothschild and Sons, J. Henry Schroder and Company, and Baring Brothers, which, with the fall of the tsarist Russian government in the March Revolution of 1917, were no longer obliged to act as covert participants in Japanese government loan issuances. In addition to these institutions, Morgan Grenfell and Company was

---

42. Ōkurashō, *Meiji Taishō zaiseishi*, pp. 368–69. The J. P. Morgan "ambassador" Thomas Lamont is seen as having played a crucial role in advising and coaching Japan's financial authorities in how to best receive foreign aid while negotiating for these new loans. See Chernow, *The House of Morgan*, pp. 232–37; E. M. Lamont, *Ambassador from Wall Street*, pp. 196–244; and Metzler, *Lever of Empire*, pp. 168–69.

admitted to the syndicate, which was now referred to as the Enlarged London Group, to communicate and coordinate the syndicate's efforts with those across the Atlantic in New York.[43]

It was through the initiative and drive of the Morgan house—in particular, its senior partners J. P. Morgan Jr. and Thomas Lamont—that J. P. Morgan of New York and its London subsidiary, Morgan Grenfell, became the vital link between the two financial markets of London and New York. The relationship between these financial capitals was reestablished for sound commercial reasons and relates to much more than just the provision of Japanese government loans. Indeed, such joint issues became the norm for business conducted with J. P. Morgan, as the parties on both sides benefited and "London alone could not provide funds on the scale required, but its participation was appreciated by New York bankers as constituting an imprimatur of quality."[44] J. P. Morgan was thus soon able to persuade Hope and Company and the First National Bank, along with two members of the old New York Group, namely Kuhn, Loeb and Company and the National City Bank, to join with them in forming a syndicate called the Enlarged New York Group, to issue Japanese government loans on the New York market.[45]

In retrospect, these could be looked upon as the halcyon days of Japan's financial courtship with New York's bankers. Indeed, for a five-year period from approximately 1923 to 1928, a host of Wall Street's finest, with J. P. Morgan front and center, eagerly sought to issue Japanese bonds. At the period's very height, J. P. Morgan Jr. and Thomas W. Lamont; Kuhn, Loeb's Mortimer L. Schiff and Otto H. Kahn; National City Bank's Charles E. Mitchell; and First National Bank's George F. Baker all received decorations the from the emperor (in absentia, except for Lamont).[46]

---

43. Suzuki, "Senkanki Rondon kinyūishijō," pp. 162–68, and Warner, *Anglo-Japanese Financial Relations*, pp. 92–93.

44. Burk, *Morgan Grenfell*, pp. 90–91.

45. Warner, *Anglo-Japanese Financial Relations*, pp. 92–93.

46. Following his audience with the emperor, Lamont and his one-time legal counsel Jeremiah Smith Jr. were invited to investigate Japanese government finances. Taking the authorities at their word, Lamont submitted a long series of pointed questions—best exemplified by "Why so much government in business?" and "How much more will it be necessary to borrow?"—for which the Japanese representatives had no satisfactory answers. Despite Japan's continued desire for J. P. Morgan's services, and Lamont's late apology for being "dreadfully frank," the relationship was never quite the

In February 1924, in accordance with proposed legislation for earthquake reconstruction payments, the 6 Percent Sterling Loan for £25 million and the 6.5 Percent Dollar Loan for $150 million were simultaneously issued on the financial markets of London and New York by their respective enlarged financial syndicates. The issue of the 6.5 Percent Dollar Loan is of particular significance, for it was the first Japanese government loan to be directed toward the New York market since 1905, and it was the first Japanese government loan to be denominated in U.S. dollars. Unlike the previous Russo-Japanese War loans of 1904 and 1905, however, the London and New York loans of 1924 were formally separated into a pound and a dollar component, at a nine-to-eleven ratio in favor of the dollar loan (that is, approximately 55 percent was raised in the New York market and the remainder was raised in London). Moreover, the terms, conditions, and popularity of the London and New York issues were also different, with the 6 Percent Sterling Loan circulating at a discount rate of 13 percent, generating a tremendous response in London, while the 6.5 Percent Dollar Loan slowly circulated at a much lower 7.5 percent discount rate in New York.[47] The emerging differentials and the popularity of the London issue encouraged members of the New York syndicate to seek resale rights in London and other European financial markets. Naturally, the members of the London syndicate bitterly opposed the resale of the 6.5 Percent Dollar Loan in London, but a face-saving

---

same again. Apart from that episode, however, the suggestion by J. P. Morgan's Russell Leffingwell that the Bank of Japan should establish closer relations with the Federal Reserve Bank of New York was met with enthusiasm. And J. P. Morgan's operation to get Japan back on the gold standard (culminating in the May 1930 loans) would be the company's greatest success and would reveal the extent of its influence. See Thomas W. Lamont Papers, Box Nos. 186-31, 187-2, 187-4, 188-12, 188-30, 189-17, 189-22, 190-6, Baker Library, Harvard University (hereafter TWL); and Benjamin Strong Papers, No. 610.2, Federal Reserve Bank of New York (hereafter, BFRB). Further research at other archives supports these circumspect views; see, e.g., Japan—Bank of Japan Correspondence, C. 261, Federal Reserve Bank of New York (hereafter, JFRB), and Russell C. Leffingwell Papers, MS 1030, Yale University Library (hereafter, RCL).

47. Subscription lists for the loan in London were filled within the first two hours of its opening. After all, Japan's fiscal and monetary policies were considered sound, its debts were scrupulously honored, and Japanese government bonds were historically, with a few exceptions, well received in London. See Warner, *Anglo-Japanese Financial Relations*, p. 94.

compromise was reached that allowed limited reselling in Amsterdam and Zurich.[48]

Within the Japanese government itself, the "Kanto earthquake loans" were not universally welcomed. Articles in newspapers and magazines claimed that the Japanese government, despite the general instability of the world's financial markets and inflationary rises in their respective interest rates, had been forced by Great Britain and the United States to accept "loans of shame" on unfavorable terms, when in reality Japan's financial weakness, specifically its need to maintain foreign specie reserves in the face of continued trade deficits, and the catalyst of the Kanto earthquake had combined to foist high-interest rates on the government's loans.[49] To complicate matters further, the loans themselves were also of a dual, or composite, nature, being made for both reconstruction and redemption purposes, as mentioned earlier. On receipt of the foreign capital, the Japanese government had allotted the great bulk of the 6 Percent Sterling Loan and the 6.5 Percent Dollar Loan to what it called an "Extraordinary Government Loan Reorganization Fund," which was used to redeem the First and Second 4.5 Percent Sterling Loans of March and July of 1905, due to be paid in 1925. In fact, of the total ¥545 million issued in accordance with the Kanto earthquake reconstruction legislation, just ¥105 million of the loan from London and ¥11 million of the loan from America, or 21 percent of the total issue amount, was actually directed toward earthquake reconstruction.[50]

The final chapter in Japanese government borrowing from foreign capital markets is very similar in character to the 6 Percent Sterling and 6.5 Percent Dollar Loans of February 1924. In May 1930 the Japanese government was compelled to raise a 5.5 Percent Sterling Loan for £12.5 million, and a 5.5 Percent Dollar Loan for $70 million (both with thirty-five-year maturities), to effect the redemption of the Second 4 Percent Sterling Loan of November 1905 (due November 1930) and refinance its international debt obligations.[51] Once again, the new enlarged financial syndicates, previously entrusted with the 6 Percent Sterling and the

---

48. Suzuki, *Japanese Government Loan Issues*, pp. 168–69, and Warner, *Anglo-Japanese Financial Relations*, pp. 93–94.

49. M. Ito, *Nihon no taigai kinyū*, pp. 147–51, and Suzuki, *Japanese Government Loan Issues*, pp. 172–73.

50. Horie, *Gaishi yunyū* , pp. 145–46.

51. See Suzuki, *Japanese Government Loan Issues*, pp. 174–79.

6.5 Percent Dollar Loans of February 1924, simultaneously issued both loans in London and New York, with an approximate nine-to-eleven ratio in the total value in favor of the dollar loan. Unlike the 1924 issues, however, these negotiations were to some extent simplified, as the concerned parties had once again (at great cost), fixed their currencies on a gold standard, which assisted the negotiation of identical interest rates and maturities for the issues on both sides of the Atlantic. Indeed, the provision of the 1930 loans was predicated on the clear understanding that Japan would employ its newly won capital to return to Anglo-American financial orthodoxy by reestablishing a gold standard to stabilize the yen's value.[52] Taken in this light, the sudden and shocking collapse of the international gold standard, the key institution of the Great Powers' political economy throughout the long nineteenth century, was seen by bellicose and increasingly influential elements within the Japanese government as the harbinger of great change. Given the new political and economic realities of the 1930s, no further loans were sought by the Japanese government until after fifteen years of war, first with China, and then, eventually, against its long-time financiers, Great Britain and the United States.[53]

---

52. TWL, 186-31, 187-2, 187-4; especially J. P. Morgan & Co. to Minister of Finance Inouye [cable], TWL, 187-2.

53. See Murakami, *Japan: The Years of Trial*, pp. 27–45.

CHAPTER 6

Municipal and Corporate Loans, 1899–1931

Municipal loans were an important source of foreign capital, particularly in the period from the adoption of the gold standard to the First World War, and in the period after the Great Kanto earthquake. Associated with Japan's then largest metropolises, the issuance of foreign loans to the "six great cities" of Honshu was entirely related to, and utterly dependent on, the fiscal needs of the national Japanese government. Indeed, tables of government and Ministry of Finance statistics often show the foreign loans of the municipalities side by side with those of the national government, as if the issuance of municipality loans was an act of the state. At the same time, the accounting of corporate bonds was treated differently, often separated from government and municipal loans. Recent research, however, emphasizes the common roles of the Japanese government, intermediary institutions, and financial syndicates in all stages of the foreign loans provided to Japanese municipalities and companies, and argues that they should be discussed together as one area of inquiry. While there is a logic to this argument, for the sake of clarity the provision of foreign capital to Japan's cities and companies is analyzed separately in this chapter from foreign loans to the Japanese state.

In 1899 the Japanese government announced a new policy of "no further increases in tax, no further increases in debt," directed in equal parts toward its electorate and the London financial market, as a desperate measure to improve domestic and foreign purchases of its own loan issues.[1] Unhappily for the government, the modernization of Japan's

---

1. Mochida, *Toshi zaisei no kenkyū*, pp. 113–14; Suzuki, *Japanese Government Loan Issues*, pp. 72–74; K. Takahashi, *Takahashi Korekiyo jiden*, pp. 752–77; and Tamaki, *Japanese Banking*, pp. 95–96.

industry required the import of foreign capital, and the corresponding increases in fiscal debt. These circumstances prompted Wakatsuki Reijiro, working on secondment from the Ministry of Finance with the newly founded Industrial Bank of Japan, to devise a method whereby the Japanese government could compensate for its revenue shortfalls by attracting foreign capital through the issuance of municipal loans. In essence, the Japanese government encouraged Tokyo, Osaka, Yokohama, and Japan's other major cities to borrow capital from foreign markets, ostensibly as a means of independently financing infrastructural and public works projects associated with the provision of water, electricity, gas, and other utilities.[2] The Industrial Bank of Japan would act to coordinate the issues and deposit foreign currencies, convertible to gold, in the Japanese government's account at the Bank of England (and elsewhere), where the funds would act as Japan's "external" gold reserve. The municipalities would then be paid out in yen with an equivalent sum of gold-convertible bank notes from the Bank of Japan.[3]

Municipal Loans from the Gold Standard to the First World War

Kobe was the first Japanese city to attract foreign capital investment when it issued the 6 Percent City of Kobe Loan for £26,000 on the London financial market in May 1899, for potable water and sewerage works (see Table 6.1). Three years later, in May 1902, Yokohama followed the Kobe example and issued the 6 Percent City of Yokohama Loan for £92,000 on the London financial market, also to be used to construct waterworks. Osaka followed suit, in June of the following year, and issued the 6 Percent City of Osaka Loan for £315,000 (with a remarkably long seventy-eight-year maturity) on the London financial market, to finance harbor repairs and reconstruction.[4] Despite these large foreign loans, representing a total of £433,000 by June 1903, there was still hesitation about Japan's commercial prospects among foreign investors, owing to the growing tension between Japan and Russia.

---

2. Mochida, *Toshi zaisei no kenkyū*, pp. 107–15.

3. Wakatsuki, *Meiji/Taishō/Shōwa sekaihishi*, pp. 124–43, and Tamaki, *Japanese Banking*, p. 100.

4. Ōkurasho henshū, *Meiji Taishō zaiseishi*, pp. 714–26; Shinjo, *History of the Yen*, p. 94; Suzuki, *Japanese Government Loan Issues*, pp. 146–62; and Tamaki, *Japanese Banking*, pp. 95–96.

Table 6.1. Japanese Municipal Loans, 1899–1927

Loan no.	Issue date	Issue market	Municipality	Interest (% per annum)	Maturity (years)	Issue amount in k¥
1	May 1899	London	Kobe	6.00	36	250
2	May 1902	London	Yokohama	6.00	23	900
3	June 1903	London	Osaka	6.00	78	3,085
4	Aug. 1906	London	Tokyo	5.00	30	14,580
5	Feb. 1907	London	Yokohama	6.00	28	3,109
6	Apr. 1909	London	Yokohama	6.00	8	648
7	May 1909	London	Osaka	5.00	29	30,220
8	June 1909	London	Nagoya	5.00	33	7,816
9	July 1909	Paris	Kyoto	5.00	29	17,550
10	July 1909	London	Yokohama	5.00	44	7,000
11	Jan. 1912	Paris	Kyoto	5.00	20	1,950
12	Oct. 1912	London, New York, Paris	Tokyo	5.00	40	89,564
13	Dec. 1912	London	Yokohama	5.00	16	1,200
14	Oct. 1926	London	Tokyo	5.50	35	58,578
15	Dec. 1926	New York	Yokohama	6.00	34	39,602
16	Mar. 1927	New York	Tokyo	5.50	34	41,408

Source: Bytheway, *Nihon keizai to gaikoku shihon*, pp. 138–39.

Issue amount in k£ [kF] {k$}	Purpose of issue	Intermediary	Issuer
26	water and sewerage infrastructure	Morse and Co.	Morse and Co.
92	water and sewerage infrastructure	S. Samuel and Co.	Capital and Counties Bank; M. Samuel and Co.
315	harbor improvement	Daisan Bank; Yasuda Bank (with S. Samuel and Co.)	Capital and Counties Bank; M. Samuel and Co.
1,500	harbor and road improvement	Industrial Bank of Japan	London Group
317	harbor improvement	S. Samuel and Co.	M. Samuel and Co.
66	gasworks infrastructure	Hongkong and Shanghai Bank	Hongkong and Shanghai Bank
3,085	water, sewerage, and tram infrastructure	Industrial Bank of Japan	London Group
800	water and sewerage infrastructure	Sale and Frazer Co.	Lazard Bros. and Co.
1,810 [45,000]	electricity, water, and sewerage infrastructure	Mitsui Bank (with Kahn and Co.)	Banque de l'Union parisienne
714	sewerage infrastructure	Industrial Bank of Japan	London Group
199 [5,000]	electricity, water, and sewerage infrastructure	Mitsui Bank (with Kahn and Co.)	Banque de l'Union parisienne
9,136	electricity infrastructure	Industrial Bank of Japan	London Group; Kuhn, Loeb and Co.; Society General Co.
122	gasworks infrastructure	Sale and Frazer Co.	Law Debenture Corp.
6,000	earthquake reconstruction	Industrial Bank of Japan (government guaranteed)	Westminster Bank; Hongkong and Shanghai Bank; Yokohama Specie Bank; Baring Bros. and Co.; Morgan Grenfell; N. M. Rothschild; J. Henry Schroeder and Co.
4,056 {19,740}	earthquake reconstruction	Industrial Bank of Japan (government guaranteed)	J. P. Morgan; Kuhn, Loeb and Co.; National City Bank; First National Bank of Commerce; Hope and Co.; Yokohama Specie Bank
4,241 {20,640}	earthquake reconstruction	Industrial Bank of Japan (government guaranteed)	J. P. Morgan; Kuhn, Loeb and Co.; National City Bank; First National Bank of Commerce; Hope and Co.; Yokohama Specie Bank

After Japan shocked the great powers by achieving a comprehensive victory in the Russo-Japanese War of 1904–1905, the import of foreign capital really became socioeconomically significant. In August 1906 Tokyo issued the 5 Percent City of Tokyo Loan for £1.5 million on the London financial market, for harbor and road improvements. In February of the following year Yokohama, also requiring funds for harbor improvement, issued the 6 Percent City of Yokohama Loan for £317,000 on the London financial market. Moreover, in April 1909 Yokohama issued another 6 Percent City of Yokohama Loan for £66,000 on the London financial market, this time for the municipal gasworks. In May 1909 Osaka issued the 5 Percent City of Osaka Loan for £3 million on the London financial market, for water purification (sewerage) and Osaka's light-railway tram service. In June 1909 Nagoya issued the 5 Percent City of Nagoya Loan for £8 million on the London financial market, for water pipelines and waste water (sewerage) infrastructure. Then, for the fourth straight month, in July 1909 Yokohama issued (again) a 5 Percent City of Yokohama Loan for £714,000 on the London financial market, this time for water purification and sewerage projects.[5]

At the same time, in July 1909 Kyoto looked toward the Paris financial market to issue the 5 Percent City of Kyoto Loan for F45 million to finance power (electricity) distribution, water supply, and the construction of sewerage works. By January 1912 Kyoto was forced to find additional funds for those above projects, and a further 5 Percent City of Kyoto Loan totaling F5 million was floated on the Paris financial market. In October 1912 Tokyo once again got in on the act and issued the 5 Percent City of Tokyo Loan for £9 million pounds, to defray infrastructure purchases related to the city's operation of its electric tram services. As a combined issue on the financial markets of London, Paris, and New York, the City of Tokyo loan was to be the largest municipal loan of the prewar period (see Table 6.1). The final loan of the period, floated on the London financial market during December 1912, was the 5 Percent City of Yokohama Loan for £122,000, once again for the development of Yokohama's municipal gas infrastructure.[6]

---

5. Ōkurasho henshū, *Meiji Taishō zaiseishi*, pp. 714–26; Shinjo, *History of the Yen*, p. 94; Suzuki, *Japanese Government Loan Issues*, pp. 146–62; and Tamaki, *Japanese Banking*, pp. 95–96.

6. Ōkurasho henshū, *Meiji Taishō zaiseishi*, pp. 714–26, and Suzuki, *Japanese Government Loan Issues*, pp. 146–62.

As detailed above, Kyoto was able to raise ₣50 million on the Paris financial market through the mediation and services of the Mitsui Bank. All the other issues of municipal loans, which totaled £16 million, were arranged through the London financial market, denominated in pounds sterling, employed a wide variety of London's financial organs, and thus demonstrated the depth of Japan's financial connection with its British ally in the prewar period of the early twentieth century. We should also note that Japan's Ministry of Finance intervened in the provision of large municipal loan issues and often insisted on the use of the Industrial Bank of Japan and its associates in London, the so-called London Group. It is for this reason that 90 percent of the of all municipal loans issued through the London financial market were financed through the Industrial Bank of Japan, or with members of the London Group.[7]

The Great Kanto Earthquake "Reconstruction Bonds"

The Great Kanto earthquake of 1 September 1923 caused widespread damage right across the Kanto region of eastern Japan. In the earthquake's aftermath, though, it was clear that Japan's capital, Tokyo, and its main port, Yokohama, had sustained the brunt of the devastation. The City of Tokyo wasted no time in contacting members of the London Group, which through intermediation of the Industrial Bank of Japan had previously issued two large loans for the city in 1906 and 1912, in regard to floating a sterling loan to finance reconstruction costs. In late 1923, however, the national government notified the regional authorities that it would, as in the past, strictly control any future issues of municipal loans. Furthermore, the national government warned that any municipality contemplating raising a foreign loan should seek the permission of both the Minister of Finance and the Minister of Home Affairs before commencing negotiations. Under these circumstances, the municipalities of Tokyo and Yokohama were forced to back away from earlier inquiries into foreign loans, thus enabling the Japanese government to push ahead with its own agenda for composite reconstruction-redemption loans: that is, the simultaneous issue of the 6 Percent Sterling Loan for £25 million and the 6.5 Percent Dollar Loan for $150 million on the financial

---

7. See Ōkurashō henshū, *Meiji Taishō zaiseishi*, pp. 321–59, and Suzuki, *Japanese Government Loan Issues*, pp. 150–57, 200–201.

markets of London and New York in February 1924 (as discussed in Chapter 5).[8]

Significantly, the Japanese government had claimed in its New York prospectus for the 6.5 Percent Dollar Loan that the funds from the February 1924 London and New York loans would provide "not only for the retirement of substantially the whole of the Japanese Government's external debt maturing prior to 1931, but also for the Japanese Government's entire estimated financial requirements in foreign markets for reconstruction work."[9] As in 1899, the Japanese government had supposedly exited the foreign market as a means to secure credit, even though it had failed to meet reconstruction costs associated with the Great Kanto earthquake (the Japanese government had claimed that foreign capital, to the tune of $300 million, was to be set aside for reconstruction work).[10] Moreover, the Japanese government's creditors, led by J. P. Morgan & Company, were not willing to turn a blind eye to the matter and pointedly reminded the Japanese government of its earlier commitment.[11] For the near future, then, further lending would have to be negotiated in the form of municipal loans, even if the state had the most pressing need of the foreign capital. As the municipality of Tokyo was keen to raise a sterling loan, the Japanese government authorized the municipality to seek a loan for £10 million to be floated on the London financial market. Although the Japanese government had appointed the Industrial Bank of Japan as the loan's intermediary, as was common practice with municipal and company loans, it should be noted that the personnel, and the issue banks of the syndicate, comprised the very same Enlarged London Group that had issued the government's February 1924 loan.[12]

Almost immediately, Tokyo's negotiations for a municipal loan stalled, with the Bank of England refusing to allow the Japanese further access to the London market during 1924. A number of issues came into play in the Bank of England's decision. First and foremost, contrary to the notion that the British government did not intervene in "private" fi-

---

8. Horie, *Gaishi yunyū*, pp. 147–48.
9. Ōkurasho henshū, *Meiji Taishō zaiseishi*, p. 369.
10. See Ōkurasho henshū, *Meiji Taishō zaiseishi*, pp. 368–69; see also Chapter 5.
11. TWL, Box 190-6, and BFRB.
12. Ōkurasho henshū, *Meiji Taishō zaiseishi*, pp. 368–69.

nancial matters, the Bank of England did, in fact, intervene when it felt that national interests were at stake, as it clearly did in the case of Tokyo's proposed municipal loan.[13] For example, during the interwar period the Bank of England was involved in the financial rescue of William Deacon's Bank, the Banca Italo-Britannica, the Anglo-South American Bank, and Frederick Huth and Company. Moreover, the Bank of England was also intimately involved in the reorganization of Britain's armaments, cotton-spinning, shipping, shipbuilding, and steel industries. But what prompted the Bank of England to intervene in a £10 million municipal loan for Tokyo when a £25 million Japanese government loan had already been sanctioned?[14] Certainly the unyielding governor of the Bank of England, Sir Montagu Norman, had some choice words—and grave doubts—about Japan's financial situation, which offended Japan's special financial delegate, Mori Kengo, but the rupture between Tokyo and London was much more serious than a mere personality clash. At the very heart of the matter were two central banks desperately attempting to reserve specie in order to reestablish their respective prewar gold standards, the Bank of England and the Bank of Japan.[15] In these circumstances, the source of conflict came to be expressed in terms of the Bank of England's insistence on "special security," or "security reserves," for Japan's foreign loans.[16]

Although it was not a matter of public record, the Japanese government's chief financial agent, the Bank of Japan, had long maintained the practice of cooperating with foreign central banks by depositing special security. Particularly in regard to special security, a secret agreement seems to have been formalized in May 1910 when the Japanese government approached the financial markets of England and France to finance the redemption of its domestic loans. In exchange for securing loans worth

---

13. See Cairncross, "The Bank of England," pp. 66–69, and Sayers, *The Bank of England*, pp. 253–71.

14. Clearly, a distinction must be drawn between the two loans. In essence, the municipal loan for Tokyo required a fresh injection of capital, while the government loan of 1924 was sanctioned to allow for the redemption of previous loans, thus preventing the Japanese government's extensive foreign borrowing from becoming a "bad debt" crisis.

15. See R. Boyce, "Central Bank Control," pp. 142–63, especially p. 147; Iida, "The Industrial Bank of Japan," pp. 129–41; and Mochida, *Toshi zaisei no kenkyū*, pp. 74–77.

16. Warner, *Anglo-Japanese Financial Relations*, pp. 94–96.

approximately ¥282 million at the very low interest rate of 4 percent, the Japanese government was forbidden to have the funds transmitted in specie, and was obligated to maintain specie deposits, commensurate with its liabilities, as security with key financial institutions in both England and France. The Japanese government's own statistics confirm that government specie held abroad (*zaigai seika*) increased sixfold, from ¥23 to ¥138 million in the 1909–1910 fiscal year. We must also consider that the Bank of Japan, after Japan's adoption of the gold standard in 1897, held a large proportion of its gold reserves overseas at the Bank of England and elsewhere, owing to the expansion of Japan's indebtedness. On the eve of the outbreak of the First World War in 1913, for example, the amount of specie held abroad by the Bank of Japan and the Yokohama Specie Bank had reached ¥241 million, or 65 percent of their total specie reserve of ¥371 million. Moreover, of the specie held abroad, a full 85 percent was in England.[17] In the context of maintaining the gold standard, the Bank of England was obviously keen to enter into an agreement with Japan's financial authorities that would compel Japan to maintain security reserves and simultaneously restrain Japan from withdrawing its specie reserves from England. The Japanese government, for its part, was willing to oblige the Bank of England's requests so long as London dominated the world's financial markets, the capital kept flowing, and Britain remained Japan's ally. After the First World War, however, with its ensuing financial upheavals and the abrogation of the Anglo-Japanese alliance, the situation had changed. Japan's financial delegates were no longer prepared even to countenance discussion of special security with their British counterparts.[18]

In late January 1926, after almost two years of difficult and at times acrimonious negotiations, the frustrated Japanese delegates played their final hand and threatened to withdraw altogether from loan negotiations. Expressing disgust with Britain's financial institutions for being either unwilling or unable to finance and underwrite their international loans, Japan's delegates sought to end the negotiations. Of course, nothing of the sort was allowed to happen, and the Bank of England finally sanctioned a face-saving loan in June 1926. At last, on 11 October 1926,

17. Kobayashi, *War and Armament Loans*, p. 186.
18. Warner, *Anglo-Japanese Financial Relations*, pp. 94–96.

the Industrial Bank of Japan and its government's long-appointed syndicate, the Enlarged London Group, issued the (Japanese) government-guaranteed Tokyo City 5.5 Percent Sterling Loan for £6 million on a very responsive London market (see Table 6.1). The conflict surrounding the negotiation of Japan's first municipal loan in fourteen years highlighted the fact that much more was at stake for the Japanese government than just providing reconstruction costs for Tokyo's public infrastructure. As with other municipal loans, the Tokyo loan was intimately related to the state's financial needs of the day, replenishing specie at the Bank of Japan's gold reserve held in London, which in turn backed its own national issue of bank notes, and accumulating enough capital to finance a restoration of the gold standard sometime in 1926 or so.[19]

As early as April 1924, the Japanese government had hinted to London's financiers that it would take its business elsewhere, to New York.[20] On concluding the London issue for the municipality of Tokyo, the same delegation, with the Industrial Bank of Japan at its helm, approached leading members of the Enlarged New York Group with the apparent aim of securing a loan to finance reconstruction costs arising from the Great Kanto earthquake disaster in Yokohama and Tokyo. In reality, it was hoped that the loan would defray reconstruction costs as well as bolster the Japanese government's foreign specie reserves—that is, in short, finish the business started by the previous City of Tokyo 5.5 Percent Sterling Loan.[21] Happily for the Japanese delegates, the Enlarged New York Group, having been formed to issue the 6.5 Percent Dollar Loan of February 1924, readily agreed to their request. Following Tokyo's London issue in October 1926, the terms and conditions of two further loans were finalized, with the Japanese government acting to "guarantee" the

---

19. M. Ito, *Nihon no taigai kinyū*, pp. 149–50, and Mochida, *Toshi zaisei no kenkyū*, pp. 72–77.

20. Warner, *Anglo-Japanese Financial Relations*, pp. 94–95. Horie and many subsequent historians claim that the October 1926 London issue marked the point at which Japanese government, municipal, and company loans switched, or transferred, from London to New York. See Horie, *Gaishi yunyū*, pp. 146–47. An examination of Japanese loan issues of the period, however, does not support the claim. In reality, Japanese loans were issued in New York well before October 1926 and Japanese loans continued to be issued in London until 1931, without a clear transition point (see Tables 5.1, 6.1, and 6.2).

21. Mochida, *Toshi zaisei no kenkyū*, pp. 74–77.

municipal issues, as it had in London, and the much-respected Yokohama Specie Bank participating in the loan as an issue bank. Less than
two months later, on 1 December 1926, the Yokohama City 6 Percent
Dollar Loan for $20 million was issued on the New York financial mar-
ket by the Yokohama Specie Bank and the Enlarged New York Group.
Then in March 1927, a full three and a half years after the Great Kanto
earthquake, the same syndicate issued a similar Tokyo City 5.5 Percent
Dollar Loan for $21 million on the same market. Presumably the mu-
nicipality of Tokyo pursued the loan at a lower interest rate in order to
match its previous London 1924 issue and, with it, receive in excess of
the £10 million, or $50 million, that it always insisted was needed for
reconstruction.[22]

Corporate Loans from the Gold Standard to the First World War

The foreign loans associated with Japan's largest and most prestigious
companies are perhaps the most well-known examples of Japan's foreign
capital imports in the late nineteenth and early twentieth centuries. Indeed, famous joint-stock companies such as Kanegafuchi Cotton Spinning Company, widely known today as Kanebo, and the great power
utilities, such as the Daido, Toho, and Tokyo electric power companies,
certainly did benefit from access to foreign capital. What is perhaps less
widely known, however, is that many of the beneficiaries of company
loans were in fact parastatal "national policy companies" (*kokusaku gaisha*) that, despite all appearances, were created and guided by the Japanese government as agents, or instruments, of the state.[23] For example,
the two financial institutions to receive corporate loans, the Industrial
Bank of Japan and the Hokkaido Colonial Bank, were both "special
banks" (*tokushu ginkō*) established by the Japanese government to per-

---

22. Ōkurasho henshū, *Meiji Taishō zaiseishi*, pp. 368–69. Mochida notes that a ru-
mor at the time suggested Yokohama's loan was at a higher 6% interest rate because it
refused capital investment from the Ministry of Finance's Deposit Bureau. See Mochida, *Toshi zaisei no kenkyū*, pp. 76–77.

23. The phrase "state management" (*kokkateki keiei*) was later replaced with the
more benign term "bureaucratic guidance" (*gyōsei shidō*), which is liberally sprinkled
throughout postwar histories of Japan's economic development.

form specific duties legislated especially for them by the state. Similarly, the South Manchuria Railway Company and the Oriental Development Company were not private companies fortunate to receive foreign investment independent of the state; rather, they were representative agents of the Japanese government in the informal, and then formal, colonies of Korea and Manchuria, and as such they were largely dependent on the state for financial capital. As with the supply of foreign loans to Japan's municipalities, the flow of foreign capital to Japanese companies was dependent on, and entirely related to, the contemporary needs of the Japanese government. Unfortunately, the crossover between state loans and company loans can obfuscate distinctions, and hence analysis, as in the case of loans to private railway companies that were soon nationalized by the Japanese government after their receipt of foreign capital. Thus we must carefully distinguish between those loans associated with Japan's private companies and the provision of foreign capital to parastatal Japanese companies, and examine the role played by foreign loans in providing capital to Japan's industries.

The extension of foreign loans to Japanese companies in many ways parallels the experience of Japan's municipal borrowing on the financial markets of London, New York, and Paris. As with the financing of municipal loans to Japan's principal cities, the brokerage and negotiation of loan issues to Japanese companies, particularly in the case of the major long-term loans, was channeled through the Industrial Bank of Japan. Indeed, the Japan's financial authorities rarely approved of corporate borrowing without Industrial Bank intermediation, and on the limited occasions that it was permitted, such as in the provision of access to the Paris financial market, it seems to have been allowed in order to deflect foreign criticism of state interference in private commercial transactions.[24] The Industrial Bank of Japan used municipal and corporate loans to replenish the Bank of Japan's foreign specie reserve held at the Bank of England, and therefore the Industrial Bank's operation of the foreign loan mechanism was crucial to the financing of Japan's foreign trade, and the operation of Japan's gold standard.[25] Under such circumstances,

---

24. See Suzuki, *Japanese Government Loan Issues*, p. 151.
25. Wakatsuki, *Meiji/Taishō/Shōwa sekaihishi*, pp. 124–43, and Tamaki, *Japanese Banking*, p. 100.

those Japanese companies without strong government connections were restrained from importing and employing foreign capital, while foreign investors were, for their part, wary of dealing with a parastatal intermediary in place of their prospective client.

It is worth recalling that Japan's first government borrowing occurred in 1870, that high-volume borrowing started with Japan's adoption of the gold standard in 1897, and that shortly after, in 1899, the first of many municipal loans were provided to Japan's principal cities. In comparison, the first foreign loan to a Japanese company was made some seven years later, in January 1906, when the Hokkaido Colliery and Coal Railway Company, eager to enlarge and upgrade its railway, mining, and shipping facilities and to repay high-interest domestic debts, issued its 5 Percent Hokkaido Colliery and Coal Railway Loan for £1 million on the London financial market, through the services of the Chartered Bank of India, Australia, and China, and brokered by the Industrial Bank of Japan (see Table 6.2). Two months later, in March 1906, the Kansai Railway Company, through the services of S. Samuel and Company and M. Samuel and Company, issued the 4.5 Percent Kansai Railway Loan for £1 million on the same London market. In the following year, the South Manchuria Railway Company was slated to issue a three-way Franco-Anglo-American loan through the services of the Industrial Bank of Japan. Owing to the financial uncertainties of that year, however, only the London financial market was thought capable of providing the necessary investors, and so, in July 1907, the first government-guaranteed 5 Percent South Manchurian Railway Loan, for £4 million, was issued on the London financial market.[26]

Foreign capital was urgently required by the South Manchuria Railway Company to purchase the material required for 480 miles of railway extensions, most notably along the Anpo Line, to further exploit the Endai coal mine; for the construction of a wharf at the Dairen (Dalian) railway station; and for other company facilities.[27] As the railway and, to a lesser extent, the electrical and mining industries were seen by Britain's financiers as appropriate areas of investment, it seems that British investment in the development of Japan's railway companies was set to

---

26. Ōkurashō henshū, *Meiji Taishō zaiseishi*, pp. 397–412.
27. Ōkurashō henshū, *Meiji Taishō zaiseishi*, pp. 397–412.

increase.[28] On 31 March 1906, however, the Japanese government passed legislation nationalizing Japan's railways and, in doing so, frustrated the investment plans of many British financial institutions, such as those of Baring Brothers.[29] Moreover, in accordance with the new legislation the loans to the Hokkaido Colliery and Coal Railway and the Kansai Railway companies were taken over and administered by the Japanese government in the same manner as other government-guaranteed loans of the period.[30]

The nationalization of the South Manchuria Railway Company, which retained its name owing to the colonial nature of its operations, in no way relieved the company of its financial shortfalls. Significantly, the Japanese government, anxious to secure international recognition of its position in Northeast China, contentiously presented the South Manchuria Railway Company as something of an investment flagship, paying scant regard to American protests (backed by railway magnate E. H. Harriman) with respect to the extension of Japanese-owned railways in China. The stockbroker Panmure Gordon discreetly located investors and privately placed the second government-guaranteed 5 Percent South Manchurian Railway Loan, for £2 million, on the London financial market in May 1908. Moreover, just seven months later, in December 1908, the third 5 Percent South Manchurian Railway Loan was issued, being identical to the second loan in every way except that the Hongkong and Shanghai Bank had taken over issuing duties from Panmure Gordon and extended the loan's maturity to twenty-four years. The second debenture was thus issued in the form of short-term bonds, and the third debenture as long-term bonds, but both debentures were used by the company to further the projects associated with the first loan of 1907. In January 1911, a fourth loan, the government-guaranteed 4.5 Percent South Manchurian Railway Loan, was issued by the company to redeem the second debenture (£2 million), upgrade its railway lines (£2 million), make harbor repairs at Dairen (£1 million), and pay for the construction costs of schools, hospitals, and dormitories

---

28. Cottrell, *British Investment*, pp. 27, 40, and Edelstein, *Overseas Investment*, pp. 37–44.

29. Warner, *Anglo-Japanese Financial Relations*, pp. 56–60.

30. See Myers, "Japanese Imperialism in Manchuria," pp. 101–32, and Young, *Japan's Total Empire*, pp. 28–46.

Table 6.2. Japanese Corporate Loans, 1906–1931

Loan no.	Issue date	Issue market	Company	Interest (% per annum)	Maturity (years)	Issue amount in k¥
1	Jan. 1906	London	Hokkaido Colliery and Coal Railway	5.00	15	9,763
2	Mar. 1906	London	Kansai Railway	4.50	20	9,763
3	July 1907	London	South Manchuria Railway	5.00	25	39,052
4	Jan. 1908	Paris	Kanegafuchi Cotton Spinning Co.	7.50	—	2,000
5	May 1908	London	South Manchuria Railway	5.00	3	19,526
6	Dec. 1908	London	South Manchuria Railway	5.00	24	19,526
7	Dec. 1908	London, Paris	Industrial Bank of Japan	5.00	25	19,526
8	Apr. 1909	Paris	Matsui Muslin Spinning Co.	6.50	—	250
9	1909	London	Keihin Electric Railway	5.50	—	2,000
10	June 1910	London	Hokkaido Colonial Bank	5.00	23	5,000
11	Jan. 1911	London	South Manchuria Railway	4.50	25	58,578
12	Mar. 1913	Paris	Oriental Development Corp.	5.00	29	19,350
13	Mar. 1923	New York	Oriental Development Corp.	6.00	30	39,919
14	June 1923	London	Tokyo Electric Light Co.	6.00	25	29,289
15	July 1923	London	South Manchuria Railway	5.00	25	39,052
16	Aug. 1924	New York	Daido Electric Power Co.	7.00	20	30,090

Issue amount in k£ [kF]{k$}	Type of issue	Intermediary	Issuer
1,000	government-guaranteed pound debenture	Industrial Bank of Japan	Chartered Bank of India, Australia, and China
1,000	government-guaranteed pound debenture	S. Samuel and Co.	M. Samuel and Co.
4,000	government-guaranteed pound debenture	Industrial Bank of Japan	London Group
204 [5,130]	franc debenture	Mitsui Bank	Banque française pour le commerce et l'industrie
2,000	government-guaranteed pound debenture	Panmure Gordon, Hill and Co.	London Group (private placement)
2,000	government-guaranteed pound debenture	Industrial Bank of Japan	Hongkong and Shanghai Bank
2,000	government-guaranteed pound debenture	Industrial Bank of Japan	London Group; Société Générale; Panmure Gordon, Hill and Co.
25.5 [640]	franc debenture	Daihyaku Bank	Banque française pour le commerce et l'industrie
204	pound debenture	Sale and Frazer Co.	Sale and Frazer Co.
510	pound debenture	Koike Co.	Sale and Frazer Co.
6,000	government-guaranteed pound debenture	Industrial Bank of Japan	London Group
1,973.7 [50,000]	government-guaranteed franc debenture	Industrial Bank of Japan	Banque Franco-Japonaise
4,089 {19,900}	government-guaranteed U.S. dollar debenture	Industrial Bank of Japan	National City Bank
3,000	pound debenture	Sale and Frazer Co.	Whitehall Trust
4,000	government-guaranteed pound debenture	Industrial Bank of Japan	Industrial Bank of Japan
3,082 {15,000}	U.S. dollar debenture	Industrial Bank of Japan	Dillon, Read and Co.

(*continued*)

Table 6.2. (continued)

Loan no.	Issue date	Issue market	Company	Interest (% per annum)	Maturity (years)	Issue amount in k¥
17	Aug. 1924	New York	Industrial Bank of Japan	6.00	3	44,136
18	Feb. 1925	London	Tokyo Electric Light Co.	6.00	23	5,858
19	Mar. 1925	New York	Toho Electric Power Co.	7.00	30	30,090
20	Mar. 1925	New York	Ujikawa Electric Co.	7.00	20	28,084
21	July 1925	New York	Daido Electric Power Co.	6.50	25	27,081
22	July 1925	London	Toho Electric Power Co.	5.00	20	2,929
23	Aug. 1925	New York	Tokyo Electric Light Co.	6.00	3	48,144
24	July 1926	New York	Toho Electric Power Co.	6.00	3	20,060
25	Dec. 1927	New York	Shinetsu Electric Power (Tokyo Electric Light Co.)	6.50	25	15,346
26	Jan. 1928	New York	Nippon Electric Power Co.	6.50	25	18,054
27	June 1928	New York	Tokyo Electric Light Co.	6.00	25	140,420
28	June 1928	London	Tokyo Electric Light Co.	6.00	25	43,934
29	Oct. 1928	New York	Oriental Development Corp.	5.50	30	39,919
30	July 1929	New York	Toho Electric Power Co.	6.00	3	22,969
31	Jan. 1931	London	Nippon Electric Power Co.	6.00	25	14,645
32	July 1931	New York	Taiwan Electric Power Co.	5.50	25	45,737

Source: Bytheway, *Nihon keizai to gaikoku shihon*, pp. 148–49.

Issue amount in k£ [kF]{k$}	Type of issue	Intermediary	Issuer
4,521 {22,000}	government-guaranteed U.S. dollar debenture	Industrial Bank of Japan	National City Bank
600	pound debenture	Sale and Frazer Co.	Whitehall Trust
3,082 {15,000}	U.S. dollar debenture	Mitsui Bank	Guaranty Trust
2,877 {14,000}	U.S. dollar debenture	Industrial Bank of Japan	Lee, Higginson and Co.
2,774 {13,500}	U.S. dollar debenture	Industrial Bank of Japan	Dillon, Read and Co.
300	British government-guaranteed pound debenture	Mitsui Trust	Prudential Life Insurance
4,931 {24,000}	U.S. dollar debenture	—	Guaranty Trust
2,055 {10,000}	U.S. dollar debenture	—	Guaranty Trust
1,572 {7,650}	U.S. dollar debenture	Mitsui Trust	Dillon, Read and Co.
1,849 {9,000}	U.S. dollar debenture	Mitsui Bank	Harris, Forbes and Co.
14,383 {70,000}	U.S. dollar debenture	Mitsui Bank	Guaranty Trust
4500	pound debenture	Mitsui Bank	Lazard Bros.; Whitehall Trust
4,089 {19,900}	government-guaranteed U.S. dollar debenture	Industrial Bank of Japan	National City Bank
2,353 {11,450}	U.S. dollar debenture	—	Guaranty Trust; Harris, Forbes and Co.; Lee, Higginson and Co.
1,500	pound debenture	Mitsui Bank	Harris, Forbes and Co.; Chase Co.; J. Henry Schroeder and Co.
4,685 {22,800}	government-guaranteed U.S. dollar debenture	Yokohama Specie Bank	J. P. Morgan; Kuhn, Loeb and Co.; National City Bank; First National Bank of Commerce

(£1 million). Predictably, the Industrial Bank of Japan was the intermediary in the fourth loan to the South Manchuria Railway Company,
and an unprecedented £6 million was raised in what was to be the largest foreign loan to a Japanese company in the period before the First
World War.[31]

In an entirely separate development, the Kanegafuchi Cotton Spinning
Company (Kanebo) became the first private Japanese company to raise
foreign capital through a debenture issue, on 11 January 1908. Kanebo,
along with the Matsui Muslin Spinning Company in April 1909, raised
loans on the Paris financial market using the Mitsui and Daihyaku
banks, respectively, as intermediaries. Tellingly, these independently negotiated loans, free from the Industrial Bank of Japan's participation,
resulted in relatively small loans for ¥2 million and ¥250,000, at unfa-
vorably high interest rates of 7.5 percent and 6.5 percent (see Table 6.2).[32]
In contrast, the Industrial Bank of Japan issued a loan for £2 million
in London to supplement its own paid-in (operational) capital reserves,
at just 5 percent interest, in December 1908. In 1909 the Keihin Electric Railway Joint-Stock Company, operating a private light-rail network
outside the field of nationalization, also raised a small ¥200,000 loan at
5.5 percent, in a similar fashion to the spinning companies, but on the
London financial market with the services of the Sale and Frazer Company. In the following year, in June 1910, the 5 Percent Hokkaido Colonial Bank Loan for £510,000 was also issued on the London financial
market.[33]

Significantly, the final loan to a Japanese company in the period before the First World War was the first 5 Percent Oriental Development
Company Loan, for ₣50 million, floated on the Paris financial market in
March 1913. The Oriental Development Company was established in 1908
to encourage Japanese agricultural colonists to migrate to Korea, in much
the same manner as an earlier generation of Japanese migrants had
colonized Hokkaido. The main force behind its conception was the Oriental Association (Tōyō kyōkai), and the goals of the company reflected

---

31. Ōkurasho henshū, *Meiji Taishō zaiseishi*, pp. 397–412.
32. Kanebo shashi henshū shitsu, *Kanebo hyakunenshi*, p. 1042.
33. Suzuki, *Japanese Government Loan Issues*, pp. 157–60, 202–3.

cabinet decisions made by the Japanese government.[34] As the Japanese government's colonial agent in Korea, having a standing similar to that of the South Manchuria Railway Company (the Japanese government's colonial agent in Manchuria), the Oriental Development Company's first loan was government-guaranteed at the then standard interest rate of 5 percent. Characteristically, the loan was brokered through the services of the Industrial Bank of Japan, although the newly established Banque Franco-Japonaise was employed as the issuer on the Paris financial market. As it turned out, it would be another ten tumultuous years before Japanese companies would once again seek the assistance of foreign investors to finance their operations.[35]

Parastatal Corporate Bond Issues between the World Wars

Fittingly, the last borrower in the prewar period from 1906 to 1913, the Oriental Development Company, was also to be the first corporate borrower in the period between the twentieth century's two distinct though connected world wars. In contrast to the United States of America, which enjoyed twenty-three years of peace between the end of the First World War and 1941, Japan was to experience only a brief thirteen-year respite, starting with the peace of November 1918 and lasting until September 1931, when elements of the Japanese army commenced hostilities in Northeast China. While the issuance of government and municipal loans was restricted in the interwar period to the financing of reconstruction costs associated with the Kanto earthquake, loan refinancing and repayments, and buttressing Japan's foreign specie reserves, foreign investment in Japan's electric power industry was to take center stage. The economic importance of Japan's

---

34. See Duus, *The Abacus and the Sword*, pp. 301–14.

35. "As with other colonial ventures calling for heavy capital investment, it was simply not possible to raise the money needed on the domestic capital markets." Duus, *The Abacus and the Sword*, p. 382. Despite oversubscription to the first government-backed domestic issue of the Oriental Development Company's stock, recession after the war with Russia created a tight domestic market for any type of large commercial credits. Under these circumstances, the corporation was forced to finance its ventures domestically with a ¥10 million loan from the Postal Savings Deposit Bureau, and internationally with a F50 million loan from Paris. See Duus, *The Abacus and the Sword*, pp. 381–83.

developing electric power industry is clearly reflected in the history of corporate loans in the interwar period. Not surprisingly, the parastatal companies—the South Manchuria Railway Company and the Oriental Development Company—and the Japanese government's international investment agent, the Industrial Bank of Japan, had priority, and were the first to issue corporate loans on the capital markets of London and New York (see Table 6.2).

Following Japan's annexation of Korea on 22 August 1910, the Oriental Development Company became an important organ in the Japanese government's colonization efforts. Initial difficulties in raising capital for the dubious enterprise of removing Koreans from their land in order to replace them with Japanese agricultural colonists were overcome only through the issuance of government-guaranteed foreign loans.[36] The second 6 Percent Oriental Development Company Loan, issued on the New York financial market in March 1923, is of particular significance as it was the first corporate loan, and the first loan among Japanese government and municipal loans, that was denominated entirely in U.S. dollars. As with the first Oriental Development Company Loan, placed in Paris just prior to the outbreak of the First World War in 1913, the corporation's second and third loans on the New York financial market were government-guaranteed debentures brokered through the services of the Industrial Bank of Japan. The National City Bank of New York issued both the second loan of March 1923 and the third loan of October 1928, for $20 million. The two loans were identical in almost every detail except that the interest rate fell from 6 percent for the 1923 issue to 5.5 percent for the 1928 issue.[37] Care should be taken in drawing conclusions from the Oriental Development Company's decision to borrow from the New York financial market: a number of economic and political factors were responsible, not the least of which was Japan's deference to the British government's sensibilities concerning Japanese actions in Korea, and in East Asia more generally. Nevertheless, in light of what followed, the Oriental Development Company's use of the New York financial market

---

36. Duus, *The Abacus and the Sword*, pp. 381–83.

37. By the time of the third loan in October 1928, the Oriental Development Company had expanded into a parastatal "multinational corporation" that, in addition to sending colonists to Korea, managed a complex set of investments and enterprises in Manchuria and other parts of Asia. See Duus, *The Abacus and the Sword*, p. 304.

clearly opened the door for a new generation of capital imports in the form of corporate loans and debentures.

Along with the Oriental Development Company, the Japanese government's colonial agent in Northeast China, the South Manchuria Railway Company, and its international investment agent, the Industrial Bank of Japan, were also able to access foreign capital markets. The South Manchuria Railway Company was very much tied to its financial backers in London, and it used that city's financial market for a fifth (and last) time in July 1923, to redeem shorter-term domestic loans, adjust its balances, and borrow a further £4 million with the government-guaranteed fifth 5 Percent South Manchurian Railway Loan. The Industrial Bank of Japan assumed all the tasks of brokering, issuing, and underwriting associated with the 1923 South Manchurian Railway loans.[38]

As the liabilities of the Industrial Bank of Japan increased, it became necessary for the bank to increase its own capital base and refinance its own domestic loans. Specifically, the Industrial Bank of Japan had to reorganize its own ledgers in a way that was acceptable to international financial institutions, for it was much more than a client of the international financial markets: it was dependent on them for its own operation.[39] A second issue of government-guaranteed Industrial Bank of Japan debentures took place on the New York financial market in August 1924, almost a full year after the Great Kanto earthquake of September 1923. The 6 Percent Industrial Bank of Japan Loan for $22 million was issued by the National City Bank to support the Japanese bank's standing as the agent of Japan's parastatal corporate loans in New York. Once again the Japanese government clearly profited from the import of foreign capital in ways above and beyond the purposes stated in the debenture brochures and portfolios of Japan's parastatal companies.[40]

---

38. M. Ito, *Nihon no taigai kinyū*, pp. 151–55.

39. Thus, in contrast to Japan's other special banks and domestic financial organs, the Industrial Bank of Japan was less able to doctor its books during the ensuing financial turmoil of the Great Kanto earthquake. See Inouye, "The Financial Crisis in Japan," pp. 436–42; Schalow, "Financial Panic of 1927," pp. 132–72; and Yukio, "Incompetence of the Bourgeoisie," pp. 109–17.

40. M. Ito, *Nihon no taigai kinyū*, pp. 151–55.

Foreign Capital and Japan's Electrification

Just as an earlier generation of foreign loans had launched Japan into the age of locomotive steam from the 1870s to the earlier part of the twentieth century, a new generation of foreign loans, in a brief period from March 1923 to July 1931, was set to propel Japan into the age of electricity. The electric power industry was very much in its infancy until the economic boom associated with the First World War precipitated domestic investment in the generation and transmission of electricity. Nevertheless, the achievements of the electric power industry were limited to urban consumers in the metropolises, and the technological advances of the domestic power industry were modest, despite their obvious historical significance. Moreover, the Great Kanto earthquake and the ensuing fires of September 1923 destroyed much of the industry's power generation and transmission infrastructure. Nevertheless, the Great Kanto earthquake was a blessing in disguise for Japan's electric power industry, for it uprooted locomotive force from its entrenched position in Japanese industry and drew attention to the potential benefits of a transition to electromotive force.[41]

Certainly private enterprise and the Japanese government had recognized the importance of financing the electric power industry well before 1923, and various electric companies had planned to raise capital through the issuance of foreign debentures well before the Great Kanto earthquake, but their plans were never realized. Without adequate financing, many pioneering electric power companies were in danger of falling behind technologically—hence the desperate need for foreign capital inputs, as exemplified by the failed loan issues of the Tokyo Electric Light Company in 1906, the Osaka Electric Light Company in 1908, and the Kinugawa Hydroelectric Company in 1912.[42] It was only late in the history of electric power development, and after the earthquake's devastation, that the Japanese government gave priority to the electric industry, giving it access to the foreign capital, particularly in the form of patents and technology, it needed to progress. The focus on electrification, however, came at a cost, as many other Japanese companies also hoped to gain access to foreign capital in the early 1920s. For example, the Industrial Bank of Japan, the Hypothec Bank of Japan, the Oriental Develop-

---

41. Horie, *Gaishi yunyū*, pp. 152–53.
42. Kikkawa, *Nihon denryokugyō*, pp. 104–9, especially p. 108.

ment Company, the Toho Electric Power Company, the Kawasaki Ship-building Company, the Tokyo Subway Company, the Keihan Electric Railway Company (not to be confused with the Keihin Electric Railway), the Hanshin Electric Railway Company, and many other companies had all planned to issue foreign debentures. Significantly, only the electric power companies and the parastatal companies were successful.[43]

The formation of the electric power industry in Japan can therefore be traced to a brief five- to ten-year period heralded by electricity's increased economic competitiveness (and the constant innovation it engendered) in the early days of the First World War. It was during the war that technological advances reduced the costs of expensive coal-generated electric power to a level below those of coal-generated steam power. Hydroelectric power was also becoming more cost-efficient, but the large costs associated with establishing hydroelectric infrastructure were prohibitive and required new sources of capital investment. The decreasing costs of coal-generated electric power encouraged the transition from steam- to electric-power generation, which in turn facilitated the wider use of electricity throughout industry and commerce. At the same time, as the war in Europe stimulated the Japanese economy and encouraged domestic investment, the Japanese government urged potential entrepreneurs and investors to pool resources in an aggressive amalgamation campaign. For the Japanese electric power industry, the result of the economic boom associated with the First World War, as modified by the state's campaign to amalgamate and merge domestic capital, was the formation of a few highly capitalized power companies, enjoying the kind of monopolistic privileges usually associated with state-owned public utilities.[44] Consequently, in the field of the generation and transmission of electric power, five big players emerged during this period.[45]

The so-called great five electric power companies, the Nippon Electric Power Company Limited, the Great Consolidated Electric Power Company Limited (also known internationally as Daido Electric), the

---

43. See Miyazaki, *Daido denryoku*, pp. 295–96.

44. To claim that the major players in the electric power industry enjoyed monopolistic privileges from the state does not deny that some forms of competition existed among the individual firms. Indeed, competition within Japan's electric industry was, in many ways, a powerful stimulus and fueled the demand for foreign capital imports. See Horie, *Gaishi yunyū*, pp. 154–55, and E. B. Schumpeter, *Japan and Manchukuo*, pp. 330–34.

45. Kikkawa, *Nihon denryokugyō*, pp. 108–9.

Toho Electric Power Company Limited, the Tokyo Electric Light Company Limited, and the Ujikawa Electric Company Limited, were to take pride of place as the electric power industry became Japan's leading industry in the decade after the First World War.[46] From 1910 to 1920 the demand for electricity grew from approximately 300 million kilowatts to 2.1 billion kilowatts, increasing by a factor of seven, and from 1920 to 1930 demand increased by a factor of five, from approximately 2.1 billion to 10.5 billion kilowatts; thus in the space of just twenty years, Japan's demand for electric power increased dramatically, by a factor of thirty-five. Prewar demand would eventually peak at around 26 billion kilowatts in the last months of 1939.[47] In the international financial markets of the 1920s, when lending to the world's electric power utilities was seen as a most attractive and sound investment, and the great five were competing to issue debentures, it was thought advantageous for Japan to be represented by only a few large companies.[48]

The Tokyo Electric Light Company was the first and the most frequent borrower of foreign capital in the Japanese electric industry of the period. In the five years between June 1923 and June 1928, the Tokyo Electric Light Company issued five separate debentures on foreign financial markets, three in London, and two in New York. The first 6 Percent Tokyo Electric Light Company Loan was floated on the London market in June 1923 for £3 million, 20 percent of which was used to redeem short-term, higher-interest domestic loans, with the remainder being invested in new power-generation technologies and infrastructure (see Table 6.2). The Sale and Frazer Company of London acted to mediate the loan, while the Whitehall Trust Company served as the issuing authority. In February 1925 the second 6 Percent Tokyo Electric Light Company Loan for a much smaller amount, £600,000, was also raised on the London market, through the services of the same financial institutions, to assist with financing additional infrastructural purchases. In August of the same year, the Guaranty Trust Company of New York issued the third 6 Percent Tokyo Electric Light Company Loan, for $24 million, on the New York market. Once again, the loan was primarily used to purchase new equipment and technologies, although a signifi-

---

46. Nakamura, *Senzenki Nihon keizai*, pp. 162–68.
47. Nakamura, *Senzenki Nihon keizai*, p. 163.
48. Kikkawa, *Nihon denryokugyō*, pp. 108–9.

cant sum was also used to repay the company's domestic, short-term debts.[49]

The fourth and fifth loans of the Tokyo Electric Light Company were quite different in nature from the earlier foreign loans, for they were simultaneously issued on the London and New York markets in a manner similar to the Japanese government's 6 Percent Sterling Loan and 6.5 Percent Dollar Loan of February 1924. The Mitsui Bank played a vital role as the intermediary in these loans, and with the cooperation of the Guaranty Trust Company of New York and the London-based Whitehall Trust, which was joined by Lazard Brothers and Company (of London), the Mitsui Bank was able to build on the earlier loans and restructure them as two large debenture issues. In June 1928, Guaranty Trust issued the New York debenture of the fourth 6 Percent Tokyo Electric Light Company Loan, for $70 million, in what was said to be "the largest foreign bond issue ever floated on the New York Stock Exchange."[50] In the same month, Whitehall Trust and Lazard Brothers both issued the London debentures of the fifth 6 Percent Tokyo Electric Light Company Loan, for £4.5 million, maintaining the previous annualized interest rate. Whereas the company's first three loans were overwhelmingly oriented toward the provision of infrastructure, the company's final two loans were directed toward the redemption of foreign debentures and the refinancing of highly leveraged and destabilizing domestic debts with shorter terms and at higher interest rates.[51]

The second most active international borrower of the great five power companies was the Toho Electric Power Company. In just under four-and-a-half years, from March 1925 to July 1929, the Toho Electric Power Company issued four separate debentures on foreign financial markets, three in New York, and one in London. The Toho Electric Power Company's first loan resembled the final New York loan of the Tokyo Electric Light Company, in that the Mitsui Bank played the role of the intermediary and the Guaranty Trust Company of New York acted as the issuer. In March 1925 the 7 Percent Toho Electric Power Company Loan for $15 million was issued in New York, at what was a relatively high interest rate, and then was immediately used by the company to purchase new

49. Kikkawa, *Nihon denryokugyō*, pp. 108–9.
50. Japan Business History Institute, *The Mitsui Bank*, p. 198.
51. Kikkawa, *Nihon denryokugyō*, pp. 108–9, and TWL, Box 186-28.

infrastructure, redeem domestic debentures, and repay short-term debts, in almost equal parts. The second debenture, the 5 Percent Toho Electric Power Company Loan for £300,000, paid for the Toho Electric Company's purchase of English technology (that is, power-generation machinery manufactured by the Metropolitan-Vickers Company) in July of the same year. Issued by the Prudential Life Insurance Company, in league with the Mitsui Trust Company, the loan was rare among the loans of the electric power industry in that it was intended solely for the purchase of infrastructure, and unique in that it was guaranteed by Britain's Ministry of Finance, and thus extended at a relatively low interest rate.[52] One year later, in July 1926, the Toho Electric Power Company issued its third debenture (the 6 Percent Toho Electric Power Company Loan), through Guaranty Trust Company of New York, for $10 million on the New York financial market. As with Toho Electric Power Company's first debenture, the company used the capital to purchase new infrastructure, redeem domestic debentures, and repay various short-term debts. The Toho Electric Power Company's fourth and final debenture occurred in July 1929. Its agent for issuing debentures in New York, Guaranty Trust, joined with Lee, Higginson Company, and Harris, Forbes and Company, to float the 6 Percent Toho Electric Power Company Loan, for $11.5 million, on the New York financial market. Unlike Toho's earlier foreign loans, however, the third American loan was placed primarily to assist in financing the redemption of the previous loans (see Table 6.2).[53]

The Great Consolidated Electric Power Company Limited, or Daido Electric, as it is most commonly known, was the first Japanese power company to borrow capital from the New York market. In August 1924, after over two years of negotiations with financiers in London and New York, Dillon, Read and Company of New York took the initiative and issued the relatively high-interest 7 Percent Great Consolidated Electric Power Company Loan, for $15 million, on the New York market. Less than a year later, in July 1925, Dillon, Read and Company issued a second, the slightly lower-rate 6.5 Percent Great Consolidated Electric Power Company Loan, for $13.5 million, on the New York market. On both occasions Daido Electric took pains to point out that the loans would be

52. Kikkawa, *Nihon denryokugyō*, pp. 108–9, 123–24.
53. Kikkawa, *Nihon denryokugyō*, pp. 108–9.

used to build new infrastructure, in the form of generating, transformer, and switching stations, and in the construction and provision of various transmission lines. The majority of the funds provided by the two loans, however, were in fact used by Daido Electric for the redemption of domestic debentures, which were intimately related to the issue of most foreign debentures, and the repayment of its short-term debts; just 9 percent of the total was left for the purchase of infrastructure.[54] Finally, it should be noted that although the Industrial Bank of Japan was largely uninvolved in the lengthy negotiation of Daido Electric's two loans, on both occasions it was nevertheless credited with the role of mediator and provided its services as an underwriter.[55]

The two remaining members of the great five, the Ujikawa Electric Company and the Nippon Electric Power Company, also had recourse to the New York financial market. In March 1925, Ujikawa Electric became the third Japanese power company to borrow from the New York financial market, with the 7 Percent Ujikawa Electric Company Loan for $14 million, employing Lee, Higginson and Company as the issuing authority and with the Industrial Bank of Japan acting as the loan's mediator and underwriter. Although the loan was modest by the standards of the day and was entirely devoted to the redemption of domestic loans, Ujikawa Electric, like Daido Electric, and Toho Electric before them, was forced to accept a relatively high interest rate on the New York market, largely owing to Japan's declining credit rating, and also the lack of foreign investor confidence in the Japanese economy given the aftermath of the Great Kanto earthquake.[56] Almost three years later, in January 1928, the Nippon Electric Power Company issued the smaller 6.5 Percent Nippon Electric Power Company Loan for $9 million through the mediation of Mitsui Bank, with Harris, Forbes and Company acting as the issuing authority. The 6 Percent Nippon Electric Power Company Loan for £1.5 million, floated in January 1931, turned out to be the final

---

54. The redemption of domestic debentures equaled approximately 46% of the total loan, and the repayment of short-term debts equaled some 39%, leaving 9% of the total to be spent on infrastructure, after subtracting 6% for ancillary foreign payments. Miyazaki, *Daidō denryoku*, pp. 295–307.

55. It was quite common for the Industrial Bank of Japan to underwrite company loans unilaterally, particularly those that no other financial institution would guarantee. See Saito, "The Industrial Bank of Japan," pp. 118–28.

56. Kikkawa, *Nihon denryokugyō*, pp. 136–42, especially p. 137.

Japanese power loan of its type issued on the London market. Once again the Mitsui Bank acted as the mediator for Nippon Electric, however the terms of the loan were, subsequent to its release on the market, unsatisfactory to the issuers, J. Henry Schroeder and Company, the Chase Company, and Harris, Forbes and Company, and so the loan was forced to be almost immediately redeemed.[57]

The five big players that emerged in the field of electric power generation in Japan during the 1920s, with the exception of Ujikawa Electric, had frequent recourse to the financial markets of London and New York. Notwithstanding the special access enjoyed by the great five, there are two interesting examples of power companies outside the group that were also granted access to foreign capital by the Japanese government. The first is the Shinetsu Electric Power Company Limited, which in December 1927, through the services of the Mitsui Trust and the Dillon, Read Companies, issued a loan for almost $8 million at an annual interest rate of 6.5 percent. Shortly after receipt of the loan's foreign capital, however, the Shinetsu Electric Power Company merged with the Tokyo Electric Light Company, the key member of the great five power companies, which assumed liability for the loan's redemption or repayment. The second is Taiwan Electric Power Company Limited, which received the last power-industry corporate loan of Japan's interwar period. In July 1931 the government-guaranteed 5.5 Percent Taiwan Electric Power Company Loan, for $23 million dollars, was issued on the New York financial market. Interestingly, given that the attempt by the Nippon Electric Power Company to raise a loan in London just six months earlier had been (embarrassingly) redeemed almost immediately after its issue, it was the Yokohama Specie Bank, rather than the Industrial Bank of Japan, that performed the role of financial mediator in what was, after all, a politically delicate loan to a parastatal company, in a Japanese colony. The reason for the anomaly was undoubtedly that the Yokohama Specie Bank was able to call on its twenty-five-year relationship with New York's premier financial institutions, namely Kuhn, Loeb and Company and National City Bank, and its more recent relationship with First National Bank and the J. P. Morgan Company, in financing the debenture. In both of these cases, therefore, the decision by the Japanese government to support its parastatal companies and the great five power companies was

---

57. Kikkawa, *Nihon denryokugyō*, p. 110.

not transgressed against but in fact maintained and strengthened. More-over, the Japanese government was able to offset its own trade deficits with the import of capital by paying the power utilities in (Japanese) yen, as it had previously done with municipal loans.[58]

Japan and the International Financial Markets

Until the outbreak of the First World War, Japanese government borrow-ing was by far the most important avenue for introducing foreign capital into the economy, accounting for some 82.5 percent of the period's total foreign capital, with borrowing by companies at 9 percent, municipal bor-rowing at 7.8 percent, and direct foreign investment accounting for the remaining 0.7 percent. After the First World War, however, the Japanese government was less able, and less inclined, to be seen as playing the lead-ing role in capital imports, and a new generation of loans extended to para-statal and private companies came to the fore, along with an increase in direct foreign investment and joint ventures. From the first foreign loan to the Meiji regime in 1870 to the last joint venture in 1939, Japanese gov-ernment borrowing accounted for 68.3 percent of the period's total foreign capital imports, with borrowing by companies increasing to 22.3 percent, municipal borrowing holding steady at 8 percent, and direct foreign in-vestment accounting for the remaining 1.4 percent (see Table 6.3).

We must consider that the overwhelming bulk of all types of foreign borrowing, some 87 percent, was denominated in pounds and issued on the London financial market, through the services of the London Group in the case of government borrowing, and mainly through the services of the Industrial Bank of Japan and the London Group in the cases of municipal and corporate loans.[59] In the period that followed the sign-ing of the Franco-Japanese Agreement of 1909, the Paris financial mar-ket emerged as the only credible competitor to the market of London, with almost 13 percent of total borrowing being denominated in francs by the time of the outbreak of the First World War.[60]

---

58. See Mochida, *Toshi zaisei no kenkyū*, pp. 72–77.

59. Between 1900 and 1913 Japanese government borrowing on the London finan-cial market was massive; approximately equal to 21% of total foreign borrowing on that market. See Suzuki, *Japanese Government Loan Issues*, p. 12.

60. The figure of 13% may require some qualification. Platt has raised concerns re-garding foreign contributions to British lending, as French investors, in contrast to

Table 6.3. Total Loan Issues and Direct Foreign Investment, 1870–1939
(units: ¥1,000)

No.	Year	Government loans	Municipal loans	Company loans	Direct foreign investment	Annual total
A	1870	4,880	0	0	0	4,880
B	1873	11,712	0	0	0	11,712
1	1897	43,000	0	0	0	43,000
2	1898	0	0	0	0	0
3	1899	97,630	250	0	108	97,988
4	1900	0	0	0	5,250	5,250
5	1901	0	0	0	0	0
6	1902	50,000	900	0	2,000	52,900
7	1903	0	3,085	0	917	4,002
8	1904	214,786	0	0	0	214,786
9	1905	829,855	0	0	150	830,005
10	1906	0	14,580	19,526	500	34,606
11	1907	224,550	3,109	39,052	5,900	272,611
12	1908	0	0	60,578	0	60,578
13	1909	0	63,234	2,250	0	65,484
14	1910	281,543	0	5,000	583	287,126
15	1911	0	0	58,578	0	58,578
16	1912	0	92,714	0	0	92,714
17	1913	106,688	0	19,350	0	126,038
18	1914	24,307	0	0	0	24,307
19	1915	29,289	0	0	0	29,289
20	1916	0	0	0	0	0
21	1917	0	0	0	1,250	1,250
22	1918	0	0	0	1,050	1,050
23	1919	0	0	0	0	0
24	1920	0	0	0	2,500	2,500
25	1921	0	0	0	0	0
26	1922	0	0	0	400	400
27	1923	0	0	108,260	4,500	112,760
28	1924	544,975	0	74,226	0	619,201
29	1925	0	0	142,186	4,000	146,186
30	1926	0	98,180	20,060	0	118,240

Table 6.3. (continued)

No.	Year	Government loans	Municipal loans	Company loans	Direct foreign investment	Annual total
31	1927	0	41,408	15,346	13,000	69,754
32	1928	0	0	242,327	2,489	244,816
33	1929	0	0	22,969	2,000	24,969
34	1930	264,463	0	0	0	264,463
35	1931	0	0	60,382	6,750	67,132
36	1932	0	0	0	2,400	2,400
37	1933	0	0	0	750	750
38	1934	0	0	0	0	0
39	1935	0	0	0	0	0
40	1936	0	0	0	0	0
41	1937	0	0	0	500	500
42	1938	0	0	0	0	0
43	1939	0	0	0	0	0
Total		2,727,678	317,460	890,090	56,997	3,992,225
Percent		*68.3%*	*8.0%*	*22.3%*	*1.4%*	*100.0%*

Source: Bytheway, *Nihon keizai to gaikoku shihon*, p. 196.

After the war, however, the once promising relationship was troubled by what were to become insurmountable difficulties. The financial market of Paris, zealously acting to protect its bondholders, closed itself to all Japanese business, owing to a disagreement between the City of Tokyo and French bondholders regarding the redemption (of the French component) of the 5 Percent City of Tokyo Loan of October 1912. In the financial confusion of the postwar period, the disagreement centered on whether the loan should be paid in gold or in paper francs, after both countries had suspended their gold standards. In every market, no defaulting debtors can borrow unless they have undertaken to meet their liabilities, and so in this case, too, the debtor was not allowed to borrow

British investors, more readily purchased bonds from foreign capital markets. Subsequent studies show that the British contribution (as opposed to that of the London capital market) has in fact been overstated, but to a modest degree. Non-British purchases of London-issued bonds varied widely, averaging from 2.5% for colonial shares, to about 16% for foreign securities. See Davis and Huttenback, *Mammon and Empire*, p. 36, and Platt, *Britain's Investment Overseas*, p. 133.

in Paris, even though the City of Tokyo was prepared to accept third-party, or international, arbitration. Moreover, the dispute, which was officially between the City of Tokyo and French bondholders, was thought sufficient reason to veto French participation in the Japanese government's conversion loans of 1930, and in those circumstances, all interwar loans to Japan from the Paris market required the authorization of the French government. Thus borrowing from the Paris market was inhibited in the interwar period, and financial cooperation between Japan and the Paris financial market was a short-lived thing.[61]

In the years after the First World War, however, New York's financial market more than made up for the loss of French credit, and indeed it overtook the London financial market as the leading supplier of foreign capital to Japan. How significant, in monetary terms, was the transfer of financial transactions from London to New York? In 1924 and 1930, two sets of Japanese government loans were divided between London and New York, totaling ¥366 and ¥443 million, respectively, with the value of the London loans being 17 percent lower than the New York issue (see Table 5.1). Similarly, of the three municipal loans floated after the Great Kanto earthquake of 1923 related to loan conversions and reconstruction funding, two were floated in New York totaling ¥81 million, with the London float worth not quite ¥59 million. That is, the value of the London loans was approximately 28 percent lower than the New York issue (see Table 6.1). It was in commercial lending to companies, however, that the New York market most clearly established its dominance. From 1923, fourteen of the twenty corporate loans of the interwar period were issued in New York, for a total of ¥550 million, and six loans in London were raised for a total of ¥136 million, with the London total being just a quarter of the New York total (see Table 6.2). Overall, Japanese borrowing from the London financial market in the period from 1923 to 1931 totaled ¥561 million, while Japanese borrowing from the New York financial market in the same period totaled ¥1,074 million, almost double the value of the London market's export of capital to Japan.

Armed with this information, it is all too easy to conclude that Japan's operations on the world's financial markets reflected fundamental changes in the contemporary realities of financial power, and to accept the time-honored argument that by the 1920s Britain's financial influence was that

---

61. Enzig, *The Fight for Financial Supremacy*, pp. 64–65.

of a "weary titan" in terminal decline.[62] In fact Britain's financiers, far from being overawed by American financial superiority, were cockily confident, especially after the American economy seemingly began to falter in the late 1920s.[63] As one very on-the-money London journalist wrote: "The experience of the last two years [1929 and 1930] has decisively proved that New York can never rise to permanent supremacy as an international financial centre. . . . The United States is too much interested in the development of her own resources to take a really keen permanent interest in international finance."[64] Indeed, it must be remembered that only a few years before the First World War, America had been deeply in debt to Britain and was, therefore, in many ways morally obliged to support its long and erstwhile creditor, both during the war and in its aftermath. It is said that at the outbreak of war in 1914, European assets in America were valued at a total of $7 billion but that after five years of war the tables had turned, with American claims on Europe reaching approximately $12 billion (Figure 6.1). The war effort of the Allied powers had required America's financial support, which had been readily provided, to the extent of $2 billion in loans and the repurchase of foreign-held American securities worth $3 million, as ultimately America needed Britain and France to secure victory.[65] Nevertheless, the United States waited until the European powers had virtually fought themselves to a standstill before entering the war. The process of the transfer of financial power from London to New York, which started for Japan with an issue in March 1923 for the Oriental Development Company—that is, no Japanese issue was wholly denominated in U.S. currency before 1923—was not complete, however, until after yet another conflagration of war in Europe.[66]

Modernization, War, and Chronic Loan "Reconstruction"

Initial borrowing by Japan after its adoption of the gold standard was undertaken expressly for the provision of infrastructure, that is, for the

---

62. See Akita, "British Informal Empire," pp. 141–56, and Cain and Hopkins, "Theory and Practice," pp. 196–220, especially pp. 211–13.

63. Withers, *War and Lombard Street*, pp. 108–9.

64. Enzig, *The Fight for Financial Supremacy*, p. 81.

65. See Green, *Banking*, pp. 97–100; Hosbawm, *Industry and Empire*, p. 126; and Fernandez-Armesto, *Millennium*, p. 419.

66. See Enzig, *The Fight for Financial Supremacy*, p. 81, and Warner, *Anglo-Japanese Financial Relations*, pp. 90–94.

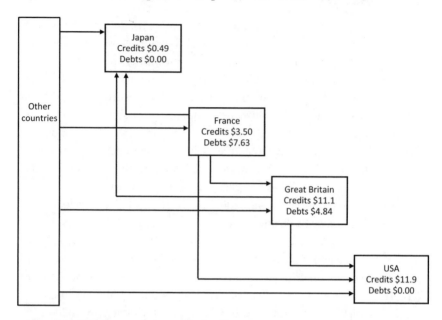

Figure 6.1. The Accumulation of Debt Claims among Wartime Allies, 1915–1920 (in billions of U.S. dollars).
Source: Bytheway, *Nihon keizai to gaikoku shihon,* p. 190.

establishment of the Yawata Steelworks, the extension of telephone service, and particularly for railway construction.[67] The outbreak of war with Russia in 1904, however, put enormous pressure on Japan's financial resources, which were already strained from the debts incurred from its earlier war against China. In this connection, the intimate relationship between the financial authorities of Britain and Japan, cemented by the signing of the Anglo-Japanese alliance in 1902, was of great benefit to Japan's war effort. Indeed, war against Russia would require vast amounts of foreign capital for armaments, and Japan had exclusive access to British capital, which it accessed in the form of government loans.[68] Such wartime financing of the Japanese government accounted for some 31 percent

67. Ōkurasho henshū, *Meiji Taishō zaiseishi,* pp. 34–49, and Spalding, *Eastern Exchange,* pp. 174–75.

68. According to Ono, Japan's total expenditure for the Russo-Japanese War was ¥1,639,267,194. See Ono, *War and Armament Expenditures,* p. 87.

of gross total government borrowing in the period from 1870 to 1930 (Table 6.3).[69] Furthermore, the debt accumulated primarily from the servicing of these wartime loans required conversion loans (at lower rates of interest), and those conversion loans, which continued to be raised until 1930, accounted for 57 percent of gross total government borrowing; in this way loans for infrastructure accounted for just the remaining 12 percent.

The British Foreign Office monitored the conversion operations and concluded in 1912 that, although Japan's national debt had increased, reaching a peak in 1910, the increase was largely owing to railway nationalization and loan conversion operations. Apart from those two factors, the trend of total interest paid on government borrowing had been downward from a peak in 1909, and if the costs of railway nationalization were exempted, interest charges on government borrowing had decreased annually (see Table 6.4). Clearly the Foreign Office was prepared to view the Japanese government's huge borrowing from London's financial market in a positive and sympathetic light, but, as the troubled episode of the Tokyo City 5.5 Percent Sterling Loan of October 1926 illustrates, after the financial upheavals associated with the First World War, Japan could no longer rely on British understanding and support.[70]

Japanese capital borrowings on the international financial markets have been characterized as "armament loans," as nearly one-third of gross total government borrowing in the 1870–1930 period was for military purposes.[71] Furthermore, the debt accumulated from the servicing of these military loans was largely responsible for the conversion loans that accounted for more than half of the total sum of borrowings in the same period. Considering the circumstances that confronted Japan subsequent to its signing of the Anglo-Japanese alliance, it should come as no surprise that a military alliance with the world's leading creditor nation, and arguably the world's premier military power, would have involved

---

69. The Anglo-Japanese alliance can thus be seen as having allowed Japan to enter into a series of wars that enabled it to take over the protection of British interests in East Asia, and eventually to attempt to achieve hegemony there. See Overlach, *Foreign Financial Control in China*, pp. 186–95.

70. MacDonald to Grey, confidential, 14 February 1912, FO 371/1388, FOJ.

71. Kobayashi, *War and Armament Loans*. It should also be noted that a large proportion of direct foreign investment was also related to the armaments industry, and that some activities, such as railway construction in Manchuria, can be seen as being related to military spending.

Table 6.4. Japanese Government Borrowing, Domestic and International, 1906–1911 (in pounds)

	A	B	C	D	E	F	G	H	I	J
	Year ending	Total in government bonds outstanding	Net increase in face value due to conversion operations	National-ized railway bonds outstanding	Total exclusive of C and D	Increase/decrease in bonds outstanding from previous year	Total interest paid	Interest on nationalized railway bonds alone	Interest exclusive of amount paid on national-ized railway bonds	Increase/decrease in interest paid compared with previous year
	31 Dec. 1906	224,047,294	—	1,894,177	222,153,117	—	10,770,125	107,826	10,662,299	—
	31 Dec. 1907	229,064,381	1,275,930	4,232,108	223,556,343	1,403,226	10,807,241	229,124	10,578,117	-84,182
	31 Dec. 1908	226,064,284	1,679,891	9,902,393	214,482,000	-9,074,343	10,652,946	507,228	10,145,718	-432,399
	31 Dec. 1909	263,941,636	1,679,891	52,886,399	209,375,346	-5,106,654	12,531,671	2,640,153	9,891,518	-254,200
	31 Dec. 1910	268,495,665	5,609,250	52,539,653	210,346,762	971,416	12,192,657	2,622,612	9,570,045	-321,473
	31 Dec. 1911	260,865,686	5,609,250	52,226,982	203,029,454	-7,317,308	11,816,416	2,606,774	9,209,642	-360,403

Source: MacDonald to Grey, confidential, 14 February 1912, FO 371/1388, in Great Britain, Foreign Office, *Japan: Correspondence* (London: Scholarly Resources, 1975), microfilm, pp. 202–4.

military loans. What, then, are the implications of the Japanese government's military loans? How and where were they used? Furthermore, what proportion of the £86 million attributed to military loans was used to purchase foreign arms, and what proportion was used to purchase the means to produce such armaments at home? The Japanese government's own sources yield surprisingly little (and often contradictory) information. Clearly a great deal of research remains to be done before the above questions can be answered comprehensively, although an extraordinary series of monographs published in 1922–1923, through the auspices of the Carnegie Endowment for International Peace, provide a firm base from which to begin just such a study.[72]

Parastatal Financing and the "Special Banks"

What is immediately striking about the issues of foreign capital to Japanese cities and companies is that, when taken as a whole, the majority of loans to Japanese cities and companies were in service of, or came to serve, the needs of the Japanese state. In reality, very few private companies benefited from foreign loans until after the First World War, whereas parastatal organizations, particularly those involved in Japan's imperialist expansion, such as the South Manchuria Railway Company and the Oriental Development Company, issued debentures guaranteed by the Japanese government (see Table 6.2). Moreover, in the period from 1899 to 1931 the Japanese government channeled the bulk of the loans—89 percent of the total amounts of municipal loans and 53 percent of corporate loans—through its own financial organ, the Industrial Bank of Japan, thus achieving the dual goal of replenishing Japan's foreign specie reserves and supplying capital to domestic industry and the cities (see Tables 6.1 and 6.2).[73]

---

72. See Ogawa, *Conscription System in Japan* and *Expenditures of the Russo-Japanese War*; Kobayashi, *War and Armament Loans*, *The Military Industries of Japan*, and *War and Armament Taxes*; Ono, *Expenditures of the Sino-Japanese War* and *War and Armament Expenditures*; and, as an overall primer, Boulding and Gleason, "War as an Investment," pp. 240–61.

73. Prior to the First World War, 86% of company loans were associated with the Industrial Bank of Japan, while only 43% of company loans were associated with the Industrial Bank of Japan in the interwar period. Most of these loans were issued as government-guaranteed debentures, except in the case of the loan to Taiwan Electric of

An examination of the operation of the Industrial Bank of Japan and its relationship with the Japanese government raises a question about the validity of the loans themselves. Were municipal and corporate loans the outcome of genuine requests from independent municipalities and private companies eager for foreign capital, or did the Japanese government carefully orchestrate the loans through its own parastatal organs, in a cynical attempt to balance its books and win support for its colonial adventurism in Asia? In seeking to answer such questions, elements from both sets of suppositions are relevant. With the amount of information we have at present, however, it is most important to stress the reality of the municipal and corporate loans, and to recognize the important role played by those loans in providing infrastructure to Japan's cities, railways, and electric power industry, while duly acknowledging the overwhelming official, or parastatal, presence of the Japanese government in all forms of foreign borrowing (87 percent by volume). Outside of the framework of the parastatal agencies, only the great five electric power companies were permitted to pursue large loans on the international financial markets, which they did frequently from June 1923 to July 1931. Finally, to emphasize the enormity of the state's role, it should be noted that of all Japan's big industrial concerns, or zaibatsu, only the Mitsui Bank and the Mitsui Trust Company were directly involved in negotiating or making use of the importation of foreign capital, and even that involvement was limited to a small number of municipal and corporate loans (Tables 6.1 and 6.2).[74] Zaibatsu apparently preferred to deal with foreign investors in other, more direct ways, as we shall see in the following chapters.

July 1931, when the Japanese government replaced the Industrial Bank of Japan with the Yokohama Specie Bank.

74. See Kikkawa, *Nihon denryokugyō*, pp. 104–9 and especially p. 127.

CHAPTER 7

Direct Foreign Investment, 1899–1939

Japanese authorities were extremely wary of foreign capital and the effects of its penetration on the domestic economy during the Meiji era. Indeed, protectionist policies were enforced until the revision of the Commercial Law (Shōgyō shūseihō) in March 1899, and direct equity investment was not only discouraged but also prohibited by law. Revision of the Commercial Law did, however, allow for foreign participation, particularly in the form of joint ventures, and so Japan ceased to be a pure loan economy to foreign investors after 1899. Nevertheless, there are only a few examples of foreign firms taking an active interest in the new market created by these legislative changes, and foreign investment in Japan accounted for a small fraction of the total foreign investment in Asia.[1] Indeed, over the forty years from 1899 to 1939 Japan did come to benefit significantly from a steady stream of direct foreign investments and some judicious joint ventures. Capitalists, companies, corporations, and entrepreneurs from the United States, Great Britain, Germany, and many other countries invested across a wide range of commerce and industry, with investments at the leading edge of technologies in the armament, automotive, electric power generation, engineering, and petrochemical

---

1. Davenport-Hines and Jones, "British Business in Japan," p. 225. For example, the total amount of direct investment from the United States in China was estimated to be twenty times greater than U.S. investments in Japan before it was drawn into war with Japan in December 1941, and the United States was the main foreign investor in Japan at that time.

industries being of particular significance to Japan's economic growth and development throughout the period.

The first direct foreign investments followed the opening of Japan's treaty ports on 1 July 1859, and many foreign companies, such as the British merchant houses Butterfield and Swire, Jardine Matheson, and S. Samuel and Company, can point to a long history of operations in Japan, and indeed throughout East Asia.[2] It must be remembered, however, that the activities of early foreign commerce and industry were "extraterritorial" and did not extend beyond the areas circumscribed by the treaty ports. For example, the Mitsubishi Iron and Steel Works of Yokohama was established in December 1875 with the financial and technical cooperation of the Boyd & Company shipyard of Shanghai, in what is thought to be one of Japan's earliest joint ventures. The enterprise enjoyed considerable success in servicing ships, however, and Boyd & Company was soon bought out by its partner in the venture, Mitsubishi, in February 1879, despite having provided half of the start-up capital. Mitsubishi was also involved in the establishment of Japan Brewery Company on 8 July 1885, which had been set up as the Spring Valley Brewery in 1870 by an American, William Copeland. The Japan Brewery Company was actually incorporated in Hong Kong for legal reasons, by T. B. Glover and M. Kirkwood, with the president of Mitsubishi, Iwasaki Yanosuke, listed as the only Japanese shareholder.[3]

It was not until the British government agreed to relinquish its extraterritoriality privileges that the Japanese government was able to revise

---

2. As related earlier, the treaty ports of Nagasaki, Hakodate, and Kanagawa (Yokohama) were opened on 1 July 1859, and the remaining ports of Hyogo (Kobe) and Niigata were opened 1 January 1868. Borton, *Japan's Modern Century*, p. 222, and Dickens and Lane-Poole, "British business in Japan," pp. 29–30. Many foreign entrepreneurs started their own companies, such as the Japan Paper Making Company (Kobe Paper Mills), run by the Americans Thomas and John Walsh in 1875, and the Osaka Iron Works/Shipyard founded by the British entrepreneur Edward H. Hunter in 1881, but these were not envisioned as joint ventures; rather, they were taken over by Japanese investors or competitors. See Morikawa, *Zaibatsu*, pp. 72, 129–30.

3. Once the legal hurdles posited by extraterritoriality were cleared, Japan's leading (and omnipresent) entrepreneur Shibusawa Eichi also became a major shareholder, and he and Iwasaki were eventually able to take over the ownership of the company. By 1907, the Japan Brewery Company was wholly in Japanese hands and firmly under the umbrella of the Mitsubishi zaibatsu, changing its name to Kirin Brewery on 23 February of that year. Kirin, *Kirin biru gojnüenshi*, pp. 1, 21–33, 55.

its international treaties with the other foreign powers and, as of 1 July 1899, conclusively put an end to the treaty port system.[4] The year 1899, therefore, has particular historical significance, for it serves as a starting point for an examination of large-scale direct foreign investment as it occurred in Japan's commercial development.[5]

Tobacco and Matches

The first large-scale joint enterprise is usually said by Japanese sources to have been undertaken in 1900, with the decision of the Murai brothers to cooperate with the American Tobacco Company.[6] In 1891 Murai Kichibei had first imported U.S. tobacco, which he rolled and sold as under the label Sunrise cigarettes in the area around Kyoto. The operation was so successful that by 1894 Murai and his brothers had established themselves as a limited partnership, and they were well on their way to becoming leading figures in Japan's tobacco industry. Some time later, the activities of the Murai brothers pricked the interest of the American Tobacco Company, which had been looking to join forces with an influential Japanese partner so it could construct a large cigarette factory in Japan and circumvent the Japanese government's planned introduction of higher tariffs on imported cigarettes after 1 July 1899.[7] After lengthy negotiations, which were subject to much public attention, both companies agreed to contribute an equal ¥5 million to the establishment of Murai Brothers and Company in 1900, in what was to become a model joint-venture enterprise in Japan (see Table 7.1).

American tobacco was imported by Murai Brothers and Company, as before, and then cut and rolled with American-made machinery at its new factory.[8] The company's Hero, Home, Sunrise, and nine other brands of cigarettes were soon engaged in fierce competition with the domestic tobacco products, such as Iwaya Company's brand of Tengu cigarettes,

---

4. See Checkland, *Britain's Encounter with Meiji Japan*, pp. 13–14, and Nish, *The Anglo-Japanese Alliance*, pp. 10–11.

5. Horie, *Gaishi yunyū*, pp. 74–82, 115–27, 156–67.

6. In fact, the first large-scale direct foreign investment in Japan was made in the previous year, 1899, when the American company Western Electric invested just over ¥100,000 in the establishment of Nippon Electric Company (NEC).

7. Cochran, *Big Business in China*, pp. 40–41, and Durden, *The Dukes of Durham*, pp. 74–76.

8. Horie, *Gaishi yunyū*, pp. 75–76.

Table 7.1. Foreign-Owned Enterprises in Japan, 1893–1939

No.	Year established	Company name (in Japan)	Start-up capital (k¥)	Foreign investor	Nationality	FDI share	FDI (k¥)	Japanese investor/ mediator	Remarks
1	1893	Japan Oil Co.	—	Standard Oil	USA	100	—		Changes name to International Oil (capital base of ¥10 million) in 1901. Japan Oil purchases the company's entire assets in 1906.
2	1899	Nippon Electric Co. (NEC)	200	Western Electric	USA	54	108	Iwadare Kunihiko, Maeda Takeshiro	Comes under the management of the Sumitomo Group of companies in 1932.
3	1900	Murai Bros. and Co.	10,000	American Tobacco	USA	50	5,000	Murai Kichibei	Japanese government nationalizes the entire tobacco industry in 1904.
4	1900	Rising Sun Oil	250	S. Samuel and Co.	UK	100	250		
5	1901	Singer Machine	—	Singer Sewing Machine	USA	100	—		
6	1902	Osaka Gas	4,000	A. N. Brady	USA	50	2,000	Asano Shoichiro	Brady family negotiates withdrawal of capital from Osaka Gas in 1925.
7	1903	Tokyo Electric Railway	—	Malcolm (details unclear)	UK	—	917		Joint venture canceled by end of 1903.

8	1905	Tokyo Electric	400	General Electric	USA	38	150	Tamura Eiji, Fukuoka Ichiro	Merges with Shibaura Electric to form Tokyo Shibaura Electric, modern-day Toshiba, in 1939.
9	1906	Oriental (Osaka) Glass Mfg.	900	private investment syndicate	UK/Belgium/France	56	500	Shibusawa Eiichi, Murai Kichibei, Nagamori Tokichiro, Okura Kihachiro	
10	1907	Japan Steel and Ordnance Works	10,000	Vickers and Armstrong Whitworth	UK	50	5,000	Hokkaido Coal and Steamship Co, Mitsui Group	
11	1907	Imperial Cotton	1,500	J. & P. Coats	UK	60	900	Murai Kichibei	
12	1909	Dunlop Far East	—	Dunlop	UK	100	—	Mitsui Bussan	
13	1910	Shibaura Electric Works	2,000	General Electric	USA	24	480	Mitsui group	Merges with Tokyo Electric to form Tokyo Shibaura Electric, modern-day Toshiba, in 1939.
14	1910	Japan Oxygen and Acetylene	103	L'Air Liquide	France	100	103		Becomes Teikoku Sanso in 1930 and falls under the management of the Sumitomo Group of companies.

(continued)

Table 7.1. (continued)

No.	Year established	Company name (in Japan)	Start-up capital (k¥)	Foreign investor	Nationality	FDI share	FDI (k¥)	Japanese investor/ mediator	Remarks
15	1910	Lever Bros. (Amaga-saki)	—	Lever Bros.	UK	100	—		Taken over by Kobe Gas in 1925; changes its name to Velvet Soap in 1926. Management taken over by the Nissan Group in 1936.
16	1910	Japan Gramo-phone	350	F. W. Hohn	USA	—	—	Japanese-American Gramophone, Japanese Gramophone Mfg.	
17	1917	Yokohama Rubber Mfg.	2,500	B. F. Goodrich	USA	50	1,250	Yokohama Electric Cable	Becomes Yokohama Tire after 1969.
18	1918	Japanese American Sheet Glass	3,000	Libby Owens Sheet Glass	USA	35	1,050	Sumitomo Kichizaemon; Mitsubishi and Sumitomo Groups	Company name changes to Japanese Sheet Glass in 1931.
19	1920	Sumitomo Electric Cable Factory	10,000	Western Electric	USA	25	2,500	Sumitomo Group	Establishes Japan Undersea Cable Company in cooperation with Fujigura Cable, and Furukawa Electric in 1932.

20	1922	Asahi Silk Textile	2,000	Vereinigte Glanzstoff Fabriken	Germany	20	400	Kita Matazo, Noguchi Shitagau	Comes under the Japan Nitrogen group during 1929. Merges with Japan Benberg Silk and Nobeoka Ammonia Silk in 1933.
21	1923	Fuji Electric Machinery	10,000	Siemens-Schukertwerke, Siemens und Halske	Germany	30	3,000	Furukawa Electric Works	
22	1923	Mitsubishi Electric	15,000	Westinghouse Electric	USA	10	1,500	Mitsubishi Shipbuilding	Increased cooperation leads to the formation of Ryobi Electric Machinery in 1930.
23	1925	Japan Ford Motor	4,000	Ford Motor	USA	100	4,000	Yokohama Specie Bank	Sale and Frazer hold exclusive retail licenses prior to 1925.
24	1927	Japan General Motors	8,000	General Motors	USA	100	8,000		Mitsui Bussan and Yanase Motor Co. hold exclusive retail licenses prior to 1927.
25	1927	Japan Victor Gramophone	2,000	Victor Talking Machine	USA	100	2,000		Mitsubishi and Sumitomo invest during 1929. Becomes part of the Nissan Group in 1937, then Tokyo Electric after 1938.

(continued)

Table 7.1. (continued)

No.	Year established	Company name (in Japan)	Start-up capital (k¥)	Foreign investor	Nationality	FDI share	FDI (k¥)	Japanese investor/ mediator	Remarks
26	1927	Daido Match Co.	6,000	Sweden Match	Sweden	50	3,000	Takigawa Gisaku	Sweden Match also invests in Asahi Match in 1923. Daido Match administered by the Nissan Group after 1932.
27	1928	Nipponophone (Columbia)	2,100	Columbia	UK/ USA	59	1,239		Becomes part of the Nissan Group in 1937; managed by Tokyo Electric after 1938.
28	1928	Toyo Babcock	1,750	Babcock and Wilcox	UK	71	1,250	Mitsui Bussan	Babcock and Wilcox had cooperative agreement with Mitsui Bussan since 1908.
29	1929	Japan Benberg Silk	10,000	J. P. Benberg	Germany	20	2,000	Japan Nitrogen Fertilizer	Merges with Japan Benberg Silk and Nobeoka Ammonia Silk to form Asahi Benberg Silk Company in 1933.
30	1931	Mitsubishi Oil	10,000	Associated Tidewater Oil	USA	50	5,000	Mitsubishi Group	
31	1931	Sumitomo Aluminium Smelting Co.	3,500	Aluminium Company of Canada (ALCAN)	Canada	50	1,750	Sumitomo Group	

No.	Year	Japanese company	Capital	Foreign company	Country			Parent/Group	Notes
32	1932	Toyo Otis Elevator	1,000	Otis Elevators	USA	60	600	Mitsui Bussan	
33	1932	Japan Undersea Cable	15,000 (2,000)	Standard Underground Cable	USA	12	1,800	Sumitomo Group	A two-step investment in Sumitomo Electric Cable allowed the formation of the ¥2 million Japan Undersea Cable joint venture.
34	1933	National Cash Register (Japan)	750	National Cash-Register	USA	100	750		Merges with Japan Cash Register in 1935 to form the Japan National Cash Register Company.
35	1937	Watson Computing-Tabulating Machine (Japan)	500	International Business Machines	USA	100	500	Shibusawa Group	
36	1939	Shibaura Cooperative Engineering	16,000	United Engineering and Foundry Co. of America	USA	—	—	Shibaura Electric Works	

Source: Utagawa and Nakamura, *Materiaru: Nihon keieishi Edoki kara genzai made*, p. 67, and corporate histories and websites (as cited in the text).
Note: FDI = foreign direct investment.

and the escapades of that "tobacco war" are quite well known in Japan, even today.[9] Murai Brothers and Company, however, enjoyed only a few short years of operation.[10] The entire tobacco industry was nationalized by the Japanese government in 1904 (and remains so today).[11] Ostensibly, tobacco's nationalization was legislated as a means to raise additional revenue for the war against Russia, but the government also undoubtedly sought to calm vocal nationalist sentiment among those opposed to the new reality of foreign entrepreneurs making profits in Japan.[12]

Although information is very scarce, it is known that the development of a match industry in Japan also aroused the interest of a group of investors from a British syndicate who joined with industrialists from the Kansai area to establish the Great Japan Match Company in 1906. Unfortunately, the details of their joint venture are obscure, and very little is known about the company's operations.[13] A second example fol-

---

9. See Otani, *Tabako Ō*, pp. 139–50.

10. After selling its factory to the Japanese government in 1904, Murai Brothers went on to form its own bank, the Murai Bank, with a paid-up capital of ¥1 million. Three years later, in 1907, Murai Kichibei established the Imperial Cotton Company as a joint venture with the British J. & P. Coats Limited (discussed in more detail later in the text), along with a group of smaller ventures that included Murai Steamship Company Limited, the Murai Mining Company, the Murai Curtain Material Company, the Imperial Printing Company, and the Japan Soap Company. In 1917 the Murai Savings Bank was established, and Murai Kichibei also became a significant landowner in Korea through his investments with the Oriental Development Company, Japan's parastatal organ in Korea. The collapse of both the Murai Bank and the Murai Savings Bank during the financial crises of the late 1920s, however, effectively put an end to the reign of the so-called tobacco king. See Duus, *The Abacus and the Sword*, p. 387; Morikawa, *Zaibatsu*, p. 125; and Otani, *Tabako Ō*, pp. 85–88, 239–45, 257–59.

11. The Tobacco Monopoly Law (Tabako senbaihō) of 1 April 1904 legislated a complete state monopoly on the sale and manufacture of tobacco, and extended beyond the government's previous monopoly on the purchase of domestic tobacco leaves, which had been introduced during the war against China. See Ogawa, *Expenditures of the Russo-Japanese War*, p. 71, and Kobayashi, *War and Armament Taxes*, pp. 30–31.

12. See Cochran, *Big Business in China*, p. 41, and Cox, *The Global Cigarette*, pp. 39–42.

13. The Great Japan Match Company was successful to the extent that it became one of the "big four" match manufacturers of the period, along with the Oriental Match Company, the Imperial Match Company, and the Chuo, or Central, Match Company.

lowed much later, in 1927, when the Sweden Match Company invested ¥3 million in a joint venture to establish the Daido Match Company.[14] The Daido Match Company is known to have rapidly established itself as one of Japan's leading match manufacturers, and was administered by the Nissan group of companies after 1932 (see Table 7.1).

Armaments and Explosives

In 1905, three British companies, Nobel Industries, Armstrong Whitworth, and Chilworth Gunpowder established the Japanese Explosive Company, with its head office in London and the company's Japanese operations centered around its factory in Hiratsuka.[15] Within a very short space of time, the Ministry of the Navy, presumably the company's largest customer, arranged to purchase the company's entire Japanese operations, and in 1908 the company became the Naval Gunpowder Workshop.[16]

One year earlier, in 1907, the Vickers and Armstrong Whitworth companies and the Hokkaido Coal and Steamship Company established Japan Steel and Ordnance Works (Nihon Seikōsho), at Muroran, in what was the first successful Anglo-Japanese joint venture.[17] As its name suggests, Japan Steel and Ordnance Works was primarily an armaments and ordnance manufacturer, with large steel manufacturing facilities. The initial investment called for a total of ¥5 million from the two British companies and the same amount from their Japanese partner, with an additional ¥2.5 million to be paid by both the British and Japanese partners in 1909 (which was also when Japan Steel and Ordnance Works received large orders for cannons from the Naval Ministry). The establishment of the joint venture was very much related to military cooperation associated with the Anglo-Japanese alliance, which was especially close between the Royal and Imperial Japanese navies, and with

---

14. The Sweden Match Company is also said to have invested in the establishment of the Asahi Match Company, but unfortunately the details of that joint venture are not clear at present.

15. Davenport-Hines and Jones, "British Business in Japan," p. 225, and Reader, *Imperial Chemical Industries*, p. 335.

16. See Sendo, *Nihon kaigun kayakushi*, pp. 25–28.

17. The Vickers and Armstrong Whitworth companies would later merge in 1928 as a result of Bank of England mediation.

the Japanese government's ardent desire to develop world-class armaments technology.[18]

Petrochemicals: Oil Exploration and Refining

The Standard Oil Company of New York had long traded in East Asia, retailing its products through the China and Japan Trading Company as "Anglo-American Oil." By 1893, however, the company decided it would attempt to realize the tremendous commercial opportunities presented by Japan's lack of an indigenous petrochemical industry. It proposed to establish a branch company in Japan to drill oil wells in the Hokuetsu region, and also to construct a pipeline from Nagaoka, in Niigata prefecture, to Ueno, near central Tokyo, with the aim of supplying oil to Japan's capital and largest city. The aims of the company were largely unrealized, however, until revisions were made to mining legislation in 1899 and 1900 allowed Standard Oil's Japanese subsidiary to engage in greater oil exploration. In the race to succeed in what was still a developing industry, the Standard Oil Company invested further capital to establish the Pacific Oil Company in 1900, and then in the following year it changed its name again, to the International Oil Company, when it took over the Zao Oil Company. The International Oil Company, with a capital base of ¥10 million, flourished while its competitors, a large group of capital-poor domestic enterprises, trailed very much behind, seemingly in disarray. Within the space of just a few years, though, a series of consolidations, mergers, and reorganizations resulted in indigenous production being dominated by two large companies: Japan Oil and Hoden Oil. In 1906 Japan Oil Company proceeded to purchase International Oil Company's entire assets, in a successful move to expel all foreign capital from domestic oil exploration in one swoop. After the purchase of International Oil, Japan Oil battled against its main rival, Hoden Oil, until the Hoden Oil Company merged with Japan Oil in 1921. As a result of the merger, the "newly strengthened" Japan Oil Company came to occupy the preeminent position in Japan's petrochemical industry.[19]

---

18. Horie, *Gaishi yunyū*, pp. 119–20, and Nagura, "Nihon Seikōsho," pp. 215–48, especially pp. 218–19.

19. Nihon Sekiyu, *Nihon sekiyu shi*, pp. 25–28, 45–50, 219–29; Horie, *Gaishi yunyū*, pp. 75, 79–81.

In 1900, Britain's S. Samuel and Company established its own petroleum company in Japan, the Rising Sun Oil Company, as a subsidiary
of the Anglo-Dutch Shell Group.[20] Ten years later, in 1910, Rising Sun
also completed construction of an oil refinery at Nishitosaki on Hakata
Bay, with the aim of refining crude oil transported from Borneo and
Java. Apparently, the low labor costs of the Japanese workforce played an
important part in the company's decision to invest in a refinery at Hakata.[21]
Not much else is known about the details of the project; however, the
Rising Sun Company had made a prudent decision and was well placed
to benefit from the technological revolution brought about by the intro-
duction of the internal combustion engine in Japan.

With the rapid growth of the Japanese automobile industry and the
growing use of the internal combustion engine in other economic fields
in the 1920s and 1930s (particularly in the fishing industry); the Japanese
petrochemical industry was faced with a dramatic increase in demand
for its petroleum products, from approximately 12 million barrels before
the First World War to 36 million barrels in 1928 and 78 million barrels
by 1934. Japan's own petroleum industry, which had refined 34 percent
of the petroleum products consumed in 1923, was unable to cope with
the increases in demand, owing in part to the country's scarce petroleum
resources, and by 1934 Japan was refining just 8 percent of the petroleum
consumed domestically. Japan's domestic petroleum companies were
scrambling to build new oil refineries, in order to refine foreign crude oil
to sell on the domestic market.[22]

Only the Mitsubishi Oil Company cooperated with foreign capital to
compete in domestic oil refining and petrochemical production. Mitsubishi Oil and the Tide Water Associated Oil Company of America,
which had sold the retail rights of its products to a Mitsubishi affiliate in
1923, came to an agreement to pay joint costs, and receive equal profits,
from the construction of a new Mitsubishi Oil refinery at Kawasaki in
1931, which is said to have involved a capital outlay of ¥10 million.[23] Tide

---

20. Davenport-Hines and Jones, "British Business in Japan," p. 222.

21. Horie, *Gaishi yunyū*, p. 122.

22. Such companies include Asahi Oil (1921), Japan Oil (1924), Kokura Oil (1924),
Mitsubishi Oil (1931), Maruzen Oil (1933), and Hayayama Oil (1935).

23. Mitsubishi Sekiyu, *Mitsubishi sekiyu gojūnenshi*, pp. 7–36, especially p. 9. The
Associated Oil Company was established in October of 1901 in California. In March
1926 it formed a separate company, called the Tide Water Associated Oil Company, in

Water Associated provided the refinery's technological inputs, on the understanding that crude oil from its wells would be refined at Kawasaki. Owing to the Japanese government's support of domestic refining, day-to-day operations went very smoothly, and the joint venture stayed free of nationalist protests.[24]

No further foreign investment was received by Japan's petroleum industry after 1931; indeed it was discouraged by the outbreak of war in China and the introduction of new legislation.[25] Nevertheless, as a result of these intense efforts in refinery construction Japan's petroleum industry captured an increased share of the market and was refining approximately 40 percent of domestically consumed petroleum products, by volume, in the late 1930s. The import of the remaining 60 percent of petroleum products, however, was held very firmly in the hands of the two giant foreign oil trusts of the period: the British-owned Anglo-Dutch Shell subsidiary Rising Sun Oil Company, and the American-owned Socony-Vacuum subsidiary Japan Vacuum Oil Company.[26]

Gas Utilities

The Osaka Gas Company is an example of a Japanese firm that attracted investment from a foreign capitalist who thought the company's projects had outstanding economic potential. Although founded in 1896, the Osaka Gas was only a company in name until the American entrepreneur Anthony N. Brady took a 50 percent share of the venture in 1902, by investing ¥2 million in the company. Even then, construction of the company's gasworks was delayed by a trenchant nationalization campaign that perceived the foreign investment as being used to create a private monopoly. In the end, however, it was clear that the Osaka Gas Company could not proceed without Brady's capital, and the weight of the American investment carried the day. Despite passing away in July 1913,

partnership with the Tide Water Oil Company of New Jersey, which was established in November 1888. These three companies, although related, were fiercely independent until they merged to form a single corporate entity in November 1936, which retained the name of their partnership from ten years before, the Tide Water Associated Oil Company. See ibid., pp. 1–6.

24. See Hein, *Fuelling Growth*, pp. 46–52.

25. See Davenport-Hines and Jones, "British Business in Japan," pp. 232–33.

26. Horie, *Gaishi yunyū*, pp. 162–64, and E. B. Schumpeter, *Industrialization of Japan and Manchukuo*, pp. 443, 774–75.

Brady was to remain the company's largest shareholder until 1925 when, for reasons that remain unclear, the Brady family negotiated the complete withdrawal of their capital from the gas company.[27]

Electric Lightbulbs and Appliances

In 1899 the Western Electric Company of America invested in the establishment of the Nippon Electric Company, commonly known today as NEC, in what can be said to be the first example of direct foreign investment in Japan's electric industry.[28] Western Electric, which was previously represented in Japan by the Takada Company, invested ¥108,000 in Nippon Electric, for what was essentially an avenue into sales and distribution of electric appliances in Japan.[29] Six years later, in 1905, Tokyo Electric and General Electric also agreed to a financial and technological linkup, whereby the General Electric Company invested ¥150,000 to increase Tokyo Electric's capital base to ¥400,000, receiving in return 1,875 of the company's 5,000 shares, the chair for a vice president, and three of the five seats on the board of directors.[30]

What drove Tokyo Electric to seek out and cooperate with General Electric, and thus reestablish itself as a joint venture, was the company's aim to produce world-class lightbulbs. Tokyo Electric had in fact been Japan's leading producer of lightbulbs since 1890, when it launched the "white hot" (*hakunetsusha*) lamp, but its own products were simply unable to compete with the superior quality of foreign-made bulbs.[31] The Japanese market was completely dominated by the products of America's General Electric and National Electric, Britain's Sunbeam Lamp and Tri-Star, Holland's Philips, and Germany's Allgemeine Elekrictäts Gesellschaft (AEG) and Siemens, all of which enjoyed brisk sales in Japan. When Tokyo Electric replaced the carbon filaments, made from

---

27. Horie, *Gaishi yunyū*, pp. 76–77, and M. Mason, *American Multinationals and Japan*, p. 26.

28. Nippon Denki, *Nippon denki nanajūnenshi*, pp. 24–56, especially pp. 50, 440.

29. Davenport-Hines and Jones, "British Business in Japan," p. 225. NEC should not be confused with the electric power generation company Nippon Electric Power Company Limited (NEPCO).

30. Toshiba sōgō kikakubu shashi, *Tōshiba hachijūnenshi*, pp. 15–31, 795. For details of the joint venture, see Toshiba, *Tōshiba gojūnenshi*, pp. 97–114, and Horie, *Gaishi yunyū*, p. 75.

31. See Toshiba, *Tōshiba gojūnenshi*, pp. 300–350.

a special type of bamboo charcoal, with tungsten filaments in its *"mazda"* lamps, however, the technological transfer of machines, tools, and materials for manufacturing tungsten bulbs allowed Tokyo Electric to enjoy an instant commercial success that would pay spectacular dividends.[32] The fact that Tokyo Electric's new epoch-making progress was based on foreign technology, with patents held by its American partner, was never left in doubt, and it is interesting to note that General Electric went so far as to insist that GE's distinctive trademark was put on all of Tokyo Electric's products. The example of the Tokyo Electric Company's cooperation with General Electric illustrates the commercial value of technology transfer. Clearly, the leasing and sharing of patents was much more important to the growth and development of the Japanese economy than is suggested by the sum total of the period's financial investments in yen.[33]

In 1910 the General Electric Company agreed to a financial and technological exchange with another Japanese electric company called Shibaura Electric Works.[34] The transaction was part of the organizational restructuring of Shibaura Electric Works as a joint venture wherein the exchange of technology and an investment of ¥480,000 on the part of General Electric were used to double Shibaura's capital base from ¥1 million to ¥2 million. General Electric became a major shareholder in the process, and received 9,900, or 24 percent, of the company's shares, and promptly passed on 4,125 shares to Tokyo Electric, its other venture in Japan. The motive behind the American investment, then, was to create a capital link between the two companies that would allow them to combine their operations.[35] In fact, the question of a merger between the

---

32. Around 1910 Tokyo Electric chose to name its new tungsten-filament lightbulbs *mazda* lamps, to distinguish them from the carbon-filament *hakunetsusha* lamp, which it had been retailing since 1890. The name *mazda*, despite being a common Japanese surname, was actually taken from the Japanese reading of the name of the Zoroastrian god of light Ahura Mazda. See Toshiba, *Tōshiba gojūnenshi*, pp. 139–42, and Horie, *Gaishi yunyū*, p. 118.

33. Horie, *Gaishi yunyū*, pp. 115–18. For more information concerning the manufacture of electric light globes, or lightbulbs, see E. B. Schumpeter, *Industrialization of Japan and Manchukuo*, pp. 544–48, and Uyeda, *The Small Industries of Japan*, pp. 266–78.

34. Dunn, *American Foreign Investments*, p. 164.

35. Toshiba sōgō kikakubu shashi, *Toshiba hachijūnenshi*, pp. 59, 795, and Horie, *Gaishi yunyū*, pp. 118–19.

two companies had been raised two years earlier, without success, so General Electric's investment provided an opportunity for the two companies to discuss merger negotiations in the future.[36]

Foreign investment in Japan's electrical appliance industry became particularly active in the period after the First World War. Increased demand for electrical appliances was such that many of Japan's most well-known appliance manufacturers were established during the interwar period. For example, the Mitsubishi Electric Machinery Company was established in January 1921, after separating from its parent company, the Mitsubishi Shipbuilding Company, based in Kobe. Two years later, in January 1923, Westinghouse Electric International provided technological assistance to the Mitsubishi Electric Machinery Company, along with a ¥1.5 million financial investment. The success of their collaborative efforts was such that, in November of 1929, they merged their retail operations in Japan and formed a new company to market their electrical products. Choosing the curious name "Ryobi" (with the "Ryo" being derived from an alternate reading of the Chinese character for the "bishi" in Mitsubishi, and the final "bi" derived from the character used in China to denote America), the new Ryobi Electric Machinery Company opened for business as of January 1930.[37]

The Fuji Electric Machinery Company, established in August 1923, provides a similar example of a joint venture in the field of electrical appliance and machinery manufacturing. Cooperation between the Furukawa Electric Works and two German companies, Siemens-Schuckertwerke and Siemens und Halske (often referred to as Siemens S & H), led to a ¥3 million financial investment in the creation of the Fuji Electric Machinery Company, with the "Fu" of Fuji, derived from the first syllable of Furukawa, and the "ji," from the Japanese pronunciation of the first syllable of Siemens, together forming the most quintessential of Japanese names. The initial start-up capital behind Fuji Electric Machinery Company was ¥10 million, with the German partners investing 30 percent of the financial capital and most of the technological capital. Indeed, the production of electrical machinery at Fuji's Kawasaki factory

---

36. Toshiba sōgō kikakubu shashi, *Toshiba hachijūnenshi*, pp. 82–94; Toshiba, *Toshiba gojūnenshi*, pp. 236–39; and Horie, *Gaishi yunyū*, pp. 118–19. The companies did in fact merge to form Tokyo Shibaura Electric in 1939.

37. Horie, *Gaishi yunyū*, p. 160.

was almost completely based on technology developed in Germany. Much later, in 1935, Fuji's telephone manufacturing factory separated from the Fuji Electric Machinery Company to become the Fuji Telegraph Manufacturing Company Limited, with a capital base of ¥6 million. Two years later, in 1937, the Fuji Telegraph Manufacturing Company, supported by its parent company, then attempted to move production offshore by investing ¥5 million in the construction of a large-scale factory complex on the Liao-tung (Liaodong) Peninsula in Northeast China.[38]

Electric Cable

Foreign investment in the related industry of electrical cable manufacturing appears to have started in September 1907, when Siemens-Schuckertwerke and Siemens und Halske were awarded a special contract by Furukawa, at the Ashio copper mine, to establish Japan's first electrical cable factory. Through building the factory, Siemens hoped to promote the sale of its own electrical cables in Japan and to compete against American cable manufacturers. Unfortunately, however, information is scarce about the joint project, and beyond its motive not much else is publicly known about the venture.[39]

In November 1920 the Sumitomo Electric Cable Factory reorganized and separated from the main Sumitomo group of companies, after receiving a large injection of technological and financial capital from the Western Electric Company of America that purportedly increasing the company's capital base to ¥10 million.[40] Having received such large-scale investment from Western Electric, Sumitomo Electric Cable was then able to attract additional investments of technological capital from Great Britain's Standard Telephone and Cable Company and Italy's Pirelli Company, and it quickly became Japan's leading producer of cables for the vital markets of communication and electric power transmission. Sumitomo Electric Cable was particularly successful at providing domestic substitutes for foreign imports, and the company's capital base was said to have increased rapidly to ¥15 million during the early 1930s. Moreover, by 1932 technical cooperation with the Standard Un-

---

38. Horie, *Gaishi yunyū*, p. 160.
39. Horie, *Gaishi yunyū*, pp. 120–21.
40. Sakudo, *Sumitomo zaibatsu*, pp. 156–57, 185, 227–29, and Hatakeyama, *Sumitomo zaibatsu setsuritsushi*, pp. 211–14, 252–54.

derground Cable Company, worth ¥1.8 million, allowed Sumitomo Electric Cable to build the world's sixth undersea, or submarine, cable factory at Osaka and establish itself as a world-class cable producer, thoroughly capable of driving out all foreign imports. In the same year, Sumitomo Electric Cable Company went on to establish the spin-off Japan Undersea Cable Company, with a capital base of ¥2 million, as part of its joint venture project, and in cooperation with new Japanese investors, the Fujigura Electric Cable Company and Furukawa Electric Works.[41]

Electrical and Mechanical Engineering

Britain's Babcock and Wilcox Company provides a prime example of direct foreign investment in Japan's electrical engineering and machinery industry during the interwar period. In 1928, the Babcock and Wilcox Company invested more than ¥1 million in the establishment of the Toyo Babcock Company, with Mitsui Bussan investing just ¥500,000 to become junior partner in the joint venture. As a leading supplier of technology associated with boilers and power (electricity) generation, the Babcock and Wilcox Company had enjoyed a long association with Mitsui Bussan that went back at least until 1908.[42]

After the "Manchurian Incident" of September 1931, when an explosion staged by Japanese military personnel near a Japanese-owned railway line was used a pretext by the local Japanese forces (the Kwantung Army) to launch an occupation of Manchuria, there are relatively few examples of foreign joint ventures and direct foreign investments in Japan. Yet in the following year, 1932, Mitsui Bussan was able to import elevator technology through entering into a joint venture with the American company Otis Elevator. The two companies worked together to establish the Toyo, or Oriental, Otis Elevator Company. Otis Elevator was the majority shareholder, contributing ¥600,000 of the initial ¥1 million investment used to create the company, in what was one of the largest foreign investments in the forty-year history under consideration in this chapter. In 1933 the National Cash Register Company, another American company, established a Japanese subsidiary of the same name with an investment of ¥750,000. Two years later, in 1935, the Japanese

---

41. Sakudo, *Sumitomo zaibatsu*, p. 309, and Horie, *Gaishi yunyū*, pp. 161–62.
42. Horie, *Gaishi yunyū*, p. 165.

subsidiary of National Cash Register merged with Japan Cash Register to form the Japan National Cash Register Company. Similarly, International Business Machines Corporation (later abbreviated to IBM) invested ¥500,000 in the formation of its own Japanese subsidiary, the Japan Watson Computing-Tabulating Machine Company in 1937. In addition, many other companies, such as Fuji Silk Reeling Company, the Oji Paper Company, the Japan Nitrogen Fertilizer Company, and the Sumitomo Group's Nippon Musical Instrument Company, are also thought to have been associated with foreign capital, but the details of their investments await further research.[43]

The Japanese company Shibaura Electric Works, mentioned earlier in relation to its financial and technological exchange with General Electric in 1910, was able to receive considerable technological assistance during March 1939. In what is thought to be the last example of a large-scale foreign investment in Japan before the outbreak of war in Europe and the Pacific, the United Engineering and Foundry Company of America, based in Pittsburgh, worked together with Shibaura Electric Works to establish a Japanese factory that would manufacture compression, rolling, and other heavy industrial machinery. While the exact sum of the American investment in the joint venture is unclear, as well as exactly what manufacturing technologies were supplied, the investment appears to have been significant, as the capital base of the new joint venture, ¥16 million, exceeded that of many other foreign subsidiaries and joint ventures operating in Japan at that time. The name of the new enterprise was the Shibaura Cooperative Engineering Company Limited.[44]

---

43. Horie, *Gaishi yunyū*, pp. 165–66. In 1923, according to R. W. Dunn, Japanese and American capitalists jointly managed and financed the establishment of the Japanese-American Engineering and Contracting Company, with a capital base of $50 million, or ¥100 million. Details of the company's operations are scarce, suspiciously so, for a company with such a large reputed capital base. Considering that a direct investment of $4 million (¥8 million) by General Motors of the United States is the largest foreign investment of the period that can be confirmed, it seems likely that the Japanese-American Engineering and Contracting Company was a smaller concern—unless eighty years of historical research has failed to identify the preeminent Japanese-American joint venture of the first half of the twentieth century. See Dunn, *American Foreign Investments*, pp. 164–65.

44. Toshiba sōgō kikakubu shashi, *Tōshiba hachijūnenshi*, pp. 80, 134–35.

In the same year, a long-anticipated merger between Shibaura Electric Works and Tokyo Electric was accomplished, and the two Japanese companies, in which General Electric was a major shareholder, merged to create the Tokyo-Shibaura Electric Company.[45] The establishment of the Tokyo-Shibaura Electric Company—known as Toshiba, from the first characters of "Tokyo" and "Shibaura"—did not interfere with the operations of Shibaura Cooperative Engineering Company. In 1944, however, Shibaura Cooperative Engineering, as a subsidiary of Tokyo-Shibaura Electric, was forced to change its name to Toshiba Heavy Industries and in so doing support the restructured Toshiba group of companies until the end of the war.[46]

Gramophones, Recording Machines, and the Wireless

In 1910 an American syndicate led by F. W. Hohn met with representatives from the Japanese-American Gramophone Company and the Japanese Gramophone Manufacturing Company to propose the merger of the two companies in order to establish a new gramophone company in Japan. Shortly after, in the same year, Japan Gramophone Company Limited was established as a joint venture, with a start-up capital base totaling ¥350,000.[47] A full seventeen years later, in 1927 U.S. capital was invested to the tune of ¥2 million to establish the completely foreign-owned Japan Victor Gramophone Company (better known in English by its initials, JVC). Two years later though, the Mitsubishi and Sumitomo conglomerates, or zaibatsu, took an interest in the company's operations and made significant organizational investments, receiving a 32 percent share in the company's stock for their efforts.[48]

In the same year that Japan Victor Gramophone was formed, 1927, the above-mentioned Japan Gramophone Company also received substantial technological and financial investment from the English arm of the American gramophone and record-manufacturing company Columbia,

---

45. Toshiba sōgō kikakubu shashi, *Tōshiba hachijūnenshi*, pp. 82–94; Toshiba, *Tōshiba gojūnenshi*, pp. 236–39; and Horie, *Gaishi yunyū*, pp. 118–19.

46. Toshiba sōgō kikakubu shashi, *Tōshiba hachijūnenshi*, pp. 134–35, and Horie, *Gaishi yunyū*, pp. 160–61.

47. Horie, *Gaishi yunyū*, p. 120.

48. See Mason, *American Multinationals and Japan*, pp. 36–41, 281.

and in 1928 a Japanese subsidiary of Columbia, the Nipponophone Company, was established.[49] By 1935, however, the Nipponophone Company had completely disengaged itself from its foreign investors. Together with Japan Victor Gramophone, in 1937 the two companies became part of the Nissan group of industries. It was under the influence of Nissan that both companies moved part of their operations into Manchuria, where the Nissan group was particularly active. Shortly after, however, Tokyo Electric Company took over the management of both companies, and it administered them as its own subsidiaries until the end of war, by which time a new round of commercial reorganization would become necessary.[50]

Finally, it is interesting to note that in 1935 Tokyo Electric Company also became involved in technical cooperation with the Radio Corporation of America (RCA), through the introduction and graces of General Electric, because it wished to use various RCA patents and improve its own wireless receivers and transmitters. After the successful merger of Tokyo Electric Company and Shibaura Electric Works (Toshiba), these technical agreements were enlarged to include fifty-nine patents and fourteen new designs for a wide variety of new technologies associated with wireless reception and transmission, the broadcasting of television, and the key component of all these technologies: electron tubes.[51]

Public Transport

One thread that runs through the entire narrative of direct investment in Japan is the great difficulty faced by non-Japanese capitalists, and identifiably foreign companies, in winning acceptance among the wider Japanese community. A Japanese company's decision to do business with non-Japanese partners, or to cooperate with foreign companies, was not taken lightly and always had the potential to become a topic of media speculation, public protest, and even government regulation. The little-known story of the Tokyo Electric Railway Company provides an interesting example of the investment climate in Japan around the turn of the twentieth century.

---

49. Davenport-Hines and Jones, "British Business in Japan," p. 230.
50. See Horie, *Gaishi yunyū*, pp. 164–65, and Mason, *American Multinationals and Japan*, p. 94.
51. Toshiba sōgō kikakubu shashi, *Tōshiba hachijūnenshi*, p. 795.

An unholy fracas erupted in January 1903 after the Tokyo Electric Railway Company accepted an investment of just under ¥1 million from an English entrepreneur named "Malcolm" (who apparently lived in Australia), by means of which he became the company's majority share-holder. Controversy reigned when it became known that Malcolm had allegedly negotiated for half of the company's executives to be English and for the chief engineer of construction to be English. Very quickly the company became the subject of intense criticism and was accused of being traitorous and immoral. Newspapers bemoaned how the Tokyo Electric Railway Company had casually sold the monopoly privileges of running a railway line, which it had been granted by the emperor in order to serve his subjects, to some unknown foreigner, without regard for any possible socioeconomic benefits to be derived from the provision of the new transport infrastructure. Given the depth of local opposition, one might have thought that there was a danger that Malcolm would take the railway back with him to Australia or England.[52] Not surprisingly, there were no further foreign investments in public transport projects, despite the fact that the Tokyo Electric Railway Company was broadly successful in its aims, and that public transport was an area in which foreign companies enjoyed great expertise and investor confidence.[53] Moreover, the Japanese government legislated to nationalize Japan's railways in 1906, thus denying investors, financial institutions, and companies the opportunity to expand the scale or scope of their investments in Japanese public transport.[54]

Rubber and Tire Manufacture

In 1909, the Dunlop Rubber Company of England established a rubber products factory in Kobe, the Dunlop (Far East) Rubber Company, which would become a leading manufacturer in Japan's rubber industry for the next thirty years.[55] In 1917 the company name was changed by adding "Joint-Stock" before Company when Dunlop entered into a joint

---

52. Horie, *Gaishi yunyū*, pp. 75–81.

53. Cottrell, *British Investment*, pp. 27, 40; Edelstein, *Overseas Investment*, pp. 37–44.

54. Warner, *Anglo-Japanese Financial Relations*, pp. 56–60.

55. Davenport-Hines and Jones, "British Business in Japan," p. 225, and Uyeda, *The Small Industries of Japan*, pp. 183–84.

venture with Mitsui Bussan as a means to meet changes legislated by the Wartime Factory Ownership Law (Kōgyō shoyūken senjihō) of that same year.[56] Also in 1917, the American tire manufacturer B. F. Goodrich and the Yokohama Electric Cable Manufacturing Company invested ¥1.25 million each in a joint venture to establish the Yokohama Rubber Manufacturing Company, the precursor of the present-day Yokohama Tire Company. Both of these rubber manufacturing companies, along with the wholly Japanese company Bridgestone, were to play an important role in supplying products to an important new area of industrial production: the Japanese automobile industry.[57]

Automobiles and Motorcycles

The Japanese automobile industry enjoyed rapid growth during the late 1920s and early 1930s. The catalyst for the production boom came in the unlikely form of the Great Kanto earthquake of September 1923, for it was not until after the earthquake that reconstruction work created the roads and highways that allowed trucks, buses, taxis, and private vehicles to be commonly used. The widespread use of motorcycles, in contrast, can be traced back to the Imperial Japanese Army's purchases of Harley Davidson motorcycles in 1912. The size of those orders, and continued interest among police and military forces in using the motorcycles, led an up-and-coming trading conglomerate, the Okura group, to purchase retail licenses from Harley Davidson in 1917. In 1931, economic depression in the United States led Harley Davidson to agree to a joint venture with the large pharmaceutical manufacturer Sankyo (which had acquired the retail rights for Harley Davidson in Japan) to form a Japanese subsidiary, Nippon Harley Davidson, or more formally in English, Harley Davidson Japan. Production licenses, blueprints, tools, dies, and associated machinery were supplied, and full production started in 1933 for the military Type 97 (or "Knucklehead"), the first wholly Japanese-made "Harley Davidson" motorcycle, colloquially known as the Rikuo (meaning "land king," or "king of the [Asian]

---

56. Horie, *Gaishi yunyū*, p. 121. In the postwar years Dunlop (Far East) joined forces with the Sumitomo Rubber Company in capital and technological tie-ups, and its Japanese operations were taken over entirely by Sumitomo during 1983. See McMillan, *The Dunlop Story*, pp. 148, 183–84.

57. See Miyamoto et al., *Nihon keieishi*, p. 186.

continent"). Just a few years later, in 1935, American staff members at the Japanese factory were advised to leave the joint venture, and Nippon Harley Davidson was renamed Sankyo Nainenki. The following year the company name was changed, once again, to Rikuo Nainenki, in recognition of the Rikuo appellation given to the Japanese motorcycles. Details of its production schedules are limited, but Rikuo manufactured approximately eighteen thousand motorcycles between 1937 and 1942, mostly for use by the military.[58]

While many foreign automobile companies were eager to conclude retail or licensing agreements with Japanese partners, Ford was the first to invest aggressively in the Japanese market, and in February 1925 the Japan Ford Motor Company Limited was established as a wholly foreign-owned subsidiary, with start-up capital totaling ¥4 million.[59] The company's Japanese factory was built in Yokohama, and the Sale and Frazer Company, widely associated with foreign finance in Yokohama since the days of the treaty ports, assisted Japan Ford in its retail operations.[60] Ford's production (conveyor) system, or "Fordism," as it was called, was introduced the following month, in March 1925, and 3,437 vehicles were assembled in the facility's first year with components imported from Ford's main factories in the United States.[61]

Ford's main competitor at that time, the General Motors Company, lost almost no time in establishing its own foothold in Japan. Japan General Motors Company Limited was established in January 1927 with an initial investment of ¥8 million, which was twice the size of Ford's investment and probably the largest single direct investment in Japan's corporate history at that time.[62] General Motors very shrewdly exploited competition for its factory's location between the rival Kanto and Kansai regions, and won significant concessions, including a four-year tax

---

58. Despite the rise of the iconic Japanese motorcycle companies such as Honda, Kawasaki, Suzuki, and Yamaha, production of classic 1930s-style Rikuo motorcycles continued as late as 1960, and stopped only when Rikuo Nainenki went into bankruptcy. See "1958 Rikuo RT2: Harley Davidson's Japanese Connection," http://www.motorcyclemuseum.org (accessed 30 April 2014).

59. Shinomiya, *Nihon no jidōsha sangyō*, p. 7.

60. Horie, *Gaishi yunyū*, p. 162, and Mason, *American Multinationals and Japan*, pp. 60–69.

61. Horie, *Gaishi yunyū*, pp. 4–7, 21; and Davenport-Hines and Jones, "British Business in Japan," p. 230.

62. Shinomiya, *Nihon no jidōsha sangyō*, pp. 7–9.

exemption, by constructing its Japanese motor works in the Kansai region, near Osaka. General Motors was able to start production at its Osaka factory in the same year, and in 1927 alone, 5,635 vehicles were assembled for sale from "knock-down" components produced in and imported from the United States.[63]

Mitsui Bussan and the Yanase Motor Company assisted General Motors in its Japanese retail operations, in an arrangement similar to that between Ford and the Sale and Frazer Company.[64] The market for automobiles in Japan was surprisingly buoyant and automobile manufacturers suffered only a relatively small downturn in demand during the worst years of the Great Depression.[65] When the Japanese government introduced legislation in 1936 requiring all automobile companies in Japan to have more than 50 percent Japanese equity or to cease production, Ford and General Motors simply withdrew, leaving Toyota, Nissan, and a whole host of smaller makers to replace them in the Japanese automobile market.[66] Nevertheless, in eleven years of its Japanese operations, Ford manufactured a total of 108,509 automobiles, with General Motors likewise manufacturing 89,047 automobiles in just nine years of production—quite a race from start to finish.[67]

Fabrics and Textiles

There are very few examples of large-scale foreign investment in Japan's textile industry, yet investment was by no means absent.[68] For example,

---

63. Shinomiya, *Nihon no jidōsha sangyō*, pp. 9, 21; Davenport-Hines and Jones, "British Business in Japan," p. 230.

64. Horie, *Gaishi yunyū*, pp. 162–63, and Mason, *American Multinationals and Japan*, pp. 69–72.

65. The Chrysler Motor Company was also interested in the Japanese market and went into partnership with three Japanese companies to establish the United Automobile Works in 1928. Production levels were very modest, with annual sales averaging around a thousand vehicles until 1934. In all, they manufactured 11,411 vehicles over seven years of production. See Shinomiya, *Nihon no jidōsha sangyō*, p. 21, and Miyamoto et al., *Nihon keieishi*, p. 188.

66. Davenport-Hines and Jones, "British Business in Japan," p. 233, and E. B. Schumpeter, *Industrialization of Japan and Manchukuo*, p. 804.

67. Shinomiya, *Nihon no jidōsha sangyō*, p. 21.

68. In the related field of sewing machine manufacture, the Singer Sewing Machine of America established its own subsidiary in Japan during 1901. See Gordon, *Fabricating Consumers*, pp. 30–56.

J. & P. Coats, in partnership with Murai Kichibei, invested ¥900,000, or 60 percent of the start-up capital of ¥1.5 million, in the establishment of the Imperial, or Teikoku, Cotton Company in 1907.[69] In 1922 the Asahi Silk Textile Company received ¥400,000 from a joint-venture with a group of German investors led by J. P. Benberg. Later, in 1929, J. P. Benberg would invest another ¥2 million, along with the Japan Nitrogen Fertilizer Company, which made an investment of ¥8 million, to establish the Japan Benberg Silk Company as a separate joint venture.[70] The Japan Benberg Silk Company then merged with Nobeoka Ammonia Silk Company, and the other German-Japanese joint venture, the Asahi Silk Textile Company, to form the Asahi Benberg Silk Company in 1933. Despite these examples of joint ventures, however, foreign investment in Japan's textile industry was of a limited nature, and was almost negligible in comparison with that evidenced in China or India.[71]

Glass, Plate Glass, and Aluminum

The Oriental Glass Manufacturing Company was established in 1906 as one of the first joint ventures in Japan's heavy industry. A Japanese syndicate contributing ¥400,000, led by such business and financial luminaries as Shibusawa Eiichi, Murai Kichibei, Nagamori Tokichiro, and Okura Kihachiro, among others, joined with a Franco-Belgian syndicate that contributed ¥400,000, and a British syndicate that contributed ¥100,000, with the aim of founding a company to produce glass for Osaka and the whole Kansai region. The multinational syndicate then went on to establish a range of "Oriental" companies, the Oriental Rubber Company, the Oriental Lumber Company, the Oriental Linoleum Company, and others, as well as the Imperial Brush Company. In addition, a related Franco-Japanese syndicate led by Nagamori Tokichiro and

---

69. Otani, *Tabako Ō*, pp. 243–46; Horie, *Gaishi yunyū*, p. 165; and Davenport-Hines and Jones, "British Business in Japan," pp. 225–26.

70. The Asahi Silk Textile Company came under control of the Japan Nitrogen Fertilizer Company in 1929, a core prewar member of the Nissan group of companies. Japan Nitrogen Fertilizer Company would later change its name to the Nitrogen Company after becoming infamous for its role in the Minamata mercury poisonings of the 1950s. See Morris-Suzuki, *The Technological Transformation of Japan*, pp. 115, 207.

71. See Horie, *Gaishi yunyū*, p. 164. For more details on the fiber and textile industry, see E. B. Schumpeter, *Industrialization of Japan and Manchukuo*, pp. 567–95, and Uyeda, *The Small Industries of Japan*, pp. 20–181.

a Mr. Hinary of France established the Oriental Compressor Company in the following year, 1907. Apart from the fact that the Oriental Compressor Company built an office in downtown Tokyo, however, very little is known about the company and the outcomes of its investors' efforts.[72] Indeed, as with many such companies, the details of their management and operations have yet to be clarified and await further study.[73]

The Japanese glass industry benefited from foreign investment in 1918, when a joint venture of the Asahi Glass Company, Mitsubishi Company Limited, Sumitomo Company Limited, and the American sheet-glass manufacturer Libby Owens resulted in the formation of the Japanese American Sheet Glass Company.[74] The American company provided the capital, in the form of patents for new sheet-glass manufacturing technology, and contributed just over ¥1 million of the company's initial capital base of ¥3 million. In a short time, the Japanese American Sheet Glass Company became Japan's second largest sheet-glass manufacturer, just behind its parent, the Asahi Glass Company. In 1931 the Japanese American Sheet Glass Company's name was changed to the Japanese Sheet Glass Company, reflecting broader political changes in Japan's corporate culture and the wider societal importance of being seen to be 100 percent "Nipponese" in 1930s Japan.[75]

The world's leading aluminum producer of the interwar period, the Aluminum Company of America (Alcoa) is said to have been involved

---

72. Horie, *Gaishi yunyū*, pp. 121–25.

73. Many cases of foreign investment in Japan still require clarification. For example, it is said that in 1909 a group of British capitalists, with the assistance of the so-called London Samurai Syndicate and one Saul Crowder and Company, purchased the Shin-Yubari Coal Mine and one-sixth of the total shares of the Moji Dock Joint-Stock Company, near Kitakyushu. The French L'Air Liquide Company established its own Japanese subsidiary and invested some ¥103,000 into its operations during 1910. Yet another example is the Lever Brothers Company's construction of a soap factory at Amagasaki, on the outskirts of Kobe, in 1910. Very little is known about the company's Japanese operations except that the soap factory was managed by the Kobe Gas Company after 1925; the Japanese subsidiary was renamed after its most famous product, "velvet soap," in the following year; and that Lever Brothers completely withdrew from Japan in 1934. See Horie, *Gaishi yunyū*, p. 122, and Yamauchi, *Nichi-ei keieishi*, pp. 151–56.

74. Sakudo, *Sumitomo zaibatsu*, pp. 192, 231, 364–65; and Hatakeyama, *Sumitomo zaibatsu setsuritsushi*, pp. 261–62, 310–11.

75. Horie, *Gaishi yunyū*, p. 164.

in a Japanese joint venture in 1926, when it held 60 percent of the shares of Toyo Aluminum Company. Owing to financial difficulties during the late 1920s, however, construction of a planned refinery was never realized.[76] And so the establishment of the Sumitomo Aluminium Smelting Company provides a final example of the important role played by direct foreign investment and joint ventures in the transfer of new technologies to Japan. In 1931 the aluminum-sheet manufacturing section of Sumitomo Copper Works separated from its parent company to start a joint venture with the Aluminium Company of Canada (Alcan). Both parties contributed a half share, and they established the Sumitomo Aluminium Smelting Company with an initial capital base of ¥3.5 million. The import of foreign "know-how" capital from Canada allowed Sumitomo Aluminium to almost immediately become the leading manufacturer in Japan's nascent aluminum industry.[77]

The study of large-scale direct foreign investment as it occurred in Japan's economic history offers some important findings in relation to the role of technology transfer in economic development. Certainly we have been able to confirm that capitalists, companies, corporations, and entrepreneurs from the United States, Great Britain, Germany, and many other countries invested across a wide range of commerce and industry by establishing subsidiaries and cooperating in joint ventures, particularly in the fields examined in this chapter. While a cursory glance at the sum total of the capital involved suggests that direct foreign investment in the Japanese economy was insignificant in comparison with other forms of indirect lending, the effects of direct investment were often disproportionate to the size of the actual financial investment. It is also important to remember that foreign capital was overwhelmingly directed toward the top end of the technology market in the heavy industries, often taking the form of patents and technology itself.[78] Moreover, monetary values alone cannot fully express the socioeconomic significance of the technologies introduced in association with the automobile, calculating

---

76. See A. Mikami, "Old and New *Zaibatsu*," p. 213, and Dunn, *American Foreign Investments*, p. 165.

77. Sakudo, *Sumitomo zaibatsu*, pp. 302–4, and Horie, *Gaishi yunyū*, p. 165.

78. See Horie, *Gaishi yunyū*, p. 126, and E. B. Schumpeter, *Industrialization of Japan and Manchukuo*, p. 612.

machines, cannons, elevators, gramophones, or even things as simple as soap, cigarettes, matches, and the tungsten lightbulb. For example, technology transfer related to electrical cable manufacturing assisted in Japan's rapid electrification and allowed the Japanese government to establish its own communications networks throughout the Japanese archipelago and later in East and Southeast Asia, owing to the import of submarine-cable technology. Similarly, the introduction of sheet-glass technology revolutionized building design and construction in Japan's sprawling cities, and larger enterprises such as oil refineries and aluminum smelters were prerequisites for the development of Japan's chemical, engineering, and manufacturing industries.

Throughout the history of foreign investment in Japan, the policies of the Japanese government were always critical to the success of foreign enterprises, and the Japanese government often took an interventionist stance—what has been described as the marginalization, or exclusion, of all non-Japanese enterprise in the Japanese economy—by limiting foreign investments in all but the most strategically important industries.[79] Concurrent with the pressures being brought to bear against foreign companies by the Japanese government, the role of the zaibatsu in controlling and using foreign capital also comes tightly into focus, especially as the Japanese economy slipped into a wartime setting. In the climate of the early Showa period (1927–1930), and particularly after the outbreak of war in China in September 1931, the foreign contribution to the economy in terms of direct capital investment and joint ventures, along with the massive imports of capital in the form of government, municipal, and company loans, was hardly acknowledged within Japan. Yet it is instructive to note that many of the industries that would come to drive the Japanese economy in the subsequent era of postwar reconstruction and rapid economic growth did, in fact, receive significant investments of foreign capital in the prewar period. For example, the manufacturers Fujitsu, Ryobi, and Toshiba, along with the Dunlop and Yokohama rubber companies and the Columbia and Victor gramophone companies, would all, once again, become leaders in their respective industries. In addition, the Mitsui, Mitsubishi, and Sumitomo groups, which had long and intimate working relationships with foreign capital,

---

79. See Davenport-Hines and Jones, "British Business in Japan," pp. 217–29, especially p. 222.

would all survive to regroup and prosper again. When considered in total, these developments seem to emphasize that no matter how politically difficult or scarce foreign investments became, there is no denying the particular significance of foreign capital investment to Japan's economic growth and development throughout the forty-year period from 1899 to 1939.

PART III

Foreign Capital and the
Postwar Japanese Economy

CHAPTER 8

Liberalization, Internationalization, and Globalization: Japan since 1945

Of great relevance to Japan's postwar socioeconomic history are three key terms: "liberalization," "internationalization," and "globalization." Putting aside for the moment any notions of their accepted "standard" definitions, let us examine them as they are used in their interrelated Japanese contexts, as markers that signify three overlapping phases in the development of commercial and financial policy in Japan's postwar economy. Starting with "liberalization," we note that it came into common usage in Japan only during the late 1950s and early 1960s, when it was a buzzword of economic policy and legislation. Written in ideograms as *jiyūka* (literally, to make or become free), liberalization now has a somewhat dated and anachronistic ring to it. Put simply, it belongs to policy debates of a different era, when the United States was clearly seen as calling the shots, and thus it is now used sparingly in the Japanese language.[1]

In many ways, the much more versatile term "internationalization" has superseded liberalization. It has been used to refer to such disparate phenomena as the Japanese economy's switch from export-led to (domestic) demand-led economic growth; the gradual diminution of Japan's "uniqueness"; and, apparently, the "sharing of the burdens of maintaining free trade and a growing world economy."[2] Most commonly, however,

---

1. Fujiwara, "Foreign Trade, Investment, and Industrial Imperialism," p. 172.
2. Higashi and Lauter, *Internationalization of the Japanese Economy*, p. 6.

intaanashonaraizeshōn refers to the historical process of integration by which Japan is becoming, owing to its own efforts, international; that is, it is conforming to established intranational standards of the modern, industrialized (and Western) economies. Outside observers have referred to the same process as being one of "permeable insulation" and stress the Japanese government's "pragmatic utilization of new rules and circumstances" that continue to promote domestic firms engaged in international competition, and to protect them against that same competition.[3] Conceptually vague, if not unsound, the term "internationalization" can be something of a misnomer, if not a deception. Nevertheless, Japan's leaders have largely shrugged off such criticisms. Japan is engaging with the world to an unprecedented degree, and it is all part and parcel of its state-driven policy of internationalization. In constant use throughout the late 1980s and 1990s, the term has more recently been contrasted with the concept of globalization.[4]

In common with the other two terms, "globalization" has been assigned ideograms in Japanese and is written as *sekaika* (to make or become global); it is commonly used to denote the spread of Japanese manufactures worldwide, which in itself reflects the progress of internationalization among economies. Dynamic, and subject to organic changes within the world economy that drives it, globalization now exists almost exclusively in Japanese academic and contemporary literature as the recent loanword *gurobaruraizeshōn*, or *gurobaruka*. As such, it takes its meaning from one aspect of the term's meaning in English that encompasses an apparently ahistorical process of unification of standards and values across all nations and cultures.[5] Critically, in the Japanese context globalization is imposed on a nation from outside, with or without its approval or consent and regardless of its own actions; hence its frequent contrast with Japan's own internal experience of internationalization.

---

3. Schaede and Grimes, "Introduction," pp. 6–8.

4. Clammer, *Japan and Its Others*, p. 31, and Higashi and Lauter, *Internationalization of the Japanese Economy*, p. 6.

5. Definitions of globalization range from the deceptively simple "integration of the world as a single market" to a complex discussion of the diverse components of globalization, internationalization, and the emerging "globalized" world. See Ferguson, *Empire*, p. 18; as primers, see Beck, *What Is Globalization?*, and Robertson, *Globalization*.

The three terms denote the principle phases of Japan's economic development since 1945: the long period of listless or even phony liberalization that culminated in the liberalization of the automotive industry and the arrival of chain stores and subsidiaries; the slightly longer period characterized by the gradual internationalization of the Japanese economy and finance; and, most recently, Japan's uneasy experiment with globalization. Significantly, these broad overarching and overlapping phases in the development of commercial and financial policy are themselves products of the Japanese experience of economic development: namely, the periods of the long postwar boom (1954–1970); the economic shocks of U.S. monetary policy, rising oil prices, and the dramatic rise in the value of the yen, which reached a climax during the halcyon years of the "bubble" economy (1971–1991); and finally, the lost years of transition and meltdown after the bubble, up until the 3/11 triple disaster (1992–2011).

A historical survey of foreign investment in Japanese finance and commerce—establishing the historical presence of the foreigner pre- and postwar—can be best understood in reference to changes signified by these three key terms and phases. The following exposition, however, aims to do more than just argue the relevancy of the terms liberalization, internationalization, and globalization. It seeks to conceptualize and explore the history of foreign investment in the finance and commerce of Japan, particularly in the period from the immediate postwar occupation to the present.

Awaiting Real Liberalization

The preparation for war, the destruction brought about by the war, and Japan's subsequent defeat all but eliminated the erstwhile foreign presence in the immediate postwar economy. While elements within the authorities of the Allied occupation (the office of the Supreme Commander for the Allied Powers) were keen to have progressive foreign (particularly American) firms investing in Japan's democratization, the postwar realities, such as the destruction of basic infrastructures and the economic malaise of high inflation, curtailed meaningful participation. In such circumstances, controlling foreign currency transactions and using foreign currency in accordance with the requirements of the national economy were the basic goals of legislation for the initial, and all subsequent, postwar Japanese governments.[6] Sovereignty was to be reasserted, through protectionist policies, across all areas of the economy; the late-Meiji experience of foreign subsidiaries and significant joint ventures was not to be repeated.

Indeed, the Japanese government's position in regard to the participation of foreign firms in the domestic economy was dramatically circumscribed in the latter part of the occupation by the Foreign Exchange and Foreign Trade Control Law of 1949 (Gaitamehō), and the Foreign Capital Law of 1950 (Gaishihō). As drafted and later revised by Japan's most zealous bureaucrats, these two laws sought nothing less than to reconfigure foreign involvement in the Japanese economy "by limiting the induction of foreign investment to that which will contribute to the self-support and sound development of the Japanese economy."[7] Given that both laws demanded that any prospective foreign investment must also contribute "to the improvement of the international balance of payments," these laws served to effectively exclude and prohibit foreign involvement in Japan's postwar economic reconstruction. Moreover, the two laws formed the legislative basis of Japan's capital controls throughout the headiest years of its high-speed postwar economic growth, helping to define (or reassert) the chauvinistic nature of Japan's industrial structure until the very last days of the bubble economy in the early 1990s.[8]

Indications that the Japanese government might be prepared to soften its position against the participation of foreign firms in the domestic economy were not clearly articulated until as late as 1967. Even then the change was largely seen as being a consequence of the debate surrounding Japan's acceptance of International Monetary Fund (IMF) Article VIII trade liberalization requirements, and its subsequent application for membership in the Organization for Economic Cooperation and Development (OECD) in 1964.[9] According to the rules prescribed by the

---

6. Adams and Hoshii, *Financial History of the New Japan*, p. 256.

7. Mason, *American Multinationals and Japan*, p. 263.

8. The Japanese government's decision to reform the Foreign Exchange and Foreign Trade Control Law in 1980 sent an important signal to the world's financial markets in regard to Japan's intentions and was a crucial precondition to the remarkable inflow of foreign capital that engendered its own financial "big bang" in the late 1990s. See Mason, *American Multinationals and Japan*, pp. 155–61.

9. As early as August 1959, U.S. Ambassador Douglas MacArthur II had pressed the Japanese government for the liberalization of trade and foreign exchange. Surprisingly, the

Japanese government's new liberalization program, fifty-fifty joint ventures between foreign and Japanese companies, rather than wholly owned (foreign) subsidiaries, were the preferred investment model for foreign capital. The relevant government minister would then give approval, provided the foreign party did not exercise a dominant influence over the joint venture's management. The criteria for ministerial approval stated that: (1) Japanese stockholders in the venture must also manage another enterprise in the same line of business as the newly established joint venture, and that those stockholders must own at least one-half of shares issued, with at least one Japanese national owning a third of the shares of the other enterprise in the same line of business; (2) at least one-half of the venture's directors must be Japanese nationals; (3) the venture's voting procedures must conform to the Japanese Commercial Code (that is, no one director should have veto power, and the unanimous consent of all board members or directors should never be required); and (4) the venture's business "should have no exceptionally detrimental effect" on any existing Japanese interests.[10] As a result, the Japanese government "routinely rejected all applications for fully-owned subsidiaries or even joint ventures in which foreigners would hold the majority share," as one indignant observer noted.[11]

The message of the new liberalization program was clearly protectionist: wherever possible, participation in the national economy was to be reserved for Japanese industry (*zehi kokusan*). In 1968, Amaya Naohiro, a senior Ministry of International Trade and Industry (MITI) bureaucrat and an important architect of Japan's industrial, investment, and trade policies put it thus: "It does a nation more harm than good to introduce free competition when the structures of industry and finance provide only a less than satisfactory environment in which free competition can flourish."[12]

Despite the severity of the governmental restrictions and the improbability of Japan's ever *providing* a satisfactory environment for free competition, a number of foreign subsidiaries and joint ventures were established, or rather *re*established, in the postwar era, owing largely to

---

move received a measure of support from Keidanren, the Japanese Business Federation—provided that Japan's economic strength was built up "to survive international competition." See Fujiwara, "Foreign Trade, Investment, and Industrial Imperialism," p. 172.

10. Adams and Hoshii, *Financial History of the New Japan*, pp. 257–58.

11. Fallows, *Looking at the Sun*, p. 59.

12. Ozaki, "Japanese Views on Foreign Capital," p. 1080.

the nationality of their parent companies and their respective technological strengths. Four of the most significant foreign enterprises, Citibank, Otis Elevator Company, National Cash Register (NCR), and International Business Machines (IBM), are American corporations whose involvement in Japan had firm prewar antecedents.

The participation of foreign enterprises in the Japanese postwar economy actually began in the first weeks and months of the Allied occupation, when National City Bank (Citibank) scrambled to reestablish branches throughout Japan in order to provide basic financial and banking services for U.S. servicemen (see Table 8.1). The patronage, and indeed protection, provided by the U.S. military at that juncture was critical to Citibank's postwar engagement with Japan.[13] In 1946, the American and Japanese joint venture Otis Elevator once again began to operate under its prewar name, Toyo Otis Elevator Company. By April 1951, Toyo Otis had restored financial and technological links with its American parent company. Similarly, another notable American and Japanese joint venture, Japan National Cash Register, restored its prewar name in 1946 and reestablished itself with capital imports from its once-estranged parent, NCR, in 1951. As a wholly owned foreign subsidiary, the Watson Computing-Tabulating Machine Company had been nationalized during the war years and was, therefore, in a more precarious situation.[14] By 1950, its American parent, IBM, had agreed to the formation of Nihon International Business Machines, with Japanese participation. IBM, however, was committed to regaining control, if not full ownership, of its Japanese subsidiary. Intense negotiations concluded with IBM agreeing to license key technologies to Japanese electronics manufacturers in return for control and majority ownership of what was renamed Nihon IBM in 1958.[15]

---

13. Cleveland and Huertas, *Citibank*, p. 218, and Mason, *American Multinationals and Japan*, p. 110.

14. In 1932 Mitsui Bussan imported leading elevator technology through a joint venture with the Otis Elevator Company of America to form the Toyo, or Oriental, Otis Elevator Company. The American company NCR established its own Japanese subsidiary of the same name in 1933; the subsidiary then merged with the Japan Cash Register Company to form the Japan National Cash Register Company two years later, in 1935. International Business Machines Corporation, the forerunner of IBM, established a subsidiary in Japan during 1937. See Chapter 7; Horie, *Gaishi yunyū*, pp. 165–66.

15. Fukao and Amano, *Tainichi chokusetu tōshi*, pp. 97–100, and Fallows, *Looking at the Sun*, p. 59.

Table 8.1. Foreign-Owned Enterprises in Japan, 1945–2009

No.	Year	Company name (in Japan)	Industry classification	Foreign investor	Nationality	FDI share (%)	Japanese investor/ mediator	Remarks
1	1945	National City Bank (Citibank)	finance	National City Bank (Citibank)	USA	100	—	Opens first branch in 1902 (Yokohama), and has 4 before leaving Japan in 1941. Returns late 1945; 6 branches by 1981.
2	1946	Toyo Otis Elevator Co.	engineering	Otis Elevator Co. of America	USA	60	Mitsui Bussan	Initially established as subsidiary of Otis Elevators in 1927. Becomes a joint venture with Mitsui Bussan in 1932.
3	1946	Japan National Cash Register Co. (NCR)	engineering	National Cash Register Co. (NCR)	USA	100	—	Initially established as a subsidiary of NCR in 1933.
4	1950	Nihon IBM	engineering	International Business Machines (IBM)	USA	100	—	Initially established as Watson Computing-Tabulating Machine (Japan), a subsidiary of IBM, in 1937.
5	1952	Yamatake-Honeywell	engineering	Honeywell Inc.	USA	50	—	
6	1952	Colliers Halifax	real estate	Pacific Architects and Engineers, and Hongkong Land	USA/ Hong Kong/ UK	100	—	The oldest foreign-owned real estate company operating in Japan.

(continued)

Table 8.1. (continued)

No.	Year	Company name (in Japan)	Industry classification	Foreign investor	Nationality	FDI share (%)	Japanese investor/ mediator	Remarks
7	1962	Bayer Yakuhin	pharmaceuticals/ chemicals	Bayer A.G.	Germany	100	—	Bayer A.G. has a long history in Japan and was actively involved in many ventures. Becomes Bayer Chemicals in 2003.
8	1962	Grace Japan	chemicals	W. R. Grace	USA	100	—	
9	1964	NSK-Warner	automotive	Borg Warner Corp.	USA	—	NSK Ltd.	NSK-Warner establishes its own American subsidiary, NSK-Warner U.S.A. Inc., in 1997.
10	1964	Simmons (Japan)	engineering	Simmons	USA	100	Tokyo Bed Manufacturers Ltd.	Simmons (Japan) becomes financially independent from its American parent in July 1987.
11	1967	CBS–Sony Records	recording/ media	Columbia Broadcasting Systems (CBS)	USA	—	Sony	Sony buys the CBS parent company in 1988.
12	1968	Nippon Texas Instruments	instruments/ integrated-circuit technology	Texas Instruments (TI)	USA	50	Sony	Becomes a wholly owned TI subsidiary in 1972.

13	1969	Aisin-Warner	automotive	Borg Warner Corp.	USA	—	Aisin	Joint venture ends in 1987.
14	1969	Koyo–Eaton Yale & Towne	automotive	Eaton Yale & Towne Inc.	USA	—	Koyo Seiko	Eaton Yale & Towne Inc. becomes Eaton Corp. in 1971.
15	1969	Koyo–TRW	automotive	TRW Inc.	USA	—	Koyo Seiko	Koyo Seiko later merges with Toyoda Engineering to become a part of the Toyota-affiliated JTEKT Group in 2005.
16	1970	Warner Bros. Pioneer	recordings/media	Warner Bros.	USA	33	Pioneer and Watanabe Productions	Watanabe and Pioneer's shares are bought out in 1978 and 1989, respectively. Becomes Warner Music Japan in 2004.
17	1971	Chrysler/Mitsubishi	automotive	Chrysler Corp.	USA	35	Mitsubishi Heavy Industries (MHI)	Joint venture continues until 1993. Financial and technical cooperation with Daimler-Chrysler from 2000 to 2005.
18	1971	GM-Isuzu	automotive	General Motors	USA	49	Isuzu Motors Ltd.	GM ownership drops to 12% in late 2002.
19	1971	Nihon–GE Plastics	chemicals	General Electric Co.	USA	33	Mitsui Chemicals and Nagase Sangyo	GE enters into three-way joint venture with Mitsui Chemicals and Nagase Sangyo.
20	1972	P&G Sunhome	consumer products/healthcare	Proctor and Gamble (P&G)	USA	33	Nippon Sunhome and Itochu Corp.	P&G enters into three-way joint venture but buys out its partners in 1978.

(continued)

Table 8.1. (continued)

No.	Year	Company name (in Japan)	Industry classification	Foreign investor	Nationality	FDI share (%)	Japanese investor/ mediator	Remarks
21	1974	Dow Chemical Japan	chemicals	Dow Chemical International	USA	100	—	Leading manufacturer of chemicals and specialty materials for science and industry.
22	1975	Motorola (Japan)	communications technology	Motorola Inc.	USA	100	—	Leading semiconductor manufacturer, involved in production of microprocessor and memory chips.
23	1979	Mazda	automotive	Ford Motor Co.	USA	27	Toyo Kogyo (Mazda)	Ford ownership increases to 33.9% in 1997.
24	1983	Sumitomo Eaton Hydraulics Co. (SEHYCO)	automotive/ engineering	Eaton Corp.	USA	50	Sumitomo Heavy Industries (SHI)	Becomes a wholly owned Eaton Corp. subsidiary in 2001 and is renamed Eaton Fluid Power Ltd.
25	1984	Chinon Industries	cameras	Eastman Kodak Corp.	USA	10	Chinon Industries	Absorbed into the Kodak Group as Kodak Japan–Digital Production Development in 2004.
26	1984	Jardine Lloyd Thompson	insurance	Jardine Group	UK/Hong Kong	100	—	Provides insurance brokering services to Japanese corporations and international banks in Japan.

27	1993	DuPont (Japan)	chemicals	DuPont	USA	100	—	DuPont Far East (established in 1961) is bought out and recapitalized by DuPont in 1993 to form DuPont (Japan).
28	1996	Ciba Specialty Chemicals	chemicals	Ciba-Geigy (Ciba Holdings Inc.)	Swiss	100	—	Becomes Ciba Japan in September 2007. Operates as a member of the German BASF Group as of April 2009.
29	1998	Merrill Lynch Japan Securities (MLJS)	finance	Merrill Lynch	USA	100	—	Recapitalized from the failed Yamaichi Securities.
30	1998	GE Edison Life Insurance	finance	General Electric Co. (Capital Services)	USA	90	Toho Mutual Life Insurance	Subsumes Toho Mutual in 2000 and Saison Life in 2002. Entire operation is sold to American Insurance Group (AIG) in 2004.
31	1999	Nissan	automotive	Renault S.A.	France	37	Nissan Motor Co.	Renault share in Nissan increases to 44.4% in 2000.
32	1999	Nissan Diesel	automotive	Renault S.A.	France	23	Nissan Motor Co.	Sweden's Volvo Group becomes Nissan Diesel's principle shareholder in 2006 and all cooperation with Nissan ceases.
33	2000	Lake Co.	finance	General Electric Co. (Capital Services)	USA	100	Lake Co.	After negotiation, GE purchases Lake Co. in entirety (Lake Co. retains its name).

(*continued*)

Table 8.1. (continued)

No.	Year	Company name (in Japan)	Industry classification	Foreign investor	Nationality	FDI share (%)	Japanese investor/ mediator	Remarks
34	2000	GE Engine Services–Japan Corp.	engineering	General Electric Co.	USA	—	ANA and IHI	Jet-engine services for commercial and military aircraft.
35	2000	Shinsei Bank	finance	Ripplewood Holdings	USA	100	—	Recapitalized from the failed Long-Term Credit Bank. Attempted merger with the Aozora Bank fails in 2010.
36	2001	Tokyo Star Bank	finance	Lone Star Equity	USA	100	Tokyo Sowa Bank	All Lone Star Equity shares purchased by Japanese investment fund Advantage Partners in 2008.
37	2001	Kansai Sawayaka (KS) Bank	finance	Nippon Investment Partners (NIP)	USA	20	Bank of Kansai	NIP set up with significant investments by major U.S. pension funds.
38	2003	Aozora Bank	finance	Cerberus Capital Management	USA	37	Softbank	Recapitalized from failed Nippon Credit Bank by Softbank-led consortium in 2000. Cerberus raises its share to 45% in 2008.
39	2006	Mandarin Oriental, Tokyo	hotels	Mandarin Oriental Hotel Group	UK/Hong Kong	100	Mitsui Real Estate	Mandarin Oriental Hotel Group presently operates one hotel in Nihonbashi, Tokyo.

	Year	Name	Sector	Acquiring company	Country	%	Target company	Notes
40	2007	Hitachi–GE Nuclear Energy	engineering	General Electric Co.	USA	20	Hitachi Ltd	GE Hitachi Nuclear Energy simultaneously established in USA with 60% GE, 40% Hitachi ownership.
41	2007	ANA Hotels	hotels	Morgan Stanley	USA	100	All Nippon Airways (ANA)	Now operating under UK's International Hotels Group.
42	2007	Sanyo Electric Credit Co.	finance	General Electric Co. (Capital Services)	USA	100	Sanyo Electric Co.	Purchased outright from Sanyo Electric Co. (name retained).
43	2007	Nikko Cordial Securities	finance	Citigroup	USA	100	Nikko Cordial Corp.	"Layered takeover" from April 2007 to January 2008.
44	2007	Cadbury Japan	food and beverage	Cadbury Schweppes	UK	100	Sansei Foods	A wholly owned Cadbury Schweppes subsidiary.
45	2008	Goodwill	human resources	Cerberus Capital Management and Morgan Stanley	USA	—	Goodwill	

Sources: Data collected from company journals, histories, newspapers, and websites. See bibliography and text for further references.

Notes: FDI = foreign direct investment. Both tangible and intangible criteria are used. An investment's scale, size, and subsequent earnings are considered alongside such intangibles as a company's prominence in its industry and the amount of media coverage it has received both in and outside of Japan. The information in this table is indicative rather than prescriptive and makes no claim to be fully comprehensive.

With parallels to IBM's experience, Texas Instruments (TI) tried to establish its own wholly owned Japanese subsidiary in the 1950s, doggedly refusing to take part in joint ventures as a minor party, as proposed by Japanese authorities. Fortunately for TI, the strength of its patented integrated-circuit (IC) technology was such that it was able to gain the advantage against the Japanese authorities by refusing Japanese companies the use of its patents and licenses.[16] The Japanese government never entirely acquiesced to TI plans, although the government and TI did finally reach a compromise in April 1968 whereby TI and Sony went into a fifty-fifty joint venture and formed Nippon Texas Instruments.

According to the agreement, Nippon Texas Instruments would limit its Japanese sales to 10 percent of the market and license its integrated-circuit patents to other Japanese manufacturers, such as Nippon Electric Company (NEC), Hitachi, Mitsubishi, and Toshiba (in other words, Nippon Texas Instruments would assist TI and Sony's main Japanese rivals). Apparently, an additional undisclosed clause allowed TI to buy back the Sony share of the joint venture after a certain face-saving period. Just four years later, in 1972, the buy-back clause was exercised and TI achieved its long-stated desire of operating as a wholly American-owned subsidiary in Japan. It was also said at the time that it was the only U.S. firm with a fully owned factory operating in Japan.[17] As the Japanese government had prescribed, joint ventures between foreign and Japanese companies were the order of the day, but few Japanese firms were successful in pursuing or attracting foreign capital investment.[18]

---

16. The Coca-Cola Company was one of the few foreign companies to establish a Japanese subsidiary in the period from 1948 to 1968. Having achieved this in June 1957, Coca-Cola Japan was seen as a trend-setting, visionary forerunner of American enterprise in Japan. See Mason, *American Multinationals and Japan*, pp. 161–73. (It should be noted, however, that Coca-Cola Japan owes its present success to a refocusing of its production and marketing on noncola products, such as sports drinks and teas, which are more profitable in the Japanese market than carbonated drinks; see www.cocacola.co.jp.)

17. Morita, Reingold, and Shimomura, *Made in Japan*, pp. 192–93.

18. Perhaps one notable exception was the joint venture between Columbia Broadcasting Systems (CBS) and Sony, which founded CBS-Sony Records in March 1967. Huge Japanese imports of foreign recordings in the late 1960s very much encouraged cooperation between Japanese and foreign record companies. See Adams and Hoshii, *Financial History of the New Japan*, p. 259.

Beyond those highly publicized and successful tie-ups, few joint ventures established in the postwar period are considered significant or are widely known.[19] Put simply, up until the late 1960s a limited foreign presence was permitted in only those areas of the economy where Japanese companies lacked the technological edge, as exemplified by the ventures involving computing and integrated-circuit technologies. Profound social and economic changes in the late 1960s, however, would make the continuance of a limited system of "licensing" untenable. Challenged externally and from within, liberalization took on a new momentum, giving rise to a string of Western-style franchises and significant foreign participation in the Japanese automotive industry.[20]

World Bank Loans

With foreign involvement in the Japanese economy so tightly regulated as to be (that it was) effectively prohibited, how did the Japanese government finance postwar economic reconstruction and, more to the point, the high-speed economic growth that distinguished it? What replaced the prewar system of financial syndicates issuing national, municipal, and corporate bonds, given what the war years had sown and reaped? The Japanese government, with considerable ingenuity, was able to protect and nurture Japanese industry and keep its leading corporate exemplars flush with yen, but outside of Japan the yen was very soft currency, at just 0.5 percent of its prewar, gold-standard exchange rate (in U.S. dollars). Where could the Japanese government find the capital it needed to bankroll the rebuilding and retooling of industry and the provision of new and revolutionary infrastructures? Given the global configuration of the postwar political economy and consequent Japan-U.S. diplomacy, the U.S. government decided that the World Bank, rather than Wall

---

19. There are undoubtedly more joint ventures from around that time. For example, Proctor and Gamble joined with Nippon Sunhome and Itochu Corporation in 1972 to form P&G Sunhome, which became a competitor in the large market for consumer goods, particularly health care products. See Fukao and Amano, *Tainichi chokusetu tōshi*, pp. 92–96.

20. Hollerman, *Japan Disincorporated*, pp. 1–49.

Street (or Lombard Street), was best placed to invest in the technological modernization of Japan's economy.[21]

Toward the end of the Allied occupation, the Japanese government recommenced negotiations for foreign loans after a twenty-year hiatus. After it joined the World Bank as a sovereign nation in August 1952, loans to Japan were quick to follow. The electric power companies of Kansai, Kyushu, and Chubu were the first to benefit, with loans from the World Bank being used to purchase steam turbines (see Table 8.2). In the years that followed, a veritable who's who of Japan's leading ferrous and nonferrous metal producers and power utilities received loans for the wholesale import of blast furnaces, coke ovens, blooming mills, plate mills, strip mills, tube mills, and hydroelectric and thermal power-generation technologies.[22] Moreover, the World Bank was particularly keen to be associated with infrastructural "development loans" and thus extended generous guidance and funding to agricultural projects, water-works, road construction (highways and expressways), and, most famously, the construction of the iconic bullet train (*shinkansen*) railway.[23]

The Japanese government's entire postwar borrowing record includes thirty-one "tied" or project-specific loans in a fourteen-year period, from 1953 to 1966 (see Table 8.2). The size of the loans varied considerably, from $1.5 million for machine tools to manufacture marine diesel engines, to $80 million for the development of the bullet train. In all, the thirty-one loans totaled $863 million. The lender was always the World Bank.[24] Domestic political opposition to international borrowing from the World Bank was circumvented by rerouting the loans through the auspices of the Development Bank of Japan as "two-step loans." That is, all industry, or nondevelopment, loans were accepted and held in U.S. dollars and then extended (or "on-lent," in financial terms) to the companies for the settlement of their international purchases. Loan repayments to the World Bank were typically scheduled to accord with long-term maturities, and the last loan was repaid in July 1990.[25]

---

21. Hayami, *Kaihatsu to Sekaiginkō*, p. 115.
22. Adams and Hoshii, *Financial History of the New Japan*, p. 480.
23. See World Bank, www.worldbank.or.jp/31project (accessed 1 May 2014).
24. Hayami, *Kaihatsu to Sekaiginkō*, p. 116.
25. World Bank, www.worldbank.or.jp/31project.

Table 8.2. World Bank Lending to Japan, 1953–1966

Loan no.	Date	Company name (beneficiary)	Project details	Contracted amount (US$ millions)
1*	15 Oct. 1953	Kansai Electric Power Co.	Tanagawa thermal power station (two turbines, 75MW)	21.5
2*	15 Oct. 1953	Kyushu Electric Power Co.	Karita thermal power station (one turbine, 75MW)	11.2
3*	15 Oct. 1953	Chubu Electric Power Co.	Yokkaichi thermal power station (one turbine, 66MW)	7.5
4*	25 Oct. 1955	Yawata Iron and Steel Co.	steel-plate production facilities	5.3
5*	21 Feb. 1956	Nippon Steel Tube Co.	seamless tube production facilities	2.6
5*	21 Feb. 1956	Toyota Motor Co.	bus and truck machine tools	2.35
5*	21 Feb. 1956	Ishikawajima Heavy Industries	marine turbine production facilities	1.65
5*	21 Feb. 1956	Mitsubishi Shipbuilding and Engineering Corp.	diesel engine production facilities	1.5
6*	19 Dec. 1956	Kawasaki Steel Corp.	hot and cold strip mills	20
7	19 Dec. 1956	Agricultural Land Development Public Corp.	agricultural development projects	4.3
8	9 Aug. 1957	Aichi Waterworks Corp.	water supply and distribution projects in Aichi prefecture	7
9*	29 Jan. 1958	Kawasaki Steel Corp. (Second loan)	1,000-ton blast furnace and coke oven	8
10*	13 June 1958	Kansai Electric Power Co. (Second loan)	Kurobe No. 4 hydroelectric power station (three turbines, 86MW)	37

(continued)

Table 8.2. (continued)

Loan no.	Date	Company name (beneficiary)	Project details	Contracted amount (US$ millions)
11*	27 June 1958	Hokuriku Electric Power Co.	Arimine hydroelectric power station (261MW)	25
12*	11 July 1958	Sumitomo Metal Industries	1,000-ton blast furnace and blooming mill	33
13*	18 Aug. 1958	Kobe Steel Ltd.	800-ton blast furnace and steel mill	10
14*	10 Sept. 1958	Chubu Electric Power Co. (Second loan)	Hatanagi No. 1 and No. 2 hydroelectric power stations (170MW)	29
15*	10 Sept. 1958	Nippon Steel Tube Co. (Second loan)	60-ton steel converter	22
16*	17 Feb. 1959	Electric Power Development Co.	Miboro hydroelectric power station (215MW)	10
17*	12 Nov. 1959	Fuji Iron and Steel Co.	1,500-ton blast furnace, converter, and blooming mill	24
18*	12 Nov. 1959	Yawata Iron and Steel Co. (Second loan)	two 1,500-ton blast furnaces	20
19	17 Mar. 1960	Japan Highway Public Corp.	Meishin Expressway (Amagasaki-Ritto)	40
20*	20 Dec. 1960	Kawasaki Steel Corp. (Third loan)	plate/slab-casting production facilities	6
21*	20 Dec. 1960	Sumitomo Metal Industries (Second loan)	combined steel mill	7

22*	16 Mar. 1961	Kyushu Electric Power Co. (Second loan)	Shin-Kokura thermal power station (156MW)	12
23	2 May 1961	Japan National Railways	bullet train (Tokaido Shinkansen)	80
24	29 Nov. 1961	Japan Highway Public Corp. (Second loan)	Meishin Expressway (Amagasaki-Nishinomiya and Ichinomiya-Ritto)	40
25	27 Sep. 1963	Japan Highway Public Corp. (Third loan)	Tomei Expressway (Tokyo-Shizuoka)	75
26	22 Apr. 1964	Japan Highway Public Corp. (Fourth loan)	Tomei Expressway (Toyokawa-Komaki)	50
27	23 Dec. 1964	Metropolitan Expressway Public Corp.	Metropolitan Expressway (Haneda-Yokohama)	25
28	13 Jan. 1965	Electric Power Development Co. (Second loan)	Kuzuryugawa hydroelectric power stations (one each in Nagano and Yugami)	25
29	26 May 1965	Japan Highway Public Corp. (Fifth loan)	Tomei Expressway (Shizuoka-Toyokawa)	75
30	10 Sept. 1965	Hanshin Expressway Public Corp.	Kobe No. 1 Expressway	25
31	29 July 1966	Japan Highway Public Corp. (Sixth loan)	Tomei Expressway (Tokyo-Shizuoka)	100

Sources: Hayami, *Kaihatsu senryaku to Sekaiginkō*, p. 116, and World Bank, www.worldbank.or.jp/31project (accessed 17 December 2012).

Notes: Asterisk indicates a two-step loan with the Development Bank of Japan. MW = megawatt. Uniquely, the World Bank's fifth heavy industrial loan was split unequally between four separate companies.

Finally, it should be stressed that, as with the Japanese experience of direct foreign investments, the significance of the World Bank loans was essentially qualitative rather than quantitative. That is, their importance relates to how they were targeted toward leading technologies for the development of infrastructure and heavy industries. Repeated assertions that World Bank loans financed less than 1 percent of total domestic investment in the postwar period, while statistically credible, thus fall wide of the mark.[26] Critically, they fail to consider and elucidate just how estranged Japan's financial relations were from the foreign capital markets during the capital-hungry years of recovery from 1953 to 1966. Given the context and configuration of the Japanese government's postwar economic policy, World Bank loans, quite simply, played a vital role in the transfer of new and revolutionary technologies and were thus crucial to the modernization of the Japanese economy.

Cracks in the Shield

The liberalization, indeed the subsequent internationalization, of the Japanese economy owes much to years of acrimonious debate between the American automotive industry and Japanese authorities, particularly the now defunct Ministry of International Trade and Industry (MITI).[27] The Japanese automotive industry was essentially on a path of autonomous development, despite receiving generous technical assistance from American and British manufacturers (particularly during the years of "special procurements" for the war in Korea in the 1950s). Nevertheless, foreign automobile manufacturers, particularly the American "big three," were subject to unyielding opposition from the Japanese authorities in their attempts to gain access to the Japanese market.

In the twenty years that followed Japan's defeat, no foreign automotive subsidiaries were tolerated, no direct ventures with existing Japanese manufacturers were accepted, and all proposed joint ventures in the automotive industry were subject to arbitrary case-by-case assessment that always seemed to end in the same negative result. During key IMF, trade liberalization, and OECD-membership negotiations in the 1960s, the Japanese government created programs ostensibly aimed at liberalizing

26. See Hayami, *Kaihatsu to Sekaiginkō*, pp. 115–23.

27. MITI was incorporated into the Ministry of Economy, Trade, and Industry (METI) during the sweeping administrative reforms of 2001.

areas of the automotive industry. International reaction to these liberalization programs, however, was "decidedly negative, and particularly so from the United States." In fact, American manufacturers saw the Japanese government's efforts as "evasive maneuvers designed to gain time and postpone a real liberalization."[28]

Trade and currency liberalization did nonetheless proceed, to the extent that in November 1963 the Japanese government liberalized fifty types of transactions in order to join the OECD.[29] In the ensuing years, trade and currency liberalization became an area of increasingly intense discussion, exacerbating earlier frictions between Japan and the United States, particularly during the years of the Nixon administration. In January 1969 the U.S. government urged the Japanese government to reexamine its liberalization policy, and in May 1969 Secretary of Commerce Maurice Stans visited Tokyo to present the Japanese government with a "number of demands" directly related to trade liberalization. The Japanese government is said to have found these demands both "contentious and offensive."[30] Nevertheless the Japanese authorities did capitulate to key U.S. demands and the liberalization process was reinvigorated, as evidenced by the relatively large number of joint ventures established between American and Japanese firms in the period from 1969 to 1971.

In the examples of joint ventures and franchises that were established, American demands, and the most intense negotiations for trade liberalization, focused on Japan's hitherto closed automotive industry. No conscionable accommodation seemed available to the contending parties, but what finally broke the deadlock was a surprise to almost everyone. In May 1965, Mitsubishi Heavy Industries (MHI) announced, seemingly out of the blue, that it had reached an understanding with the Chrysler Corporation to establish two joint ventures in Japan, one for

---

28. Adams and Hoshii, *Financial History of the New Japan*, pp. 258–59.

29. Adams and Hoshii, *Financial History of the New Japan*, p. 250. For example, these changes allowed foreigners leaving Japan to change yen for foreign currencies, provided the amount did not exceed the limits of the foreign currency taken into Japan, and beginning in April 1964, Japanese citizens were allowed to travel overseas "for pleasure" for the first time since the early 1930s. It is interesting to note the extent to which Japan, as a capitalist nation seeking OECD membership, had institutional characteristics in common with countries of the Communist bloc.

30. Adams and Hoshii, *Financial History of the New Japan*, p. 245.

vehicle import and export, and one for automobile manufacture. MHI would own 65 percent and Chrysler 35 percent of the new joint ventures. Incredibly, there was no immediate negative reaction from the Japanese authorities.[31] Apparently, MHI had "studiously avoided" informing MITI of its plans and, owing to tensions with the United States in regard to cooperation in the automotive industry, the Japanese government could not prevent the linkup. In the end, only one venture between MHI and Chrysler, what was essentially a badge-swapping exercise in vehicle import and export, was concluded in 1971. Irrespective of its merits, MHI's audacious behavior cleared the way for further negotiations between Ford and Toyo Kogyo (Mazda), and between General Motors (GM) and Isuzu Motors. Whether MHI's agreement with Chrysler did anything to improve non-Japanese perceptions of Japanese business is debatable; in many ways the Japanese were portrayed as being just as "inscrutable" as ever.[32] Still, it is important to note that Japanese liberalization programs did, during a brief initial phase in 1969, lead to a number of notable joint ventures established in the area of automotive parts: Aisin-Warner in transmissions; Koyo Eaton Yale & Towne in axles; and Koyo-TRW in steering (see Table 8.1).[33]

The arrivals of Japan's first foreign chain stores, subsidiaries, and fast-food franchises, in the form of Kentucky Fried Chicken in July 1970, Mister Donut in April 1971, and McDonald's in May 1971, were also a

---

31. Which, in turn, has led to speculation that the Chrysler-MHI relationship had MITI's secret blessing. Both companies were manufacturers of armored personnel carriers, tanks, and other military vehicles, and it is tempting to speculate that in the run-up to the war in Vietnam they were both looking to develop common manufacturing platforms, as had been done during the Korean War. Further investigation of the confidential Chrysler-MHI negotiations is required before anything definite can be stated in print.

32. This is exemplified by the experiences of American financial operator T. Boone Pickens when he accumulated a 23% stake (bigger than that of Toyota's) in the automotive lighting manufacturer Koito in 1988, apparently with the intention of becoming a company director and changing the company's sales and pricing policies (presumably biased to favor its main client, Toyota). Pickens was ultimately seen as being a stooge, albeit one that would attract U.S. attention, for the "greenmailer" Watanabe Kitaro, as he purchased his shares from Watanabe and sold them back to Watanabe once it was clear that Koito would not acknowledge his petitions. See Fallows, *Looking at the Sun*, p. 209; Johnson, *The Banking Keiretsu*, pp. 173–76; Murphy, *The Weight of the Yen*, pp. 49–51.

33. Adams and Hoshii, *Financial History of the New Japan*, p. 258.

part of the Japanese government's concessions to American demands for liberalization. Moreover, by May 1973 the Japanese government was announcing "100 percent liberalization," albeit with delayed schedules and significant "industry exceptions."[34] Riding on the coattails of the automotive industry's tentative liberalization, these now ubiquitous franchises set the Japanese stage for the further development of foreign subsidiaries. The image, if not necessarily the substance, of Western-style enterprise in Japan was thus being redefined.

Preparations and Preconditions

While trade and currency liberalization can be traced back to late 1958, Japan's premier financial institutions were not formally asked to prepare for liberalization by the government until 1967. It was also around this time that major banks, like Mitsui Bank, were pursuing the "internationalization" of their "global business." The issue of internationalization was seen by the Japanese banks in the simplest of terms. The main threat was the possible entrance of non-Japanese banks into the domestic market and the main opportunity was the possibility of expanding their own businesses abroad. Consequently, their vision of "internationalization" cynically revolved around cooperating with foreign partners in foreign countries, without extending quid pro quo concessions at home.[35] Significantly, discussions of internationalization did not include the revision of existing domestic banking practices or the adoption of international financial codes. In fact, internationalization did not require any fundamental internal or operational change at all: it was essentially an external process, foreign to the world of Japanese banking and finance. In this climate, therefore, larger Japanese banks responded to the government's request to internationalize by asking for permission to open new branches (and follow Japanese manufacturers) overseas, arguing that rapid expansion in foreign trade necessitated the allocation of foreign branches. These requests heralded an end to the long-held monopoly of the Bank of Tokyo, formerly the Yokohama Specie Bank, in Japan's external finances. At the same time that Japanese banks were arguing for their need to expand their own operations offshore, they were

---

34. Henderson, *Foreign Enterprise in Japan*, p. 20.
35. Japan Business History Institute, *The Mitsui Bank*, p. 162.

also rigorously urging their government to maintain strict entrance procedures for outsiders in the domestic banking market, and worked to limit foreign participation in Japanese financial services.

At this point, it is helpful to briefly review the issue of foreign participation in Japanese finance. As of 30 June 1971, the apogee of old-school, postwar banking, some seventy-two foreign banks had ninety-two branch offices in Japan.[36] It is interesting to note that recently, as of 18 October 2012, some fifty foreign banks were said to be operating in Japan. The vast majority of these institutions are limited to operating representative branch offices, with only two, Citibank Japan and J. P. Morgan Chase Bank, having full Japanese Banking Association membership and privileges.[37] Furthermore, among those fifty or so financial institutions, only Citibank Japan is publicly committed to establishing anything like a national network of branches and ATMs in Japan.[38] It is reasonable, given the legendary saving propensity of the Japanese, to expect that the number of foreign banks operating in Japan will increase in the near future. Nevertheless, strict regulations on entrance will ensure that their growth is less than dramatic, and that their total number will only reapproach the levels of the 1970s. In this way, Japan's internally driven internationalization will be allowed to run its own course, against the tide of globalization.

The rise of ever-larger financial conglomerates—that is, the dramatic consolidation of Japan's megabanks—may be seen as another long-term response to the combined pressures to become "international," and hence

---

36. Adams and Hoshii, *Financial History of the New Japan*, p. 478.

37. The figure of fifty foreign banks operating in Japan is in dispute. During 2008 the number varied from forty-four to forty-eight, although some websites listed more. See the Japanese Banking Association's website, www. zenginkyo.or.jp (accessed 23 December 2012).

38. In July 2007, Citibank N.A. formed a new wholly owned subsidiary called Citibank Japan and announced plans to double its number of retail branches "over the next few years." By 2008 Citibank Japan had opened thirty-one branches, with twenty-one of them in the Kanto region. See "Citibank Japan Opens with Eyes on Retirees," *Japan Times* (hereafter, *JT*), 3 July 2007. HSBC, the British multinational bank (and descendant of the Hongkong and Shanghai Bank), had planned to establish seven branches across during Japan by 2008, and possibly up to thirty-five thereafter, but it has dramatically downsized its operations in recent years. See "HSBC to Open Seven Branches in Japan, Hire 270 People," *JT*, 13 December 2007, and "HSBC Opens Two Private Banking Outlets," *JT*, 1 February 2008.

resist globalization. The merger of the two large city banks Dai-Ichi and Nippon Kangyo in 1973 is generally seen as the first step toward the modern reorganization of Japan's financial institutions.[39] It is possible to argue, however, that financial consolidation began much earlier, in a series of phases or waves that started during the war years from 1931 to 1945; or the interwar years of financial scandal from 1923 to 1928, with 1927 being the key point; or indeed during the reorganization of the national banking system from 1883 to 1898. If we are to understand Japan's present financial environment, we must consider that the recent institutional reorganization that is the current tangled web of interbank ownership, acquisitions, and holdings, is also the product of something referred to in Japanese as the *biggū ban*, or big bang.

---

39. Japan Business History Institute, *The Mitsui Bank*, p. 163.

CHAPTER 9

The "Big Bang" and Beyond, 1996–2011

On 11 November 1996, the cabinet of Prime Minister Hashimoto Ryūtarō laid out a plan of basic policy reform designed to reinvigorate Japanese financial markets and put the Tokyo financial market on a par with the New York and London markets by 2001.[1] This would be a Japanese version of the London financial market's wholesale deregulatory "big bang" (a new creation of increased financial activity); and its catchwords were "free, fair, and global."[2] The Japanese big bang experiment to liberalize its financial markets was not introduced, however, until the end of 1997, when Yamaichi Securities, Japan's fourth-largest securities broker, along with Sanyo Securities, had failed; Hokkaido Takushoku Bank was heading toward collapse; and several other small and medium-size Japanese banks and securities companies were about to be, or had already been, declared bankrupt or insolvent.[3] Thus, the explosive big bang of policy change was in reality preceded by a profound, if muffled, financial im-

---

1. Calls for reforming Japan's financial market date back to 1985 and joint U.S.-Japan discussions on exchange rates, and to the internationalization of the yen. See Grimes, "Internationalization as Insulation," p. 50, and Higashi and Lauter, *Internationalization of the Japanese Economy*, p. 231.

2. Y. Ito, "The Japanese Version of the Big Bang," http://arfaetha.jp/.ycaster.com /chat/index (accessed 2 May 2014). Ironically, the "big bang" revolution of the London financial market proved to be something of a disappointment. See Kindleberger, *Financial History of Western Europe*, p. 447.

3. The reforms mark the end of the practice among large, solvent groups of gathering up smaller, vulnerable institutions (the "convoy system"), which had mitigated against the failure of commercial banks from 1946 to the collapse of Hokkaido Takushoku Bank in 1997. See Rose and Ito, "M&As in Japanese Banking," pp. 150–53.

plosion. The Japanese government's new "free market/free trade" reforms promised the "removal of limitations on entry into banking, securities, and insurance business and incorporation of the principle of free competition," all promulgated with a broad timetable of gradual implementation, designed to satisfy core international standards in terms of legal, accounting, and supervisory practices.[4] No guarantees were provided for non-Japanese institutions, and lengthy revisions to the law failed to specify *exactly* what the laws meant, but clearly the financial market's Japanese participants were to prepare for internationalization.[5] For the first time in Japan's postwar history, foreign firms were to be encouraged to operate in the larger Japanese economy, apparently in the commanding heights of finance itself.

The Japanese Experience of the Big Bang Reforms

Let us first briefly examine the working results of Japan's new big bang policy. On 24 November 1997, Yamaichi Securities was forced to close its doors and declare bankruptcy. In what was the first case in which a foreign firm was permitted to take over and operate a domestic firm in Japan's securities market, the American brokerage house Merrill Lynch took control of Yamaichi Securities to form Merrill Lynch Japan Securities in July 1998 (see Table 8.1). It immediately set about reorganizing Yamaichi Securities' former business operations, closing down branch offices and retrenching staff. At that time, many Japanese observers expressed surprise and disgust at the decision to allow the sale of Yamaichi Securities to a foreign firm, suggesting that the government was selling the "family silver," if not the crown jewels. Indeed, just seven years after its purchase, in 2005, Merrill Lynch Japan Securities' performance had improved to the extent that it had eclipsed that of Nomura Securities' and its other rivals to become the most profitable securities firm operating in Japan. In these circumstances, Merrill Lynch's sudden turnaround

---

4. Horiuchi, "The Big Bang," pp. 234–38. See also Malcolm, *Financial Globalisation*, pp. 110–28.

5. The amount of documentation compiled by the Ministry of Finance relating to the revision of the laws was massive, totaling 2,129 pages and weighing some 4.4 kilograms. See Y. Ito, "The Japanese Version of the Big Bang," http://arfaetha.jp/.ycaster .com/chat/index (accessed 2 May 2014).

of Yamaichi Securities heightened speculation about the details, motives, and wisdom of its sale to Merrill Lynch in the first place.[6]

Significantly, the Hokkaido Takushoku Bank's very public collapse on 17 November 1997 was not accompanied by a foreign bailout of any kind. Quite remarkably, despite the Ministry of Finance's failure to enforce a merger between the Hokkaido Takushoku and the Hokkaido Banks in March 1997, no other countermeasures were openly tabled or approved.[7] Apparently not all of Japan's financial institutions were seen as being the same. It was as if Hokkaido Takushoku Bank's long history as a parastatal "special" bank precluded the possibility of foreign assistance or ownership.[8]

The corresponding situation among Japan's premier long-term credit and debenture banks serves as a striking parallel. The well-established postwar banking system, in which there were three major institutions that provided long-term loans to Japan's industries, unraveled with alarming speed in the last years of the twentieth century when, on 23 October 1998, the National Diet passed the Financial Reconstruction Law to provide "special, public management" (that is, bailout funds) to those financiers in danger of bankruptcy. One of the three major long-term lenders, the Long-Term Credit Bank (LTCB), established in 1952, was immediately nationalized, audited, and readied for a quick "reprivatization." Despite a credible bid offered by the Chuo Mitsui Trust and Banking Corporation, LTCB was purchased for a larger bid of ¥121 billion by a consortium of foreign (mainly U.S.) banks, led by Ripplewood Holdings, in March 2000. LTCB was renamed Shinsei Bank in June 2000 and immediately disposed of its worst debts (leaving many of its erstwhile clients, such as the Dai-Ichi Hotel Group and Sogo depart-

---

6. Grosse, *Thunderbird on Global Business*, pp. 25–27.

7. Technically the Hokkaido Takushoku Bank only "suspended operations" on 17 November 1997 as it approached outright default. See Cargill, Hutchison, and Ito, *Financial Policy and Central Banking*, p. 25.

8. Later, Prime Minister Koizumi Junichiro's frequent calls for "drastic reform" (*bappontekina kaikaku*), particularly in relation to the privatization of Japan's Postal Savings Bank, would elicit the same passionate defense by Japan's financial and political elites of Japanese-only "national" business, exposing one of their greatest fears: foreign capital, unrestrained and rampant. "All Eyes on Japan Post as Privatization Begins," *JT*, 29 September 2007, and "Wariness Greets Start of Postal Privatization: Private-Sector Concerns," *JT*, 2 October 2007.

ment store chain, insolvent); it then abruptly traded in its long-term credit license for a commercial banking license in 2004.[9]

The Nippon Credit Bank (NCB), established in 1957, was also nationalized under similar circumstances in December 1998. Rechartered from the remnants of the parastatal "special" Bank of Chosen (Korea), NCB initially resisted foreign assistance and was purchased by a Japanese consortium, led by Softbank, in June 2000; in January 2001 it was renamed the Aozora Bank.[10] Less amenable than Shinsei Bank to jettisoning its bad debts (and client base), the Aozora Bank's modest performance, tied with its inability to win regulatory approval to become the investment arm of the Softbank Corporation, led Softbank to sell its stake to the U.S. private-equity firm Cerberus Capital Management in September 2003. Further shadowing Shinsei Bank, the Aozora Bank was rechartered as a commercial bank in April 2006. Continued difficulties allowed Cerberus to increase its stake in Aozora to 45.5 percent of the bank's shares, underlining the depth of foreign participation in the bank's rehabilitation.[11]

With the exception of the treatment received by Hokkaido Takushoku Bank, the trend of permitting foreign firms to revitalize Japan's financial organs—which started with the redemption of Yamaichi Securities by Merrill Lynch, and was sanctified by the Japanese government's big bang policy—has continued to a significant degree. Alongside many "new" foreign entrants, conspicuously, Lehman Brothers and the Zurich Insurance Group in 1986, a number of Japanese banks, securities firms, and particularly insurers have been obliged to seek outside help in

---

9. The ideograms for Shinsei signify "new life" or "newly (re)born." "¥202 Billion Offered for Shinsei Stake," *JT*, 21 November 2007; "Flowers Back for a Second Bite of Shinsei Bank," *JT*, 13 February 2008; and "Ex-LTCB Execs Get Another Hearing," *JT*, 20 February 2008.

10. The ideograms for Aozora denote a nebulous "blue sky" of presumably fine weather. Initially, Softbank held a controlling 37.5% stake in Aozora, with Orix (approximately 15%), other Japanese companies, and the Japanese government holding the remainder of shares. See Corporate Information, www.aozorabank.co.jp (accessed 2 May 2014).

11. "Aozora 'Open' to Takeover Talks," *JT*, 5 November 2007; "Aozora, Sumitomo Agree on Broad Tieup," *JT*, 21 November 2007; and "Cerberus to Raise Stake in Aozora," *JT*, 5 March 2008.

recapitalizing and restructuring their operations.[12] For example, Tokyo Sowa Bank was purchased from the Japanese government by the U.S. private equity firm Lone Star for ¥35 billion ($331 million) in January 2001 and became Tokyo Star Bank.[13] Less than a month later Kansai Sawayaka (KS) Bank became the first foreign-funded bank to operate in the Kansai region.[14] It should also be noted that many other financial institutions in Japan have received similar help from domestic sources after intimating that they might have to look outside Japan for financial assistance.[15]

If the progress of Japan's financial reorganization was initially slow and turgid, there can be no doubt that after the crash of the bubble economy in early 1991, and during the "bad loans crisis" from 1997 to 2004, the pace of financial reorganization and consolidation quickened alarmingly. By 2007, three financial institutions, the Bank of Tokyo–Mitsubishi UFJ (MUFJ), Sumitomo Mitsui Banking Corporation (SMBC), and Mizuho Holdings (Mizuho and Mizuho Corporate Banks [MHFG]), had emerged preeminent among Japan's mega "city" banks, with only two others (Resona and Saitama Resona Banks) holding elite

---

12. Goldman Sachs and Aflac, which established Japanese subsidiaries in January and October of 1974, respectively, were among the first foreign firms in their fields to do a significant amount of business in Japan. Financiers and insurers, including Lehman Brothers, the Zurich Insurance Group, and many others, came later. See Paprzycki and Fukao, *Foreign Direct Investment in Japan*, pp. 163–71, and Rose and Ito, "M&As in Japanese Banking," pp. 153–55.

13. "Tokyo Star to Get New Owner," *JT*, 14 December 2007.

14. Nationalized in 1999, Kofuku Bank was recapitalized by Nippon Investment Partners (NIP), a partnership set up by W. L. Ross and several major U.S. pension funds, when it invested ¥24 billion to purchase Kofuku Bank's ailing business. The Bank of Kansai subsequently purchased 80% of NIP's holdings, and then merged with Kofuku to form KS Bank. See American Chamber of Commerce in Japan, www.accj .or.jp/doclib/fdi/1069040587.pdf (accessed 23 March 2010).

15. The nationalized Ashikaga Bank provides an interesting example. The fear that Tochigi prefecture's leading regional bank might be run by foreigners is reported to have been behind the Financial Service Agency's rejection of foreign bids for that struggling bank. See "Banks Offer ¥310 Billion for Ashikaga," *JT*, 18 November 2007; "Auction for Ashikaga Bank Reduced to Field of Two as Foreign Bids Nixed," *JT*, 22 November 2007; and "Two Ashikaga Offers," *JT*, 23 November 2007. Resona, the holding company of Resona Bank and Saitama Resona Bank, was also "considering" the allocation of shares to foreign institutions before its merger with Daiwa. See "Resona, Daiichi Mutual Close to Major Tie-up Deal," *JT*, 18 June 2007.

city-bank status, followed by a long line (a veritable "march of the dwarves") of some 109 regional banks.[16]

Automotive Industry

Having examined the results of the big bang reforms, we must also consider that the gist of these reforms among financial institutions—and, critically, the acceptance and use of foreign capital—was mirrored by profound changes in the automotive industry. Indeed, thirty years after the first joint ventures in the automotive industry, a "strategic alliance" between Japan's second-largest automaker, Nissan, and the French giant Renault changed the Japanese automobile industry, or at least how it came to be perceived: it was now (at last) open, cooperative, and, of course, very "international."

On 27 March 1999, Renault joined with the Nissan Motor Company to create the fourth largest automaker in the world, with Renault investing ¥605 billion ($5 billion) by taking a 37 percent equity stake, and corresponding voting rights, in Nissan, and a 22.5 percent stake in Nissan Diesel, with corresponding voting rights. These measures served to reduce Nissan's overall indebtedness, estimated at more than ¥2 trillion ($17 billion), to more manageable levels. In addition, a mutual agreement allowed Renault to purchase Nissan's European financial subsidiaries for a total of approximately ¥38 billion ($320 million) at a later date.[17] According to the deal, Nissan would be allowed to buy into Renault when it was financially able, although Nissan's holdings in Renault would not entitle it voting rights under French law. Nissan would buy a 15 percent stake in Renault, which in turn would increase its own stake in Nissan to 44 percent. In addition, to give the alliance more independence, the French government announced it would reduce its stake in Renault from 44 percent to 25 percent through a public sell-off of its shares.[18]

---

16. "Financial conglomerates" may be a more helpful term than "financial institutions," as Japan's mega city banks have (since 2000) reincorporated themselves as holding companies that offer commercial, corporate, insurance, investment, securities, and trust banking, along with other financial services. See Japanese Bankers Association, www.zenginkyo.or.jp (accessed 2 May 2014).

17. See "Nissan Renault Form $5.4 Billion Alliance," www.dieselnet.com/news /1999/03nissan.php (accessed 25 February 2014).

18. See "Renault Buys into Nissan," http://news.bbc.co.uk/2/hi/business/304675.stm (accessed 25 February 2014).

To strengthen Nissan's management and ensure the return to profit, Carlos Ghosn, then executive vice president of Renault, was appointed chief operating officer of Nissan in April 1999, starting something of a media "love affair" with Japan. According to Nissan hagiography, Ghosn's team put together a "turnaround plan" in three months, based primarily on input from young Nissan workers. The Ghosn plan "electrified" the Japanese automobile industry by parting with its established conventions: that is, it closed five plants; bucked keiretsu protocols, such as the seniority and lifetime employment systems; and retrenched or retired some 21,000 workers worldwide during the first few years of Ghosn's tenure. Despite controversies over such policies, of critical importance to all parties, the Ghosn plan did turn Nissan's fortunes around almost immediately.[19] Indeed, the alliance has proved to be profitable to both of the automakers as well as strategically successful, as that they now share plants and distribution networks, build common platforms, and are developing common components and engines, with each company leading engine design in its respective areas of expertise: Renault in diesel and Nissan in gasoline.[20] Japan's other multinational automakers have adopted similar international policies in-house, while outwardly eschewing the future possibilities of joint ventures or strategic alliances with foreign competitors.

Chain Stores, Franchises, and Subsidiaries

In addition to the entrance of Renault into Japan's automobile industry, the rise of chain stores, franchises, and subsidiaries has reinvigorated the image and substance of Western-style enterprise in Japan. Since the late 1990s, a relatively small number of highly visible and widely recognized franchises have, almost without exception, transformed the appearance of modern Japanese cities and suburbs (see Table 9.1). Fast food franchises like Kentucky Fried Chicken and McDonald's came first, in July 1970 and May 1971, respectively, as a result of earlier liberalization. Thereafter, however, despite all the indications of a boom economy throughout the 1980s, as acknowledged by the arrival of Disney when it opened a theme-park franchise on Tokyo's outskirts in April 1983, there was something of a hiatus in franchise development. Paradoxically, it

---

19. Paprzycki and Fukao, *Foreign Direct Investment in Japan*, pp. 140–43.

20. See Nancy DuVergne Smith, "Nissan-Renault Alliance Faces Down a Few Challenges," www.web.mit.edu/newsoffice/2004/ghosn.html (accessed 25 February 2014).

Table 9.1. Foreign Franchises and Subsidiaries in Japan, 1953–2011

Business category	Date established	Country of origin
Food and beverage		
Coca-Cola Company	June 1957	USA
A&W Restaurants	Apr. 1963	USA
Dunkin' Donuts	Apr. 1970	USA
Kentucky Fried Chicken	July 1970	USA
Mister Donut	Apr. 1971	USA
McDonald's	May 1971	USA
Godiva Chocolatier	Apr. 1972	Belgium
Denny's Japan	Nov. 1973[a]	USA
31 (Baskin-Robbins) Ice Cream	Dec. 1973	USA
Hard Rock Café Japan	July 1983	USA
Häagen-Dazs	Aug. 1984	Netherlands
Red Lobster Japan	Nov. 1987	USA
Pizza Hut	May 1991	USA
Nihon Subway	Oct. 1991	USA
Starbucks	Oct. 1995	USA
Burger King	Apr. 1996[b]	USA
Tully's Coffee	May 1998	USA
T.G.I. Friday's Japan	Nov. 1998	USA
Outback Steakhouse Japan	Apr. 2000	Australia
Pierre Marcolini (chocolate)	Aug. 2002	Belgium
Doughnut Plant	May 2004	USA
Cold Stone Creamery	May 2005	USA
Krispy Kreme Doughnuts	Dec. 2006	USA
Bill's (pancakes)	Mar. 2008	Australia
Grom (gelato)	Apr. 2009	Italy
Eggs 'n Things	Oct. 2009	USA
Retail: fashion (apparel, shoes) and brand merchandising		
Nihon L'Oréal	Apr. 1963	France
Estée Lauder	Apr. 1967	USA
Avon	Nov. 1968	USA
DAKS Simpson	Apr. 1970	UK
Mary Quant	Nov. 1970	UK
Tiffany & Co.	Apr. 1972	USA
Wella Japan	Sept. 1972	Germany (USA)

(*continued*)

Table 9.1. (continued)

Business category	Date established	Country of origin
Boucheron	Apr. 1973	France
Louis Vuitton	Mar. 1978	France
Clinique	Apr. 1978	USA
Amway	May 1979	USA
Chanel	Apr. 1980	France
Nike	Oct. 1981	USA
Levi Strauss & Co.	Nov. 1982	USA
Hermès Japan	Apr. 1983	France
Agnès B.	Dec. 1983	France
Folli Follie	Apr. 1985	Greece
Laura Ashley	Feb. 1986	UK
Etro	Apr. 1988	Italy
New Balance Japan	Dec. 1988	USA
United Arrows	Oct. 1989	USA
The Body Shop	June 1990	UK
Coach	Jan. 1991	USA
Miu Miu	Mar. 1991	Italy
Bulgari	Apr. 1991	Italy
Le Creuset	Apr. 1991	France
Eddie Bauer	Dec. 1993	USA
Gap	Dec. 1994	USA
Giorgio Armani Japan	Apr. 1995	Italy
Vivienne Westwood	Sept. 1996	UK
Tag Heuer	July 1997	Switzerland
Zara	Aug. 1997	Spain
Adidas	Feb. 1998	Germany
Burberry	Dec. 2000	UK
Katherine Hamnett	Apr. 2001	UK
Gucci	June 2001	Italy
Dolce & Gabbana	Aug. 2001	Italy
Converse Japan	Apr. 2002	USA
Diesel	Apr. 2002	Italy
Birkenstock	May 2002	Germany
Paul Smith	Oct. 2002	UK
Fendi	Nov. 2002	Italy

Table 9.1. (continued)

Business category	Date established	Country of origin
Berluti	Nov. 2002	France
Puma	Feb. 2003	Germany
Prada	June 2003	Italy
Cartier	July 2003	France
Christian Dior	Dec. 2003	France
Kate Spade	Apr. 2004	USA
Yves Saint Laurent	Apr. 2005	France
Patrizia Pepe	Sept. 2005	Italy
Chloe	Jan. 2006	France
Bottega Veneta	Feb. 2006	Italy
Marimekko	Mar. 2006	Finland
Polo Ralph Lauren	Apr. 2006	USA
Topshop	Sept. 2006	UK
Ugg	Oct. 2006	Australia
H&M (Hennes & Mauritz)	Aug. 2007	Sweden
Balenciaga Japan	Jan. 2008	Spain
L'Occitane	May 2008	France
Kitson Japan	Aug. 2008	USA
Lush Japan	Oct. 2008	UK
Theory	Mar. 2009	USA
Forever 21	Apr. 2009	USA
Abercrombie & Fitch	Dec. 2009	USA
J. Lindeberg	Apr. 2010	Sweden
American Eagle	Apr. 2011	USA
Supermarkets, consumer goods, wholesale, and convenience stores		
7-Eleven	Nov. 1973	USA
IKEA Japan	Apr. 1974[c]	Sweden
Lawson	Apr. 1975	USA
Hotspar	Apr. 1977	Netherlands
Circle K Sunkus	Mar. 1980	USA
Toy R Us	Nov. 1989	USA
am/pm Japan	Apr. 1990	UK
Sports Authority	Aug. 1995	USA
Office Depot	May 1996	USA
Costco	Apr. 1999	USA

(*continued*)

Table 9.1. (*continued*)

Business category	Date established	Country of origin
Metro Cash & Carry	Nov. 2002	Germany
Carrefour	Apr. 2001[d]	France
Seiyu (Wal-Mart)	May 2002[e]	USA
Tesco	Apr. 2007	UK
IT: media, music, and communications technology		
Nihon Samsung	Apr. 1953	Korea
Intel	Apr. 1976	USA
LG Japan (Lucky Group)	Jan. 1980	Korea
Tower Records	Dec. 1981	USA
Apple	June 1983[f]	USA
Microsoft Japan	Feb. 1986	USA
Nokia Japan	Apr. 1989	Finland
HMV	Feb. 1990	UK
Willcom	Oct. 1990	USA
Yahoo Japan	Jan. 1996	USA
Fox International Channels	Feb. 1998	USA
Hewlett-Packard Japan	July 1999	USA
Amazon Japan	Nov. 2000	USA
Sony Ericsson	Oct. 2001	Sweden
Google Nihon	Nov. 2001	USA
Cinema complexes and theme parks		
Tokyo Disney Resorts	Apr. 1983	USA
Warner Mycal Cinemas	Oct. 1991	USA
Universal Studios Japan	Dec. 1994	USA

Sources: Data collected from company journals, histories, newspapers, and websites. See bibliography and text for further references.

Notes: This table incorporates both tangible and intangible criteria. An investment's scale, size, and subsequent earnings are considered alongside such intangibles as a company's prominence in its respective industry and the amount of media coverage it has received both in and outside of Japan. The information in this table is indicative rather than prescriptive and makes no claim to be fully comprehensive.

a. Denny's Japan becomes a subsidiary of Seven & I Food in 2007.

b. Burger King withdraws from Japan in March 2001; returns in June 2007.

c. Ikea withdraws from Japan in 1986; returns in July 2002.

d. Carrefour withdraws from Japan in March 2005.

e. Seiyu has been wholly owned by Wal-Mart since June 2008.

f . Apple has a network of showrooms in Japan by 2006.

seems, the pace of franchise development did not pick up until Japan was on the cusp of a profound economic downturn (which suggests we should look more deeply into the conditions of the U.S. and global economy at that time). Pizza Hut arrived in November 1994, and Starbucks stormed in from October 1995. Burger King first arrived in April 1996, only to withdraw by March 2001 and then make a second attempt on the Japanese market in June 2007.[21] Setting up shop in December 2006, the Krispy Kreme doughnut franchise is one of the period's amazing success stories, and the remarkable popularity of the franchise has encouraged many more franchises to try branching out into Japan.[22]

The popularity of these franchises, along with their attractiveness to both foreign license holders (franchise owners) and Japanese investors, warrants further attention, much of it outside the bounds of the present discussion. Suffice it to say, Japanese consumers appear to desire an internationalized domestic market that offers goods and services informed by recent changes in foreign fashion and trends. For Japanese investors, competition to invest in foreign franchises often exists to the extent that foreign license holders (franchise owners) can invest human capital without having to risk the financial capital needed to pay the exorbitant start-up costs associated with doing business in Japan. While these franchises undeniably serve as potent and ubiquitous symbols of Western or American-style capitalism, they are, nonetheless, joint ventures requiring extensive inputs of local, Japanese capital.

Moreover, we must recognize that the rise of chain store franchises, often born of a native desire to internationalize the Japanese market, does, in turn, reflect concurrent phases of globalization impinging on the architecture and configuration of the domestic market. That is, the rise of chain store franchises, and their remarkable progress, is symptomatic and indicative of wider global trends, as best exemplified by the arrival of information technology (IT) and dot.com commerce between 1996 and 2006 (see Table 9.1). These franchises, the newest flagships of American enterprise, driven by the so-called IT revolution, were relatively quick to establish Japanese subsidiaries. Without significant Japanese

---

21. Burger King Japan is a joint venture between the multinational confectioner and food corporation Lotte and the management consulting firm Revamp. See "Burger King Stages Return under New Management Realities," *JT*, 7 June 2007.

22. Lotte and Revamp also invested in the Krispy Kreme franchise. See "Tenacity, Chance Imported Krispy Kreme Craze," *JT*, 11 December 2007.

rivalry, Microsoft's first international office was opened in Japan on 1 November 1978, Yahoo Japan started up in January 1996, Amazon Japan started in November 2000, and in late 2003 Apple opened its first Apple Store in Japan (the first outside of the United States), which quickly developed into a network of stores and showrooms throughout Japan by 2006.

The success of these "global" American technology franchises, however, has not been duplicated across the board. In retail supermarkets, for example, the French giant Carrefour marched into Japan in April 2001 only to strategically withdraw by March 2005, leaving behind just its brand name; Wal-Mart experienced difficulties for nearly a decade after its purchase of Seiyu in 2002; and Tesco's tentative entry in 2007 underscores the fact that large foreign retailers have yet to prove themselves in the field.[23] The apparent internationalization, and indeed globalization, of the Japanese market defies easy generalization. Scratch below the surface of the "Japanese market" that greets—or confronts—foreign enterprise, and things are not nearly as intelligible, nor as Western, as they first appear.

Enter Globalization

The Japanese government today appears to be promoting the "openness" of its public (and now privatizing) utilities to partial ownership by foreign investors and institutions, despite reports of its first "negative FDI [foreign direct investment] inflows" since the financial turmoil of 1989.[24] Once unthinkable, such an about-face would never have been contemplated before the Japanese government divested itself of its premier funds late in 2007 (the Postal Savings System [PSS] and the interrelated Trust Fund Bureau [TFB], through its contributions to the Fiscal Investment

---

23. "Carrefour, Wal-Mart Battle for Chinese Market Share," *JT*, 4 March 2008. "Wal-Mart Set to Pay ¥100 Billion to Take Over Ailing Seiyu," *JT*, 23 October 2007, and "Wal-Mart Raises Seiyu Stake to 95% to Speed Up Retailer's Turnaround," *JT*, 6 December 2007. "Tesco Opens First Supermarket in Japan," *JT*, 26 April 2007.

24. With FDI at around 2% of GDP, compared with 22% in the United States and 38% in Great Britain, the Japanese government announced it would like to see FDI inflow double by 2010. See "Japan Finally Warms to Vulture Culture," *JT*, 27 April 2007. The figures from 2006 show Japan, almost alone in Asia, attracting less foreign capital, despite a worldwide increase (38%) in trans-national FDI. See "Foreign investment in Japan negative in 2006," *JT*, 17 October 2007.

and Loan Program [FILP]) and thus starved itself of its traditional, readily available sources of domestic capital.[25]

The apparent easing of the Japanese government's position, particularly with regard to foreign investment in Japan's utilities, has not been augmented by corresponding legislative reform, a liberalization program, or a distinct policy of deregulation. Under existing foreign exchange law, non-Japanese entities seeking to purchase a stake of 10 percent or more in electric utilities, and in other companies related to "public order" and "national security," require government approval.[26] The Japanese government is empowered under the law to recommend, or order, foreign investors to alter or terminate their acquisition plans, or ultimately to deny approval. Intriguingly, it is claimed that every year "Japan receives about 100 such applications from foreign entities under the system, [and] none of them has so far been rejected," according to an unnamed official at the Ministry of Economy, Trade, and Industry (METI).[27] Nevertheless, the notion that appears to be espoused here—that hundreds of eager foreign equity firms are, at present, receiving approval to buy into Japanese utilities—is pure fiction, or perhaps wishful thinking, and does not accord with the recent machinations and workings of foreign capital.[28]

Clearly, there was an upsurge in foreign activity across the Japanese market during the 2007–2008 financial year (see Table 8.1).[29] Morgan Stanley carried out Japan's largest real estate purchase by a foreign investor

---

25. For further discussion of the Postal Savings System, its organs, and its funds, see Cargill and Yoshino, "The Postal Savings System," pp. 201–30, and Ishi, "Government Credit Program," p. 88.

26. Almost all Japanese companies are able to argue, if so inclined, that their business relates to public order and national security. Foreign investment houses therefore view the foreign exchange law as a major impediment to potential foreign investment in Japanese firms.

27. The British Children's Investment Fund, known as TCI, served as the test case when it attempted to raise the value of its holdings in J-Power from 9.9% to 20%. It appears TCI was locked out, and we must consider that the investment capital needed (a stake upward of 10% in most Japanese utilities would cost in excess of $2 billion, according to my enquiries) could itself deter or curtail potential applications. See "British Fund Faces Limit on Its Stake in J-Power," *JT*, 6 April 2008.

28. Earlier studies have also pointed out the disconnect between the reality of FDI statistics and the rhetoric of Japanese government agencies. See, for example, Lawrence, "Low Levels of Inward Investment," p. 100.

29. The Japanese financial year starts on 1 April and finishes on 31 March of the following calendar year.

when it took over the hotel chain subsidiary of All Nippon Airways for ¥281.3 billion in April 2007.[30] Goldman Sachs, in competition with Morgan Stanley, also planned to invest a similar amount (¥200 billion) in real estate during 2007, in order to increase its investment in Japanese properties, estimated at ¥2 trillion since 1998.[31] In finance, the General Electric group acquired Sanyo Electric Credit, the financial wing of the Sanyo Electric Company, in May 2007.[32] Interestingly, the trade in buying and selling Japanese banks went both ways, as the Japanese investment fund Advantage Partners prepared, in May 2007, to take over Tokyo Star Bank, and in fact completed a "friendly buyout" of it in March 2008.[33] Furthermore, one of the world's leading beverage and confectionary groups, Britain's Cadbury Schweppes, successfully purchased Sansei Foods in July 2007 and subsequently turned the Japanese company into a wholly owned subsidiary, Cadbury Japan.[34]

Significantly, there is also mounting evidence of profound institutional change occurring amid all of this increased foreign activity. Undoubtedly Citigroup's layered takeover of Nikko Cordial Corporation (from April 2007 to January 2008) was one of the most closely scrutinized financial transactions of recent times. By aggressively expanding its corporate and retail operations, with Nikko Cordial's cooperation, Citigroup hoped to become the preeminent banking and securities manager of Japan's enormous savings base.[35] With Japanese investors and

---

30. "ANA to Sell 13 Domestic Hotels to Morgan Stanley," *JT*, 18 June 2007.

31. "Goldman Makes ¥200 Billion Bet on Property Boom Here," *JT*, 4 October 2007.

32. Full details of this transaction are unclear, but it was undoubtedly significant, valued in the hundreds of billions of yen. See "GE Takes Over Sanyo Electric Credit," *JT*, 11 May 2007.

33. "Advantage Partners May Get Tokyo Star Bank," *JT*, 11 May 2007, p. 8; "Advantage to Launch Bid for Tokyo Star Bank," *JT*, 5 February 2008; and "Lone Star Group Firm Allegedly Hid ¥14 Billion," *JT*, 1 April 2008.

34. "Cadbury Gets Sansei," *JT*, 21 July 2007.

35. "Citigroup Bid for Nikko Opposed," *JT*, 27 April 2007; "Citigroup Bags Nikko Cordial for ¥920 Billion," *JT*, 28 April 2007; "Citigroup to Complete Nikko Cordial Acquisition," *JT*, 3 October 2007; "Nikko Wins OK for Citigroup Linkup," *JT*, 20 December 2007; "Nikko Cordial Now Citigroup Subsidiary," *JT*, 30 January 2008; "Citibank, Nikko to Integrate in May," *JT*, 13 February 2008; and "Citigroup to Realign in Japan Over Next Two Years," *JT*, 12 March 2008.

retirees increasingly using "overseas financial products" (the so-called carry trade in the yen), and with further liberalization of Japan's regulatory system expected, foreign fund managers have been keen to enter the Japanese market.[36] Unprecedented in Japan's postwar period, the Franco-Belgian bank Dexia (Credit Local) S.A. is actively extending loans to municipalities, prefectures, and even regional banks.[37] Moreover, in January 2008 Mizuho Bank became the first Japanese bank to invest with Indian lenders, in this instance the state-run Bank of India, to fund large infrastructure projects and concerted industrial development in the corridor between New Delhi and Mumbai.[38] Increased international cooperation of this nature can be expected to continue as Japanese banks, with the world's largest savings pools languishing in nonperforming, practically zero percent interest–paying bank accounts, are eager to invest in higher-yielding assets.[39]

In a climate in which overseas investors are said to have doubled the value of their holdings over the past decade or so, investment funds have profited by aggressively buying into Japanese companies and using their large shareholdings to pressure managers for payouts, along with making vociferous demands for higher dividends and board representation.[40] In this regard, the colorful activities of Steel Partners merit particular attention. Labeled as an "abusive acquirer" by the Tokyo High Court, the U.S. fund has, since 2003, attempted a number of highly publicized, unsolicited bids for iconic Japanese companies, such as Myojo Foods, Tenryu Saw, Bull-Dog Sauce, and Sapporo Beer, all without apparent success. Undeterred, a "misunderstood" Steel Partners, seeking to "educate" Japanese managers, continues to lobby the management of its more recent

---

36. "Aussie Fund Managers Targeting Japan," *JT,* 6 July 2007, and "Expanding Japanese Economy Attracting Fund Managers," *JT,* 21 July 2007. The global financial crisis forced Citibank to revisit its acquisition. See Alison Tudor, "Citigroup Back Flips to Put Nikko Cordial on Sale," *Wall Street Journal,* 20 January 2009; www.theaustralian.com.au/archive/business-old/citi-to-sell-japan-brokerage/story-e6frg9ox-1111118606285 (accessed 26 May 2014).

37. "Franco-Belgian Bank Looking for Struggling Cities," *JT,* 11 May 2007.

38. "Mizuho Claims First Tieup between Japanese, Indian Lenders," *JT,* 26 June 2007.

39. "Cadbury Gets Sansei," *JT,* 21 July 2007.

40. "Japan Finally Warms to Vulture Culture," and "Expanding Japanese Economy Attracting Fund Managers," *JT,* 21 July 2007.

acquisitions with proposals to achieve larger profits and thus reward shareholders with larger returns.[41]

The unprecedented, and at times unwanted, foreign demand for Japanese shares has provided welcome help to some surprising beneficiaries. For example, the scandal-ridden Goodwill, the "leading human resources provider" that allegedly violated Japan's employment laws, announced that it would raise approximately ¥20 billion in funds from a foreign consortium led by Cerberus and Morgan Stanley, in March 2008. Arguably, in Japan's new post–big bang environment of increased international competition, the message to failing managers is: foreign assistance (in a pinch) can help protect against failure (if not national disgrace).[42]

Post–big bang Japan is also, at least in outward appearances, becoming more competitive. As we have seen, foreign capital is heavily involved in the development of franchises, joint ventures, strategic alliances, mergers, and acquisitions in the Japanese market.[43] Within the context of Japanese capitalism, therefore, events such as the first successful hostile takeover of a Japanese company by another Japanese company, and the first "unsolicited tender offer" against a listed Japanese firm to succeed in Japan, signify real change in the workings of the Japanese market.[44] Still, no amount of "Tokyo liberalism" was ever is likely to allay criticism from neoliberal quarters. On 1 May 2007, the Japanese government acceded to requests from U.S. business groups and the Office of the U.S. Trade Representative and authorized the introduction of the takeover technique of "triangular mergers."[45] On meeting with President George Bush, Prime Minis-

---

41. "Tenryu Saw Latest Target to Elude Steel Partners," *JT*, 6 July 2007; "Steel Partners Woos Sapporo with New Business Proposals," *JT*, 9 November 2007; "Steel May Seek Noritz Management Reshuffle," *JT*, 30 January 2008; and "Sapporo to Reject Steel's Buyout," *JT*, 5 February 2008. See also Schaede, *Choose and Focus*, pp. 120–25.

42. "Goodwill to Raise Funds from Foreign Consortium," *JT*, 12 March 2008.

43. There was an exponential increase in mergers and acquisitions in recent years, with an unprecedented 2,775 deals being recorded in Japan during 2006. See "Japan Finally Warms to Vulture Culture," *JT*, 27 April 2007.

44. The real estate developer TOC Company was taken over by the so-called real estate investment fund K. K. DaVinci in a hostile bid. See "DaVinci Set to Clinch First Hostile Takeover," *JT*, 21 July 2007. The investment arm of Ken Corporation took over the used-car dealer Solid Group—significantly, with the indispensable help of Lehman Brothers (Japan). See "Ken's Hostile Bid Wins Listed Firm," *JT*, 14 December 2007.

45. A triangular merger allows the subsidiary of a foreign firm in Japan the right to effect a takeover of a Japanese company "by swapping new shares issued by the parent

ter Shinzo Abe called attention to his government's decision to allow Japanese subsidiaries of foreign multinationals certain takeover rights, only for Bush to demand further explanation. An exasperated Abe gasped, "This is a measure which the United States strongly requested. . . . I faced lots of criticism that . . . it would open the path for giant U.S. companies to absorb Japanese companies," while an unimpressed Bush quizzed him about the anomalies of takeovers in Japan. One can only wonder whether the intentions of Citigroup were breached in their troubled discussion.[46]

Conceptualizing Japan's Post–Big Bang Reforms

Having discussed how, in what ways, and to what ends Japan's financial and commercial markets have come to accept and accommodate foreign capital, and thus have become more "international" in recent times, it is now necessary to consider what this change means. We also need to consider how Japan's new political economy relates to the interplay between indigenous internationalization and externally driven globalization, and explain why these processes are important to social scientists.

Quite apart from the common perception of a long-suffering Japan burdened with ineffective political-bureaucratic leadership, unable to conceptualize outside the boundaries of the old "Japan, Inc." and U.S.-style neoliberal models, Japan offers the interesting paradox of a nation where ideological conservatism has often served as the principal instrument for organizing radical institutional transformation.[47] Certainly, profound socioeconomic changes attributed to the "restoration" movements of the Meiji and Showa eras were driven by an ideological conservatism, but could this conservatism be acting as a force for radical institutional change in today's Japan? In this regard, not enough attention has been paid to the importance and pace of financial reform.

The financial situation of Japan in the years since 1996 no longer suggests a picture of "institutional rigidity and reluctant change" but one of

---

for all or a sizeable portion of the target's shares without using any cash to fund the acquisition." See "Bush Asked Abe to Explain Triangular Mergers," *JT,* 14 May 2007. Citigroup subsequently used a triangular merger to acquire complete control of Nikko Cordial in December 2007. See "Citigroup to Complete Nikko Cordial Acquisition," *JT,* 3 October 2007; "Nikko Wins OK for Citigroup Linkup," *JT,* 20 December 2007; and "Nikko Cordial Now Citigroup Subsidiary," *JT,* 30 January 2008.

46. "Bush Asked Abe to Explain Triangular Mergers," *JT,* 14 May 2007.

47. See Metzler, "Japan's Long Stagnation," p. 665.

prompt institutional and legislative reformation.[48] Institutional reform is exemplified by the promulgation of the new Bank of Japan Law in June 1997, the establishment of the Resolution and Collection Corporation in October 1998, the Japanese government's quick decision to recapitalize the Deposit Insurance Corporation with a new balance of ¥60 trillion (the approximate size of the government's annual budget) in October 1998, and the government's sudden nationalization of, and subsequent injection of liquidity into Japan's most corrupt, frail, and reckless financial organs (in the form of huge amounts of public funds during the early months of 1999). It must be remembered, it was around this time (February 1999) that the Bank of Japan initiated its bold, untried monetary reform, the zero-interest-rate policy (ZIRP). Amid an air of general uncertainty, the government's brusque introduction of a reworked legal definition of nonperforming loans (with forced public disclosure of losses backed by criminal sanctions), and its augmentation of the Financial Supervisory Agency with the Financial Planning Bureau of the Ministry of Finance, in order to establish the Financial Services Agency (FSA-Kinyūchō) in July 2000, reflected the pronounced and prompt administrative and legislative changes of the late 1990s.[49]

In addition, in the last year of the twentieth century a hitherto unthinkable consolidation of the government's ministries was enacted, culminating (in a highly symbolic act) with the venerable moniker of the "Ministry of Finance" being discarded as of 2001. Then, in April 2001, the ministry's successor (sometimes rendered in English as the Finance Ministry) was divested of its control of the world's largest financial institution, the Postal Savings Bank and its Trust Fund Bureau/Fiscal Investment and Loan Program contributions, in effect cutting it out of the Japanese government's "alternate budget." In April 2001 the cause of structural reform was underscored by the appointment of Koizumi Junichiro as prime minister, a bellicose and strident proponent of reform,

---

48. Quoted phrase taken from Amyx, *Japan's Financial Crisis: Institutional Rigidity and Reluctant Change*. Metzler also makes a similar point, yet characterizes Japan's political leadership as lacking vision, and enigmatically asks, did "the Japanese government in its muddling-through way prevent the greatest debt-deflation crisis in recent history from turning into a great depression?" See Metzler, "Japan's Long Stagnation," pp. 664–66.

49. Cargill, Hutchison, and Ito, *Financial Policy and Central Banking*, pp. 51–62, 75, 96–101; Metzler, "Japan's Long Stagnation," p. 661.

even if that reform was often vague and ill-defined.[50] Intransigent conservatism within in his own party, the Liberal Democratic Party (LDP), no doubt transmogrified the reforms that Koizumi and his cadre had envisioned. Nevertheless, at least in a financial sense, the inertia of earlier reforms carried the day, and ultimately Koizumi presided over the privatization of a number of banks and would set in motion the privatization (over a ten-year period from October 2007) of the world's largest single source of public funds: Japan's Postal Savings (or Yucho) Bank. Surely, in light of Japan's modern history, there is a case for dismissing post-bubble notions of an unchanging and indeed unchangeable Japan, limping, if not crippled by its inability to adapt and grow.[51]

---

50. Metzler, "Japan's Long Stagnation," pp. 662–63.

51. Some take the argument further: for example, Schaede argues persuasively that during the period between 1998 and 2006 Japanese business reached a "strategic inflection point" that irreversibly changed many of the fundamentals that inform and influence our conception of Japan's postwar economy. See Schaede, *Choose and Focus*, pp. 253–60.

Conclusion

The economic growth and development of the Japanese economy was profoundly affected by the financial and monetary reforms enacted in the period from the Meiji Restoration, in 1868, to the adoption of the gold standard in 1897. From the outset, *Investing Japan* has argued that it was those processes that provided the necessary conditions for Japan's adoption of the gold standard. Indeed, Chapter 1 demonstrated how the Meiji regime reformed the financial and monetary systems of the preceding Tokugawa *bakufu*, which had been compromised by the onset of large-scale foreign trade and the consumption of Japan's precious metal currencies. The first chapter also demonstrated how, despite its attempt to adopt a gold standard in 1871, the Meiji regime was forced by foreign interests to retain a silver standard in the treaty ports. Furthermore, it noted how, in 1875, the regime's further attempt to address the depletion of its specie by replacing the silver yen with the *bōeki gin* trade yen failed to stem the outflow of Japanese gold and silver and, in 1878, compelled the regime to accept the Mexican silver dollar as legal tender. Significantly, one Mexican silver dollar was made equal to the value of either one silver yen or one gold yen, confirming Japan's adoption of a bimetallic standard. Chapter 1 also documented how the issue, and overissue, of paper currency intensified the financial and monetary problems of the Meiji regime, which had resorted to printing paper money to finance the commutation of pensions and to establish national banks.

The second half of Chapter 1 examined the institutions that were set in place to resolve those problems, namely the Yokohama Specie Bank and the Bank of Japan. In so doing, it analyzed how the program for the redemption of currency, in the so-called Matsukata deflation, facilitated the reintroduction of currency convertibility between notes and specie, so that by 1890 Japan's currency had been stabilized and unified by transferring to a depreciating, de facto silver standard. Finally, we saw how those financial and monetary reforms provided the basis for the adoption of the gold standard in Japan.

Chapter 2 focused on Japan's transition to a gold standard in the context of the world market's demonetization of silver. Initially the discussion detailed how the European economies revolutionized and transformed their respective monetary systems in a way that rejected silver as the measure of the standard of value in favor of gold. It then examined the reaction of the Meiji regime to the depreciation of silver relative to gold through the establishment of the Coinage Investigation Commission. The analysis focused on the commission's findings, which reflected the political intrigues of the period, especially those recommendations that conflicted with that clique of the Meiji oligarchy of which Matsukata was a senior member. Against this background, Chapter 2 illustrated how that same clique managed to change the composition of the Coinage Investigation Commission to circumvent "unfavorable" findings, and how Matsukata was able to use the indemnity from the Sino-Japanese War as the specie reserve necessary for the adoption of the gold standard. Finally, the chapter traced the passage of the gold standard legislation, the Coinage Law of 1897, through the Diet, outlining the form in which the gold standard was adopted in Japan.

Chapter 3 focused on the more general question of how the adoption of the gold standard allowed Japan to attract and utilize foreign capital. Noting the roles that the Matsukata deflation and the Sino-Japanese War played in stimulating the Japanese economy, and the successful introduction of the Coinage Law of 1897, Chapter 3 highlighted the consequences of the pivotal decision to adopt the gold standard. In particular, it illustrated how the gold standard facilitated the growth and development of the Japanese economy by helping Japan forge financial links with Britain that were intimately associated with the progress of the twenty-year Anglo-Japanese alliance (as explored in Chapter 4). Further, it demonstrated how the transfer to the gold standard ensured the stabilization of the international value of Japan's currency; created international and domestic confidence in trading with Japan; accelerated large-scale importation of capital in the form of modern technologies;

and, most important, promoted the massive increase in foreign investment of the late Meiji era. In sum, Chapter 3 argued that the adoption of
the gold standard in 1897 was a central component in the unprecedented
economic growth and development that Japan experienced in the late
Meiji period.

Foreign Capital in the Prewar Japanese Economy

After highlighting how Japan's adoption of the gold standard facilitated
the import of foreign capital, the task then turned to conceptualizing
and quantifying the amount of capital borrowed by Japan's government,
municipalities, and companies in the period from 1870 to the outbreak
of the Second World War in 1939. Critically, the size and frequency of
Japanese-government borrowing sheds new light on fiscal priorities during that period, and on the government's financial position in relation to
the import of foreign capital (Table C.I; see also Tables 5.1 and 6.3). Initially, foreign capital was needed to defray the costs associated with the
Sino-Japanese War and to finance the provision of basic infrastructure.
Waging the Russo-Japanese War then required a huge amount of foreign
capital from 1904 to 1905, and the inability of the Japanese government to
repay these and previous loans necessitated a series of conversion loans in
1907, 1910, 1924, and 1930. Finally, we noted that costs associated with the
nationalization of Japan's railways required short-term borrowing in the
financial markets of both London and Paris from 1913 to 1915. In total,
Japanese government borrowing in the period from 1870 to 1939 reached
a gross sum of ¥2,728 million (see Tables 5.1 and 6.3).

Loans extended to municipalities were most significant during 1902,
1909, 1912, and for earthquake reconstruction in 1926 and 1927, and totaled ¥317 million (see Table 6.1). Likewise, corporate loans, most notably to the South Manchuria Railway Company, totaled some ¥890 million.[1] Loans issued for electric power companies were the dominant
form of Japanese borrowing in the interwar period, totaling ¥523 million
and accounting for some 59 percent of the total amount loaned to Japanese
companies in the 1899–1931 period (see Table 6.2). When we combine
those figures with the approximate total of ¥57 million in direct foreign

---

1. British loans to the South Manchuria Railway Company alone totaled ¥176 million, or £18 million; hence it was often said that the British paid for Japan's railways in
China. See Overlach, *Foreign Financial Control in China*, pp. 186–95.

Table C.1. Total Merchandise Imports and Balance of Trade versus Total Capital Imports, 1870–1939

No.	Year	Total merchandise imports (k¥)	Trade balance (k¥)	Total capital imports (k¥)	Capital imports as percent of trade balance	Capital imports as percent of merchandise imports
		a	b	c	c/b	c/a
A	1870	33,741.6	−19,198.6	4,880.0	−25.42%	14.46%
B	1873	27,617.3	−6,475.2	11,712.0	−180.87%	42.41%
1	1897	231,960.1	−56,072.8	43,000.0	−76.69%	18.54%
2	1898	294,377.6	−115,804.0	0.0	0.00%	0.00%
3	1899	234,675.0	−8,652.5	97,988.0	−1,132.48%	41.75%
4	1900	300,832.5	−85,870.4	5,250.0	−6.11%	1.75%
5	1901	268,626.4	−8,042.8	0.0	0.00%	0.00%
6	1902	281,831.8	−9,804.5	52,900.0	−539.55%	18.77%
7	1903	328,145.0	−27,655.6	4,002.0	−14.47%	1.22%
8	1904	383,950.7	−52,402.5	214,786.0	−409.88%	55.94%
9	1905	499,501.9	−167,338.7	830,005.0	−496.00%	166.17%
10	1906	431,521.6	2,012.4	34,606.0	1719.63%	8.02%
11	1907	505,688.0	−63,533.7	272,611.0	−429.08%	53.91%
12	1908	453,332.2	−65,788.7	60,578.0	−92.08%	13.36%
13	1909	406,790.3	18,009.8	65,484.0	363.60%	16.10%
14	1910	498,521.0	−23,570.7	287,126.0	−1218.15%	57.60%
15	1911	553,390.0	−87,264.1	58,578.0	−67.13%	10.59%
16	1912	664,658.8	−117,100.2	92,714.0	−79.17%	13.95%
17	1913	779,073.9	−127,749.5	126,038.0	−98.66%	16.18%
18	1914	633,397.5	−22,865.3	24,307.0	−106.31%	3.84%
19	1915	563,391.2	169,665.6	29,289.0	17.26%	5.20%
20	1916	794,532.8	379,442.3	0.0	0.00%	0.00%
21	1917	1,088,306.8	575,147.3	1,250.0	0.22%	0.11%
22	1918	1,744,849.9	269,342.9	1,050.0	0.39%	0.06%
23	1919	2,335,751.7	−179,158.2	0.0	0.00%	0.00%
24	1920	2,502,716.3	−491,509.6	250.0	−0.05%	0.01%
25	1921	1,730,487.1	−433,223.2	0.0	0.00%	0.00%
26	1922	2,023,027.9	−337,522.9	400.0	−0.12%	0.02%
27	1923	2,119,996.2	−622,649.0	112,760.0	−18.11%	5.32%

(continued)

Table C.1. (continued)

No.	Year	Total merchandise imports (k¥)	Trade balance (k¥)	Total capital imports (k¥)	Capital imports as percent of trade balance	Capital imports as percent of merchandise imports
		a	b	c	c/b	c/a
28	1924	2,597,717.4	−725,670.0	619,201.0	−85.33%	23.84%
29	1925	2,734,699.6	−356,780.3	146,186.0	−40.97%	5.35%
30	1926	2,563,637.3	−444,727.5	118,240.0	−26.59%	4.61%
31	1927	2,359,130.8	−294,041.7	69,754.0	−23.72%	2.96%
32	1928	2,372,999.4	−334,904.8	244,816.0	−73.10%	10.32%
33	1929	2,389,175.3	−171,517.3	24,969.0	−14.56%	1.05%
34	1930	1,680,314.1	−161,740.1	264,463.0	−163.51%	15.74%
35	1931	1,319,405.8	−140,194.5	67,132.0	−47.88%	5.09%
36	1932	1,524,521.0	−67,225.2	2,400.0	−3.57%	0.16%
37	1933	2,017,503.9	−85,434.8	750.0	−0.88%	0.04%
38	1934	2,400,494.6	−142,414.0	0.0	0.00%	0.00%
39	1935	2,618,406.0	−15,254.0	0.0	0.00%	0.00%
40	1936	2,927,975.3	−130,376.5	0.0	0.00%	0.00%
41	1937	3,954,725.6	−635,905.3	500.0	−0.08%	0.01%
42	1938	2,836,327.5	60,427.0	0.0	0.00%	0.00%
43	1939	3,127,475.7	805,444.2	0.0	0.00%	0.00%

Source: Bytheway, *Nihon keizai to gaikoku shihon*, p. 198.

investment in the period from 1899 to 1939, we see that Japan's total import of foreign capital reached a staggering figure of ¥3,992 million (see Table 6.3).

We can then compare the total value of capital imports to the total value of Japan's imports of merchandise. For example, capital imports averaged 41 percent of the total value of Japan's commodity imports in the decade prior to the outbreak of the First World War, and 7.4 percent in the decade prior to the Manchurian Incident and subsequent war in China. Moreover, in the same two ten-year periods capital imports averaged 361 percent and 50 percent of the balance of payments deficits recorded in those two periods. The enormity of Japan's import of foreign capital, particularly in the lead-up to the First World War, needs to be acknowledged in clear and unqualified terms (Figure C.1).

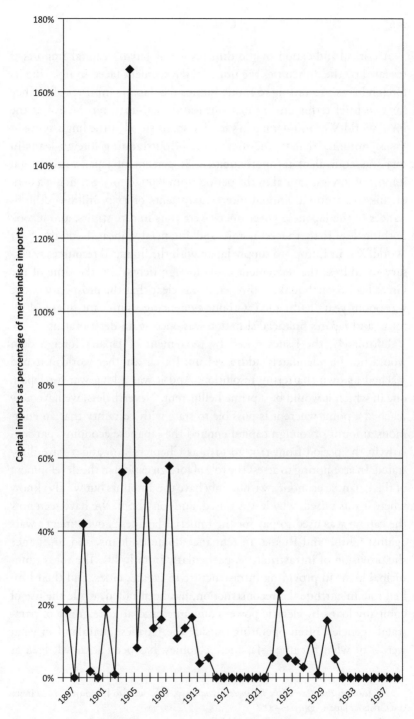

Figure C.1. Total Capital Imports versus Total Merchandise Imports, 1897–1939.
Source: Bytheway, *Nihon keizai to gaikoku shihon*, p. 199.

A critical indication of the dimensions of Japan's capital imports is revealed by the difficulties the imperial government faced in repaying its foreign loans. According to Inoue Junnosuke, Japan's minister of finance for two brief terms during 1923–1924 and 1929–1931, on the eve of the First World War in 1913, Japan's foreign loans stood at the huge figure of ¥1,941 million. That is, the total value of outstanding foreign loans in 1913 was equivalent to approximately 85 percent of Japan's gross total import of foreign capital in the period from 1897 to 1913. Servicing a debt of this size required annual interest payments of ¥130 million.[2] The finances of the Japanese government were thus in dire straits, and it took nothing less than the economic and financial upheavals of the First World War in Europe to supply Japan with the financial resources necessary to address the repayment of its foreign debts.[3] By the time of the Great Kanto earthquake, however, it was clear that the prosperity of the war-boom years had ended without evidencing significant financial reform, and Japan's financial situation was once again deteriorating.

Ultimately, the issues raised by repayment of Japan's foreign debt would not be adequately addressed until after another world war had reached its own shattering resolution. And it was a long war for Japan, one in which it would be a prime belligerent. Nevertheless, we have now reached a point where it is possible to state with certainty that an enormous amount of foreign capital entered the Japanese economy, particularly in the period from 1897 to 1931, as Chapters 5, 6, and 7 have illustrated. In attempting to assess the role of foreign capital in the development of the Japanese economy, we not only have the amounts but we also know where it was raised, why it was raised, and for whom. We have seen how the capital was used to pay for the imperial Japanese government's wars against China and Russia, to refinance domestic loans, and to finance the provision of infrastructure, particularly in railways. The role of municipal loans in providing infrastructure to Japan's cities, and their limited role in earthquake reconstruction, has been noted, while the use of company loans by electric power companies and an elite group of parastatal agencies, often operating outside the Japanese mainland in what were—or what became—Japanese colonies, has been acknowledged as

---

2. J. Inouye, *Problems of the Japanese Exchange*, p. 229. See also J. Inouye, "The Financial Crisis in Japan," pp. 436–42.

3. Warner, *Anglo-Japanese Financial Relations*, p. 81.

an important component of Japanese imperialism. In addition, the important role in the Japanese economy played by direct foreign investments and joint ventures has also been clarified.

In light of Japan's utter defeat in the Second World War, it might be asked: Was the prewar import of foreign capital really significant? Indeed for some educators, economists, social commentators, and many others inside Japan, fifteen years of war and destruction had, by the end of 1945, reduced the Japanese economy to an all-encompassing zero, and it was from this so-called zero point, in the embers of 1945, that the modern Japanese economy was born. According to their conception of Japanese history, inquiring into the economic past before 1945, however interesting, is seen as being of little value. But much lies conveniently buried beneath ashes of war, and the characterization of the "modern" Japanese economy as a veritable phoenix has obfuscated historical inquiry and analysis.[4]

The creation and destruction of capital, however, is much more than a simple flow of money and materials; it also involves technological transfer and intellectual endeavor. In this sense, Japan, as a country that had long enjoyed "generous hospitality and liberal treatment" at the hands of the foreign banking, business, and financial communities, was able to have the experience of building and operating such things as locomotive and electric railways; telegraph and telephone networks; ports and docks; water, gas, and sewage systems; armaments and steelworks; and a whole host of industries.[5] Moreover, it was through the introduction of foreign capital and technology that the Japan of 1859, which was completely overawed by the "black ships" of the nineteenth-century steam revolution, would take a leading place in the introduction and development of the electricity revolution of the twentieth century, and now faces the challenges of the information revolution in the twenty-first

---

4. The claim is not explicitly stated by most authors; rather, it is implicit in their sweeping generalizations about, or their silence in regard to, the pre-1945 economy. Typically, Japanese-language texts exclusively address the postwar economy in their treatment of "modern" Japanese economic history, as do many English language studies.

5. The quotation is taken from Stern, *United States in International Banking*, p. 350, a consideration of Japan's failure to reach an amicable agreement with its long-time creditors in the period before the Second World War. See also Warner, *Anglo-Japanese Financial Relations*, pp. 104–7.

century. Rather than dismiss what happened before 1945 as unimportant, therefore, we must study what has happened in Japan's complete modern history, in terms of both change and continuity, and consider how it relates to the present. In that context, *Investing Japan* has focused on the dynamic growth and development of the Japanese economy in a remarkable period of "openness" that peaked in the period from 1897 to 1931, after a much longer period of relative isolation, and finds that the introduction of foreign capital had important implications for the operation of Japan's imperialism, and a most profound effect on the modernization of Japan.

Foreign Capital and the Postwar Japanese Economy

As noted in relation to the prewar economy, investigating the history of foreign investment in postwar Japan demands intense scrutiny of the policies and role of the Japanese state. Prior to 1945 the imperial Japanese government often took a chauvinistic, interventionist stance against foreign-owned enterprises operating in the Japanese economy; as is widely acknowledged. Surprisingly, what is less understood is that foreign participation in the Japanese economy after the Second World War was, in many ways, more restricted than it had been prior to the 1930s. Lending from the World Bank was judicially applied to large-scale infrastructural projects and extended to the metals and power-generation industries, but it was not until the late 1960s, after many years of acrimony and bickering, that the Japanese economy can be meaningfully thought of as having been in any way liberalized to accommodate foreign capital. And it must be said that even then, foreign investment was largely limited to the establishment of franchises and subsidiaries in the food, beverage, and retail sectors, and joint ventures in the automotive industry.[6]

Economic downturn and the desperate need for external inputs of capital in the 1990s, after unprecedented economic prosperity in the 1980s, proved to be the wedge that opened the Japanese market to a greater foreign presence, with the neoliberal "big bang" revisions to Japan's banking and financial laws representing its hallmark. Japan's markets can now be said to be more "international" than ever, in that there is a greater non-Japanese presence across the economy. Significantly, much of the international pres-

---

6. We should also acknowledge that it was not until Japan had achieved impressive economic growth throughout the 1960s that it came to be thought of as an "attractive market" for foreign investors. See Ozaki, "Japanese Views on Foreign Capital," p. 1071.

ence is in fact American in origin. That does not imply, however, that there has been a profound, irreversible change in, or an Americanization of, the Japanese business environment. Rather, it recognizes a long history of American-led investment in the Japanese market that in many ways reached its culmination in the ten-year period from 1998 to 2008. Indeed, it was arguably during the decade or so before the global financial crisis of 2008 that the direct foreign investment of capital in the Japanese economy became most conspicuous and significant, as exemplified by the vigorous activities of such corporations as Citibank, Merrill Lynch, and Renault (see Tables 8.1 and 9.1). As for the future, foreign participation in the finance and commerce of Japan is expected to continue, albeit at much subdued levels in the immediate future, owing to the evolving financial crisis in Europe and North America, worldwide economic depression, and the earthquake, tsunami, and nuclear disaster of 11 March 2011. Within Japanese capitalism itself, the foreign investment of capital has experienced its own remarkable growth and development, and that, too, is an important sign that Japan is in flux and changing more quickly, and with more profundity, than is generally acknowledged.

Postscript

The earthquake and tsunami that struck eastern Japan on 11 March 2011 were profound natural disasters. The missing and dead, some 25,000 people, tell only part of the story. Many thousands were injured or in need of urgent medical care, hundreds of thousands were displaced or relocated in the ensuing months, and most of the families who live, or lived, along the Pacific coast of northeastern Japan lost all or part of their livelihood and economic means of support, if not their homes and land. Their rice fields were salted with seawater, their boats were left high and dry, and the wreckage of their towns was strewn across the Pacific and littered the harbors and frontages of once proud ports. A natural disaster of these dimensions is clearly large enough to challenge the abilities of any modern state, even the world's third largest economy.

Tragically, though, the dominant narrative that emerged from perhaps the world's largest seismic event was not one of earthquake and tsunami, but that of a nuclear disaster triggered by a series of tsunamis crashing into one of Japan's oldest nuclear power stations, at Fukushima. Within the first few days, three detonations told everyone what no one wanted to hear: three reactors in operation at the facility had, despite the increasingly strident denials of the Japanese government, not only melted down but were in fact melting *through*. Subsequent international detection of nuclear contamination and key radioactive isotopes suggested that, were it not for prevailing winds pushing airborne radioactive pollutants out over the northern Pacific—Japan's twenty-first-century "divine wind" (*kamikaze*)—the Japanese archipelago would have almost certainly been cut in two by nuclear fallout, with large parts of neighboring Niigata prefecture, as well as Fukushima prefecture, being rendered uninhabitable by nuclear contaminants and reactor detritus. Even so, Japan has at least three nuclear reactors hemorrhaging radiation (and one in danger of toppling over), located close to its political and economic core in the regions from Kanto to Kansai, where just over half of all Japan's people now live. Moreover, Japan has only just begun to consider the specter of what widespread nuclear contamination might mean to its mid- and long-term economic and demographic structure. The high number of casualties associated with the 2011 Tōhoku earthquake and tsunami may pale in significance compared with later deaths caused by cancers and other illnesses associated with exposure to nuclear contaminants and radioactive particles. One thing seems sure: the pace of Japan's depopulation is set to accelerate throughout the twenty-first century.

Indeed, a disturbing array of socioeconomic issues has been brought to the fore by the triple disaster. The Japanese government and its key representative institutions struggled to grasp the immediate implications of the earthquake and tsunami, they failed to act with the alacrity that the circumstances demanded, and, most critically, they were unable to respond effectively to the new and emerging threats the nuclear disaster presented. Not only were Japan's politicians found to be wanting, but the bureaucracy itself was shown to be self-serving, ineffective, and deeply compromised by its long-known, widely criticized, yet still largely unaltered symbiotic relationship with industry and big business. That politicians and bureaucrats were exposed as being impotent and ineffectual is perhaps hardly surprising, but most tellingly, the machinery and mechanisms of Japan's postwar economic "miracle" also seem to have lost their prestige and power. The "Japan, Inc." brand has been tarnished. Japan's largest electric power provider been shown to be incompetent, and the foundations of many of Japan's leading institutions have been discredited and undermined as well.

Beyond the apportioning of blame and responsibility in response to the unfolding events since 11 March 2011, there is the question of the financial and monetary costs. Relief requires money, but *reconstruction requires investment*. Who or what can save Japan? Which agencies will be charged with the task of rebuilding and reconfiguring Japan's northeastern economies in Tōhoku? And the quintillion-yen question: How is this all going to be paid for? Since the mid-1980s Japan has been the world's largest creditor nation (and remains so as *Investing Japan* goes to press), but the exchange-rate exigencies that fueled Japan's recent transformation from debtor to creditor nation have masked a long and significant, if little-studied, history of chronic foreign borrowing. A longer-term historical view suggests that the Japanese government is going to be hard-pressed to finance the massive costs associated with reconstruction and nuclear contamination, while also maintaining its leading creditor status, when its sovereign debts are the world's highest, leveraged at some 225 percent of its annual GDP. At present, some 95 percent of Japan's sovereign debt is held by Japanese institutional investors and households, with non-Japanese entities holding the remaining 5 percent, but given the magnitude of the challenges confronting Japan's national government, the deeper questions become can the internal mechanisms for directing domestic savings into national investments be reconfigured to fund reconstruction, or is a demographically challenged Japan in fact rapidly nearing the limits of its domestically controlled debt financing regime? Will foreign capital once again be imported to effect the reconstruction of the nation, or perhaps judiciously raised to ease the most pressing exigencies of nuclear decontamination and cleanup? The history presented in *Investing Japan* suggests that some mixture of those two options will be adopted, and the questions point to an enduring and fundamental problem in modern Japanese capitalism: the financing of investment in the nation's future.

As bad as things almost certainly are for Japan today, there are grounds for hope. The Japanese people faced some of the most daunting threats that the nineteenth and twentieth centuries could throw at any nation and somehow managed to do much more than merely survive. Indeed, remarkably, Japan has in many ways thrived. Consider its prospects in the last days of the Tokugawa *bakufu*: perhaps more so than in Japan's present circumstances, its institutions were shown to be ineffective and irrelevant; hence the Meiji Restoration and the birth of a new Japan. Moreover, the vistas from the last days of the Greater Japanese Empire must have had some disturbing parallels to the present. Certainly there was no obvious reason for Japanese confidence in August 1945—and very little indication of the tremendous economic growth and development that was to come.

Now, more than at any other time in their history, there is an urgent need for the Japanese people to acknowledge the significance of their long and enduring relationship with foreign capital, to rethink and reflect on its relevance and importance in their contemporary economy and daily lives. *Investing Japan* shines a light on the reality of Japan's underappreciated history of cooperation, hard work, and shared endeavor with foreign capital and international enterprise. Given the desperate need for innovation and new technologies, and the appalling magnitude of the challenges that Japan now confronts, the opportunities provided by the foreign investment of capital need to move beyond today's deeply qualified acceptance and be confidently seized for tomorrow. Of course, a historian's cap is not to be confused with the cloak of a prophet; nevertheless, it seems that foreign investment in the Japanese economy will very likely be a key determinant in any economic and financial successes that Japan might enjoy in its twenty-first-century future.

Bibliography

Primary Sources

BRITISH FOREIGN OFFICE (JAPAN)

Great Britain, Foreign Office. *Japan: Correspondence*. London: Scholarly Resources, 1975. Microfilm.

Foreign Office Folios: 1901–2, FO 46/563; 1903–5, FO 46/672; 1905, FO 46/673; 1905–6, FO 371/85; 1911–12, FO 371/1137; 1911–12, FO 371/1140; 1915, FO 371/2384; and 1915, FO 371/2388. In National Archives (United Kingdom), London.

BRITISH SESSIONAL PAPERS

Great Britain, House of Commons. *Sessional Paper*. New York: Readex Microprint, 1967. Microfilm.

UNITED STATES SENATE

U.S. Senate. 61st Cong., 2nd sess. (1909–1910). Vol. 37, Senate Doc. No. 586. Washington, DC: Government Printing Office, 1911.

ARCHIVAL COLLECTIONS

Daily Accounts, C1/44 to C1/64, Bank of England Archives, London.

Histories of the Bank—Prof. R. S. Sayers Research Papers by B/E Staff, ADM33/10–11, Bank of England Archives, London.

Letter Book No. 25, G23/70, Bank of England Archive, London.

Japan—Bank of Japan Correspondence, C.261, Federal Reserve Bank of New York.

Japan—Miscellaneous, Hongkong and Shanghai Bank, HSBC Group Archives, London.

Japan—Miscellaneous, Morgan Grenfell Collection (Deutsche Bank), London Metropolitan Archives, London.

Japan—Miscellaneous, XI/III/681a, Rothschild Archive, London.

Thomas W. Lamont Papers, Box Nos. 185–90, Baker Library, Harvard University.

Russell C. Leffingwell Papers, MS 1030, Yale University Library.

Benjamin Strong Papers, No. 610.2, Federal Reserve Bank of New York.

Secondary Sources (Articles and Monographs)

Adams, T. F. M. *A Financial History of Modern Japan*. Tokyo: Research, 1964.

Adams, T. F. M., and I. Hoshii. *A Financial History of the New Japan*. Tokyo: Kodansha, 1972.

Adler, C., and M. L. Schiff. *Jacob H. Schiff: His Life and Letters*. Vols. 1 and 2. New York: Kessinger, 2003.

Akita, S. "British Informal Empire in East Asia, 1880–1939: A Japanese Perspective." In *Gentlemanly Capitalism and British Imperialism: The New Debate on Empire*, edited by R. E. Dumett, pp. 141–56. London: Longman, 1999.

Alcock, R. *The Capital of the Tycoon: A Narrative of a Three Years' Residence in Japan*. Vol. 2. London: Harper and Brothers, 1863.

Allen, G. C. *A Short Economic History of Modern Japan*. Rev. ed. London: Allen and Unwin, 1972.

Alley, R. "Gold, the Pound Sterling and the Witwatersrand, 1886–1914." In *Evolution of the World Economy, Precious Metals and India*, edited by P. B. Bertola, J. McGuire, and P. D. Reeves, pp. 97–122. New Delhi: Oxford University Press, 2001.

Amyx, J. A. *Japan's Financial Crisis: Institutional Rigidity and Reluctant Change*. Princeton, NJ: Princeton University Press, 2004.

Andreades, A. *History of the Bank of England, 1640 to 1903*. 4th ed. London: Frank Cass, 1966.

Baba, M., and M. Tatemoto. "Foreign Trade and Economic Growth in Japan: 1858–1937." In *Economic Growth: The Japanese Experience since the Meiji Era*, edited by L. Klein and K. Ohkawa, pp. 162–96. Homewood, IL: Richard D. Irwin, 1968.

Bagchi, A. K. "Anglo-Indian Banking in British India: From the Paper Pound to the Gold Standard, 1821–1931." *Journal of Imperial and Commonwealth History* 13, no. 3 (1985): 231–57.

———. "Substitution between Council Bills and Silver Imports during the Period of the Depreciating Rupee in British India." Paper presented at the Precious Metals, the World Economy and India Conference, Curtin University, Perth, Australia, 11–12 July 1993.

Bagehot, W. *Lombard Street*. London: John Murray, 1873.

Balachandran, G. "The Gold Exchange Standard and Empire: India, 1900–1940." In *Evolution of the World Economy, Precious Metals and India*, edited by P. B. Bertola, J. McGuire, and P. D. Reeves, pp. 199–229. New Delhi: Oxford University Press, 2001.

Bank of Japan. *Money and Banking in Japan*. Tokyo: Economic Research Department—Bank of Japan, 1964.

Bartlett, C. J., ed. *Britain Pre-eminent: Studies of British World Influence in the Nineteenth Century*. London: Macmillan, 1969.

———. *British Foreign Policy in the Twentieth Century*. London: Macmillan, 1989.

———. *Defense and Diplomacy: Britain and the Great Powers*. Manchester: Manchester University Press, 1993.

Baster, A. S. J. *The Imperial Banks*. Reprint. New York: Arno Press, 1977.

———. *The International Banks*. Reprint. New York: Arno Press, 1977.

Bayoumi, T. *Modern Perspectives on the Gold Standard*. Cambridge: Cambridge University Press, 1996.

Beasley, W. G., "From Conflict to Co-operation: British Naval Surveying in Japanese Waters, 1845–82." In *The History of Anglo-Japanese Relations*, vol. 1: *The Political-Diplomatic Dimension, 1600–1930*, edited by I. Nish and Y. Kibata, pp. 87–106. London: Macmillan, 2000.

———. *Great Britain and the Opening of Japan, 1834–1858*. Reprint. Folkestone, UK: Japan Library, 1995.

———. *The Meiji Restoration*. London: Oxford University Press, 1973.

———, ed. *Selected Documents in Japanese Foreign Policy, 1853–1868*. London: Oxford University Press, 1955.

Beck, U. *What Is Globalization?* Cambridge: Polity Press, 1997.

Beloff, M. *Britain's Liberal Empire: 1897–1921*. London: Methuen, 1969.

Bertola, P. B. "Cyclical Developments in Gold Mining at Kalgoorlie: 1893–1944." In *Evolution of the World Economy, Precious Metals and India*, edited by P. B. Bertola, J. McGuire, and P. D. Reeves, pp. 123–52. New Delhi: Oxford University Press, 2001.

———. "Kalgoorlie, Gold, and the World Economy, 1893–1972." Ph.D. diss., Curtin University, 1993.

Bordo, M. D. *The Gold Standard and Related Regimes*. Cambridge: Cambridge University Press, 1999.

———. "The Gold Standard: The Traditional Approach." In *A Retrospective on the Classical Gold Standard, 1821–1931*, edited by M. D. Bordo and A. J. Swartz, pp. 23–120. Chicago: Chicago University Press, 1984.

Bordo, M. D., and F. Capie, eds. *Monetary Regimes in Transition*. Cambridge: Cambridge University Press, 1993.

Born, K. E. *International Banking in the 19th and 20th Centuries.* New York: St. Martin's Press, 1983.

Borton, H. *Japan's Modern Century.* New York: Ronald Press, 1955.

Boulding, K. E., and A. H. Gleason. "War as an Investment: The Strange Case of Japan." In *Economic Imperialism*, edited by K. E. Boulding and T. Murkerjee, pp. 240–61. Ann Arbor: University of Michigan Press, 1972.

Boyce, R. "Britain's Changing Corporate Structure and the Crisis of Central Bank Control in the 1920s." In *Finance in the Age of the Corporate Economy*, edited by P. L. Cottrell, A. Teichova, and T. Yuzawa, pp. 142–63. Aldershot, UK: Ashcroft, 1997.

Broadberry, S. N., and N. F. R. Crafts. *Britain in the International Economy, 1870–1939.* Cambridge: Cambridge University Press, 1995.

Brown, I. "Siam and the Gold Standard, 1902–1908." *Journal of Southeast Asian Studies* 10, no. 1 (1979): 381–99.

Brown, W. A. *England and the New Gold Standard, 1919–1926.* London: King and Son, 1929.

Bryan, S. *The Gold Standard at the Turn of the Twentieth Century: Rising Powers, Global Money, and the Age of Empire.* New York: Columbia University Press, 2010.

Burk, K. "Money and Power: The Shift from Great Britain to the United States." In *Finance and Financiers in European History, 1880–1960*, edited by Y. Cassis, pp. 359–69. Cambridge: Cambridge University Press, 1992.

———. *Morgan Grenfell 1838–1988: The Biography of a Merchant Bank.* Oxford: Oxford University Press, 1989.

Bytheway, S. J. "Japan's Adoption of the Gold Standard: Financial and Monetary Reform in the Meiji Period." In *Evolution of the World Economy, Precious Metals and India*, edited by P. B. Bertola, J. McGuire, and P. D. Reeves, pp. 79–96. New Delhi: Oxford University Press, 2001.

———. "Kinhonisei jidai niokeru Nichigōkan no kin bōeki, 1897–1931 nen" (Australian gold exports to Japan during the era of the gold standard, 1897–1931). *Nihon University Journal of Business* 76, no. 4 (2007): 41–53.

———. *Nihon keizai to gaikoku shihon: 1858–1939* (The Japanese economy and foreign capital). Tokyo: Tōsui, 2005.

Cain, P. J., and A. G. Hopkins. *British Imperialism*, vol. 1: *Innovation and Expansion, 1688–1914.* London: Longman, 1993.

———. "The Theory and Practice of British Imperialism." In *Gentlemanly Capitalism and British Imperialism: The New Debate on Empire*, edited by R. E. Dumett, pp. 196–220. London: Longman, 1999.

Cairncross, A. "The Bank of England and the British Economy." In *The Bank of England, Money, Power and Influence, 1694–1994*, edited by R. Roberts and D. Kynaston, pp. 57–82. Oxford: Clarendon Press, 1995.

Cargill, T. F., M. M. Hutchison, and T. Ito. *Financial Policy and Central Banking in Japan*. Cambridge, MA: MIT Press, 2000.

Cargill, T. F., and N. Yoshino. "The Postal Savings System, Fiscal Investment and Loan Program, and Modernization of Japan's Financial System." In *Crisis and Change in the Japanese Financial System*, edited by T. Hoshi and H. Patrick, pp. 201–30. Boston: Kluwer, 2000.

Carosso, V. P. *The Morgans: Private International Bankers, 1854–1913*. Cambridge, MA: Harvard University Press, 1987.

Chamberlain, M. E. *Pax Britannica? British Foreign Policy, 1789–1914*. London: Longman, 1988.

Checkland, O. *Britain's Encounter with Meiji Japan, 1868–1912*. London: Macmillan, 1989.

Chernow, R. *The House of Morgan*. London: Simon and Schuster, 1990.

———. *The Warburgs: The Twentieth-Century Odyssey of a Remarkable Jewish Family*. New York: Vintage, 1993.

Clammer, J. *Japan and Its Others: Globalization, Difference and the Critique of Modernity*. Melbourne: Trans Pacific Press, 2001.

Clapman, J. *The Bank of England: A History, 1797–1914*. Vol. 2. Cambridge: Cambridge University Press, 1958.

Clemment, E. W. *A Handbook of Modern Japan*. Chicago: A. C. McClurg, 1903.

Cleveland, H. van B., and T. F. Huertas. *Citibank, 1812–1970*. Cambridge, MA: Harvard University Press, 1985.

Cochran, S. *Big Business in China: Sino-Foreign Rivalry in the Cigarette Industry, 1890–1930*. Cambridge, MA: Harvard University Press, 1980.

Collins, M. *Money and Banking in the UK: A History*. London: Croom Helm, 1988.

Cortazzi, H. *Mitford's Japan*. London: Athlone, 1985.

Cottrell, P. L. "The Bank of England in Its International Setting, 1918–1972." In *The Bank of England: Money, Power and Influence 1694–1994*, edited by R. Roberts, and D. Kynaston, pp. 83–139. Oxford: Clarendon Press, 1995.

———. *British Investment in the Nineteenth Century*. London: Macmillan, 1975.

Cox, H. *The Global Cigarette: Origins and Evolution of British American Tobacco, 1880–1949*. Oxford: Oxford University Press, 2000.

Crawcour, E. S. "Economic Change in the Nineteenth Century." In *The Cambridge History of Japan*, vol. 5: *Nineteenth Century*, ed. M. B. Jansen, pp. 569–617. Cambridge: Cambridge University Press, 1989.

———. "Industrialization and Technological Change, 1885–1920." In *The Cambridge History of Japan*, vol. 6: *Twentieth Century*, edited by P. Duus, pp. 385–450. Cambridge: Cambridge University Press, 1988.

——. "The Tokugawa Heritage." In *The State and Economic Enterprise in Japan*, expanded ed., edited by W. W. Lockwood, pp. 17–44. Princeton, NJ: Princeton University Press, 1968.

——. "The Tokugawa Period and Japan's Preparation for Modern Economic Growth." In *The Industrialization of Japan*, edited by W. J. Macpherson, pp. 3–15. Oxford: Basil Blackwell, 1994.

Crow, C. *He Opened the Door of Japan: Townsend Harris and the Story of His Amazing Adventures in Establishing American Relations with the Far East.* New York: Harper and Brothers, 1939.

Crowley, J. B. *Japan's Quest for Autonomy: National Security and Foreign Policy, 1930–1938.* Princeton, NJ: Princeton University Press, 1966.

Crowther, G. *An Outline of Money.* London: Thomas Nelson and Sons, 1940.

Curzon, G. N. "The Conditions in Which the Alliance Can Continue: A Plea for Sympathy with Each Other's 'Thoughts, Wishes and Hopes.'" *New East* 1, no. 1 (1917): 19–20.

Cusumano, M. A. *The Japanese Automobile Industry: Technology and Management at Nissan and Toyota.* Cambridge, MA: Harvard University Press, 1985.

Dale, P. N. *The Myth of Japanese Uniqueness.* New York: St. Martin's Press, 1986.

Davenport-Hines, R. P. T., and G. Jones. "British Business in Japan since 1868." In *British Business in Asia since 1860*, edited by R. P. T. Davenport-Hines and G. Jones, pp. 217–44. Cambridge: Cambridge University Press, 1989.

Davis, L. E., and R. A. Huttenback. *Mammon and the Pursuit of Empire: The Political Economy of British Imperialism, 1860–1912.* Cambridge: Cambridge University Press, 1986.

Dayer, R. A. *Bankers and Diplomats in China, 1917–1925: The Anglo-American Relationship.* London: F. Cass, 1981.

De Cecco, M. *Money and Empire.* Oxford: Basil Blackwell, 1974.

Dickins, F. V., and S. Lane-Poole. *The Life of Sir Harry Parkes.* Vol. 2. London: Macmillan, 1894.

Dopfer, K. "Reconciling Economic Theory and Economic History: The Rise of Japan." *Journal of Economic Issues* 19, no. 1 (1985): 21–73.

Droppers, G. "Monetary Changes in Japan." *Quarterly Journal of Economics* 12 (1897–98): 153–85.

Dumett, R. E. "Exploring the Cains/Hopkins Paradigm: Issues for Debate; Critique and Topics for New Research." In *Gentlemanly Capitalism and British Imperialism: The New Debate on Empire*, edited by R. E. Dumett, pp. 1–43. London: Longman, 1999.

Dunn, R. W. *American Foreign Investments.* Reprint. New York: Arno Press, 1976.

Durden, R. F. *The Dukes of Durham, 1865–1929.* Durham, NC: Duke University Press, 1975.

Dutton, J. "The Bank of England and the Rules of the Game under the International Gold Standard." In *A Retrospective on the Classical Gold Standard, 1821–1931,* edited by M. D. Bordo and A. J. Swartz, pp. 173–202. Chicago: Chicago University Press, 1984.

Duus, P. *The Abacus and the Sword: The Japanese Penetration of Korea, 1895–1910.* Berkley: University of California Press, 1995.

———. "Japan's Informal Empire in China, 1895–1937." In *The Japanese Informal Empire in China, 1895–1937,* edited by P. Duus, R. H. Myers, and M. R. Peattie, pp. xi–xxix. Princeton, NJ: Princeton University Press, 1989.

Edelstein, M. *Overseas Investment in the Age of High Imperialism.* New York: Columbia University Press, 1982.

Eichengreen, B. "Editor's Introduction." In *The Gold Standard in Theory and History,* edited by B. Eichengreen, pp. 1–35. New York: Methuen, 1985.

———. *Golden Fetters: The Gold Standard and the Great Depression, 1919–1939.* Oxford: Oxford University Press, 1992.

Emi, K. *Government Fiscal Activity and Economic Growth in Japan, 1868–1960.* Tokyo: Kinokuniya, 1963.

Enzig, P. *The Fight for Financial Supremacy.* London: Macmillan, 1931.

Ericson, S. J. *The Sound of the Whistle: Railroads and the State in Meiji Japan.* Cambridge, MA: Harvard University Asia Center, 1996.

Fallows, J. *Looking at the Sun: The Rise of the New East Asian Economic and Political System.* New York: Pantheon, 1994.

Ferguson, N. *Empire: The Rise and Demise of the British World Order and the Lessons for Global Power.* London: Allen Lane, 2002.

———. *The House of Rothschild: The World's Banker, 1849–1999.* Vol. 2. New York: Viking Penguin, 1999.

Fernandez-Armesto, F. *Millennium: A History of the Last Thousand Years.* New York: Touchstone, 1995.

Feuerwerker, A. "Japanese Imperialism in China: A Commentary." In *The Japanese Informal Empire in China, 1895–1937,* edited by P. Duus, R. H. Myers, and M. R. Peattie, pp. 431–38. Princeton, NJ: Princeton University Press, 1989.

Fletcher, W. M. "Japanese Banks and National Economic Policy, 1920–1936." In *Banking in Japan,* vol. 2: *Japanese Banking in the High-Growth Era, 1952–1973,* ed. W. M. Tsutsui, pp. 251–84. London: Routledge, 1999.

Ford, A. G. "Notes on the Working of the Gold Standard before 1914." In *The Gold Standard in Theory and History,* edited by B. Eichengreen, pp. 141–65. New York: Methuen, 1985.

Fox, G. *Britain and Japan, 1858–1883.* Oxford: Clarendon Press, 1969.

Fraser, H. F. *Great Britain and the Gold Standard.* London: Macmillan, 1933.

Fratianni, M., and F. Spinelli. "Italy in the Gold Standard Period, 1861–1914." In *A Retrospective on the Classical Gold Standard, 1821–1931,* edited by M. D. Bordo and A. J. Swartz, pp. 405–54. Chicago: Chicago University Press, 1984.

Friedberg, A. L. *The Weary Titan*. Princeton, NJ: Princeton University Press, 1988.

Fujise, K. "Kokusai kinhonisei to sekai shijō" (The international gold standard and world markets). In *Kokusai kinhonisei to chuōginkō taisaku* (The international gold standard and central banking policy), edited by K. Fujise and A. Yoshioka, pp. 1–28. Nagoya: Nagoya University Press, 1987.

Fujiwara, S. "Foreign Trade, Investment, and Industrial Imperialism in Postwar Japan." In *Japanese Capitalism since 1945: Critical Perspectives*, edited by T. Morris-Suzuki and T. Seiyama, pp. 166–206. New York: M. E. Sharpe, 1989.

Fukao, K., and Amano, T. *Tainichi chokusetu tōshi to Nihon keizai* (Direct foreign investment and the Japanese Economy). Tokyo: Nihon Keizai Shinbun, 2004.

Gallarotti, G. M. *The Anatomy of an International Monetary Regime: The Classical Gold Standard, 1880–1914*. Oxford: Oxford University Press, 1995.

———. "The Scramble for Gold: Monetary Regime Transformation in the 1870s." In *Monetary Regimes in Transition*, edited by M. D. Bordo and A. J. Swartz, pp. 1–15. Cambridge: Cambridge University Press, 1994.

Gordon, A. *Fabricating Consumers: The Sewing Machine in Modern Japan*. Berkeley: University of California Press, 2012.

Goto-Shibata, H. "Anglo-Japanese Co-operation in China in the 1920s." In *The History of Anglo-Japanese Relations*, vol. 1: *The Political-Diplomatic Dimension, 1600–1930*, edited by I. Nish and Y. Kibata, pp. 224–54. London: Macmillan, 2000.

Grabowski, R. "A Historical Reassessment of Early Japanese Development." In *The Industrialization of Japan*, edited by W. J. Macpherson, pp. 241–56. Oxford: Blackwell, 1994.

Green, E. H. H. *Banking: An Illustrated History*. Oxford: Phaidon, 1989.

———. "The Influence of the City over British Economic Policy, c. 1880–1960." In *Finance and Financiers in European History, 1880–1960*, edited by Y. Cassis, pp. 193–218. Cambridge: Cambridge University Press, 1992.

Grimes, W. W. "Internationalization as Insulation: Dilemmas of the Yen." In *Japan's Managed Globalization: Adapting to the Twenty-First Century*, edited by U. Schaede, and W. W. Grimes, pp. 47–76. New York: M. E. Sharpe, 2003.

Grosse, R. E. ed. *Thunderbird on Global Business Strategy*. New York: John Wiley and Sons, 2000.

Hadley, E. *Antitrust in Japan*. Princeton, NJ: Princeton University Press, 1970.

Hall, J. W., and M. B. Jansen, eds. *Studies in the Institutional History of Early Modern Japan*. Princeton, NJ: Princeton University Press, 1968.

Halliday, J. *A Political History of Japanese Capitalism*. New York: Pantheon, 1975.

Hamashita, T. "A History of the Japanese Silver Yen and the Hongkong and Shanghai Banking Corporation, 1871–1913." In *Eastern Banking*, edited by F. H. H. King, pp. 321–49. London: Athlone Press, 1983.

Hanashiro, R. S. *Thomas William Kinder and the Japanese Imperial Mint, 1868–1875*. Leiden: Brill, 1999.

Hara, T. "Nichi-fuginkō (1912–1954) no keieishi" (A management history of the Banque Franco-Japonaise, 1912–1954). *Waseda Shōgaku* 382 (October 1999): 139–92.

Hatakeyama, H. *Sumitomo zaibatsu setsuritsushi no kenkyū* (Research into the establishment of the Sumitomo Zaibatsu). Tokyo: Dobunkan, 1988.

Hawtrey, R. G. *Bretton Woods for Better or Worse*. London: Longman, 1946.

———. *A Century of Bank Rate*. 2nd ed. London: Frank Cass, 1962.

Hayami, Y. ed. *Kaihatsu senryaku to Sekaiginkō* (The World Bank and development strategies). Tokyo: Chisen, 2003.

Hein, L. E. *Fuelling Growth: The Energy Revolution and Economic Policy in Postwar Japan*. Cambridge, MA: Harvard University Press, 1980.

Henderson, D. F. *Foreign Enterprise in Japan: Laws and Policies*. Chapel Hill: University of North Carolina Press, 1973.

Higashi, C., and G. P. Lauter. *The Internationalization of the Japanese Economy*. Boston: Kluwer, 1990.

Hirshmeier, J. *The Origins of Entrepreneurship in Meiji Japan*. Cambridge, MA: Harvard University Press, 1964.

H.R.H. Prince Arthur. "A Message from H. R. H. Prince Arthur of Connaught." *New East* 1, no. 1 (1917): 1.

Hoare, H. *The Appreciation of Gold and Its Connexion with the Depression of Trade*. London: Edward Stanford, 1886.

Hoare, J. "The Era of Unequal Treaties, 1858–99." In *The History of Anglo-Japanese Relations*, vol. 1: *The Political-Diplomatic Dimension, 1600–1930*, edited by I. Nish and Y. Kibata, pp. 107–130. London: Macmillan, 2000.

———. *Japan's Treaty Ports and Foreign Settlements: The Uninvited Guests, 1858–1899*. Folkestone, UK: Japan Library, 1994.

Hollerman, L. *Japan Disincorporated: The Economic Liberalization Process*. Stanford, CA: Hoover Institution Press, 1988.

Honjo, E. *The Social and Economic History of Japan*. New York: Russell and Russell, 1965.

Hont, I., and M. Ignatieff, eds. *Wealth and Virtue: The Shaping of Political Economy in the Scottish Enlightenment*. Cambridge: Cambridge University Press, 1983.

Horie, Y. *Gaishi yunyū no kaiko to tenbō* (A recollection and consideration of the importation of foreign capital). Tokyo: Yuhikaku, 1950.

Horiuchi, A. "The Big Bang: Idea and Reality." In *Crisis and Change in the Japanese Financial System*, edited by T. Hoshi and H. Patrick, pp. 233–52. Boston: Kluwer, 2000.

Hosbawm, E. J. *The Age of Empire, 1875–1914*. London: Guild Publishing, 1987.

———. *The Age of Extremes, 1914–1991*. London: Abacus, 1994.

———. *Industry and Empire: An Economic History of Britain since 1750*. London: Weidenfeld and Nicholson, 1968.

———. *On History*. London: Abacus, 1997.

Hsu, Un Yuen. "The Need and Method of Immediate Reforms in the Currency of China." *Economic Journal* 20, no. 78 (June 1910): 222–35.

Huber, J. R. "Effects on Prices of Japan's Entry into World Commerce after 1858." *Journal of Political Economy* 79, no. 3 (1971): 614–28.

Hume, D. "On the Balance of Trade." In *The Gold Standard in Theory and History*, edited by B. Eichengreen, pp. 39–48. New York: Methuen, 1985.

Hunter, J. "Bankers, Investors and Risk: British Capital and Japan during the Years of the Anglo-Japanese Alliance." In *The Anglo-Japanese Alliance, 1902–1922*, edited by P. P. O'Brien, pp. 176–98. London: RoutledgeCurzon, 2004.

Iida, T. "The Industrial Bank of Japan during the Inter-war Period." In *Finance in the Age of the Corporate Economy*, edited by P. L. Cottrell, A. Teichova, and T. Yuzawa, pp. 129–41. Aldershot, UK: Ashcroft, 1997.

Inkster, I. "Meiji Economic Development in Perspective: Revisionist Comments upon the Industrial Revolution in Japan." In *The Industrialization of Japan*, edited by W. J. Macpherson, pp. 143–66. Oxford: Blackwell, 1994.

———. "Prometheus Bound: Technology and Industrialization in Japan, China and India Prior to 1914—A Political Economy Approach." *Annals of Science* 45 (1988): 399–426.

———. *Science and Technology in History: An Approach to Industrial Development*. London: Macmillan, 1991.

———. "Science, Technology and Economic Development: Japanese Historical Experience in Context." *Annals of Science* 48 (1991): 545–63.

Inouye, J. "The Financial Crisis in Japan." In *Problems of the Pacific*, edited by J. B. Condliffe, pp. 436–42. Chicago: University of Chicago Press, 1928.

———. *Problems of the Japanese Exchange, 1914–1926*. London: Macmillan, 1931.

Inouye, K. "Attitude of Germany after the War: The Question of the Renewal of the Alliance." *New East* 1, no. 1 (1917): 22.

Inouye, Y. "From Unequal Treaty to the Anglo-Japanese Alliance, 1867–1902." In *The History of Anglo-Japanese Relations*, vol. 1: *The Political-Diplomatic*

Dimension, 1600–1930, edited by I. Nish and Y. Kibata, pp. 131–58. London: Macmillan, 2000.

Ishi, H. "The Government Credit Program and Public Enterprises." In *Public Finance in Japan*, edited by T. Shibata, pp. 81–102. Tokyo: University of Tokyo Press, 1986.

Ishibashi, T. "Kin yushutsu kaikin ronshi" (A history of the debate on lifting the gold export ban). *Toyo keizai shinpō* 1340, no. 16 (March 1929): 539–62.

Itagaki, T., S. Okuma, and K. Ukita. "The History of Political Parties in Japan." In *Fifty Years of New Japan*, 2nd ed., vol. 1, edited by S. Okuma, pp. 133–93. New York: Kraus. 1970.

Ito, M. *Nihon no taigai kinyū to kinyū seisaku: 1914–1936* (Japan's financial policy and foreign finances). Nagoya: Nagoya University Press, 1989.

Ito, T. *The Japanese Economy*. Cambridge, MA: MIT Press, 1992.

Jansen, M. B., and G. Rozman, eds. *Japan in Transition: From Tokugawa to Meiji*. Princeton, NJ: Princeton University Press, 1986.

Japan Business History Institute. *The Mitsui Bank: A History of the First Hundred Years*. Tokyo: Mitsui Bank, 1976.

Johnson, H. J. *The Banking Keiretsu*. Chicago: Probus, 1993.

Jonung, L. "The Swedish Experience under the Classical Gold Standard, 1873–1914." In *A Retrospective on the Classical Gold Standard, 1821–1931*, edited by M. D. Bordo, and A. J. Swartz, pp. 361–404. Chicago: Chicago University Press, 1984.

Kajima, M. *A Brief Diplomatic History of Modern Japan*. Rutland, VT: Charles E. Tuttle, 1965.

———. *The Diplomacy of Japan, 1894–1922*. Vol. 1. Tokyo: Kajima, 1976.

Kamiyama, T. *Meiji keizai seisakushi no kenkyū* (Research into the history of Meiji economic policy). Tokyo: Haniwa, 1995.

Kanebo shashi henshū shitsu. *Kanebō hyakunenshi* (The hundred-year history of Kanebo). Tokyo: Kanebo, 1988.

Kann, E. *The Currencies of China*. Shanghai: Kelly and Walsh, 1926.

Kato, T. "Development of the Monetary System." In *Japanese Society in the Meiji Era*, edited by K. Shibusawa, pp. 212–13. Tokyo: Toyo Bunka, 1958.

Kato, Y. "The Opening of Japan and the Meiji Restoration, 1837–72." In *The History of Anglo-Japanese Relations*, vol. 1: *The Political-Diplomatic Dimension, 1600–1930*, edited by I. Nish and Y. Kibata, pp. 60–86. London: Macmillan, 2000.

Keene, D., trans. *Essays in Idleness*. New York: Columbia University Press, 1967.

Kelly, A. C., and J. G. Williamson. *Lessons from Japanese Development*. Chicago: University of Chicago Press, 1974.

Key, B. M. *The Long-Term Capital Pattern of Capital Movement in Japan, 1868–1936*. Singapore: Eurasia Press, 1977.

Keynes, J. M. *Indian Currency and Finance*. London: Macmillan, 1913.

―――. "The Significance of the Gold Points." In *The Gold Standard in Theory and History*, 2nd ed., edited by B. Eichengreen and M. Flandreau, pp. 131–39. London: Routledge, 1997.

Kikkawa, T. *Nihon denryokugyō no tenbō to Matsunaga Yasuzaemon* (The Japanese electric power industry and Matsunaga Yasuzaemon). Nagoya: Nagoya University Press, 1995.

Kindleberger, C. P. *A Financial History of Western Europe*. 2nd ed. New York: Oxford University Press, 1993. First published 1984 by Allen and Unwin, London.

―――. *The World Economy and National Finance in Historical Perspective*. Ann Arbor: University of Michigan Press, 1995.

―――. *The World in Depression, 1929–1939*. Berkeley: University of California Press, 1973.

King, F. H. H., with C. E. King and D. J. S. King. *The History of the Hongkong and Shanghai Banking Corporation*, vol. 2: *The Hongkong Bank in the Period of Imperialism and War, 1895–1918*. New York: Cambridge University Press, 1988.

Kirin. *Kirin biru kabushiki gaisha gojūnenshi* (A fifty-year history of the Kirin Beer Company). Tokyo: Kirin, 1957.

Kobayashi, U. *The Military Industries of Japan*. New York: Oxford University Press, 1922.

―――. *War and Armament Loans of Japan*. New York: Oxford University Press, 1922.

―――. *War and Armament Taxes of Japan*. New York: Oxford University Press, 1923.

Kuznets, S. *Modern Economic Growth: Rate, Structure, and Spread*. New Haven, CT: Yale University Press, 1966.

Lamont, E. M. *The Ambassador from Wall Street: The Story of Thomas W. Lamont, J. P. Morgan's Chief Executive: A Biography*. Boston: Madison, 1994.

Laughlin, J. L. "The Gold Standard in Japan." *Journal of Political Economy* 5 (December 1896–September 1897): 378–83.

―――. "Report on the Adoption of the Gold Standard in Japan." *Journal of Political Economy* 8 (December 1899–September 1900): 424–27.

Lawrence, R. Z. "Japan's Low Levels of Inward Investment: The Role of Inhibitions on Acquisitions." In *Foreign Direct Investment*, edited by K. A. Froot, pp. 85–111. Chicago: University of Chicago Press, 1993.

Lebra, J. C. *Okuma Shigenobu*. Canberra: Australian University Press, 1973.

Lensen, G. A. *Russia's Japan Expedition of 1852 and 1855*. Westport, CT: Greenwood Press, 1955.

Lockwood, W. W., ed. *The Economic Development of Japan*. Expanded edition. Princeton, NJ: Princeton University Press, 1968.

Louis, R. *British Strategy in the Far East, 1919–1939.* Oxford: Clarendon, 1971.

Lowe, P. *Britain in the Far East: A Survey from 1819 to the Present.* London: Longman, 1981.

———. *Great Britain and Japan, 1911–15.* London: Macmillan, 1969.

Lythe, S. G. E. "Britain, the Financial Capital of the World." In *Britain Preeminent: Studies of British World Influence in the Nineteenth Century*, edited by C. J. Bartlett, pp. 31–53. London: Macmillan, 1969.

Mackenzie, C. *Realms of Silver.* Reprint. New York: Arno Press, 1978.

Macpherson, W. J. *The Economic Development of Japan, c. 1868–1941.* London: Macmillan, 1987.

Malcolm, J. D. *Financial Globalisation and the Opening of the Japanese Economy.* London: RoutledgeCurzon, 2001.

Mason, M. *American Multinationals and Japan: The Political Economy of Japanese Capital Controls, 1899–1980.* Cambridge, MA: Harvard University Press, 1992.

Mason, W. E. "The Labor Theory of Value and Gold." *History of Political Economy* 14, no. 4 (1982): 543–58.

Masuda, T. "The Foreign Trade of Japan and Its Future Prospects." In *Fifty Years of New Japan*, 2nd ed., vol. 1, edited by S. Okuma, pp. 620–46. New York: Kraus, 1970.

Matsukata, M. "Japan's Finance." In *Fifty Years of New Japan*, 2nd ed., vol. 1, edited by S. Okuma, pp. 359–89. New York: Kraus, 1970.

———. *Report on Post-Bellum Financial Administration in Japan.* Tokyo: Government Press, 1903.

———. *Report on the Adoption of the Gold Standard in Japan.* Tokyo: Government Press, 1899.

———. "Teikoku zaisei" (Imperial finances). In *Kaikoku gojūnenshi* (Fifty years of new Japan), vol. 1, edited by S. Okuma, pp. 211–54. Tokyo: Shueisha, 1907.

Mayers, F., N. B. Dennys, and C. King. *The Treaty Ports of China and Japan.* London: Trubner and Co., 1867.

McCloskey, D. N., and J. R. Zecher, "How the Gold Standard Worked, 1880–1913." In *The Gold Standard in Theory and History*, edited by B. Eichengreen, pp. 63–80. New York: Methuen, 1985.

McGouldrick, P. "Operations of the German Central Bank and the Rules of the Game." In *A Retrospective on the Classical Gold Standard, 1821–1931*, edited by M. D. Bordo and A. J. Swartz, pp. 311–60. Chicago: Chicago University Press, 1984.

McGuire, J. "India, Britain, Precious Metals and the World Economy: The Role of the State between 1873 and 1893." Paper presented at Precious Metals, the World Economy and India Conference, Curtin University, 11–12 July 1993.

———. "India, Britain, Precious Metals and the World Economy: The Role of the State between 1873 and 1893." In *Evolution of the World Economy,*

Precious Metals and India, edited by P. B. Bertola, J. McGuire, and P. D. Reeves, pp. 179–98. New Delhi: Oxford University Press, 2001.

McKay, A. *Scottish Samurai: Thomas Blake Glover, 1839–1911.* 2nd ed. Edinburgh: Cannongate, 1997.

McLean, D. "The Foreign Office and the First Chinese Indemnity Loan, 1895." *The Historical Journal* 16, no. 2 (1973): 303–21.

McMaster, J. "The Japanese Gold Rush of 1859." *Asian Studies* 19 (1960): 273–87.

McMillan, J. *The Dunlop Story: The Life, Death and Re-birth of a Multi-National.* London: Weidenfeld and Nicolson, 1989.

Meiji zaiseishi henshūkai. *Meiji zaiseishi* (Meiji financial history). Vols. 2, 8, and 9. Tokyo: Yoshikawa Hirofumikan, 1972.

Metzler, M. *Lever of Empire: The International Gold Standard and the Crisis of Liberalism in Prewar Japan.* Berkeley: University of California Press, 2006.

———. "Toward a Financial History of Japan's Long Stagnation, 1990–2003." *Journal of Asian Studies* 67, no. 2 (May 2008): 653–66.

Mikami, A. "Old and New *Zaibatsu* in the History of Japan's Chemical Industry: With Special Reference to the Sumitomo Chemical Co. and the Showa Denko Co." In *Development and Diffusion of Technology: Electrical and Chemical Industries*, edited by A. Okochi and H. Uchida, pp. 201–23. Tokyo: University of Tokyo Press, 1980.

Mikami, R. *Edo no kahei monogatari* (Monetary stories from Edo). Tokyo: Toyo keizai, 1996.

Mitsui. *The 100 Year History of Mitsui and Co., Ltd.* Tokyo: Mitsui, 1977.

Mitsubishi Sekiyu. *Mitsubishi sekiyu gojūnenshi* (A fifty-year history of the Mitsubishi Oil Company). Tokyo: Mitsubishi Sekiyu, 1981.

Miyamoto M., T. Abe, M. Utagawa, M. Sawai, and T. Kikkawa. "*Nihon keieishi: Nihonkei kigyō keiei no hatten, Edo kara Heisei he* (Japanese management history: The development of Japanese-style business management from the Edo period to the Heisei present). Tokyo: Yuikaku, 1995.

Miyazaki, R., ed. *Daidō denryoku kabushiki gaisha engakushi* (A history of the Daido Electric Company). Tokyo: Yumani Shoten, 1999.

Mochida, N. *Toshi zaisei no kenkyū* (Research into city finances). Tokyo: Tokyo University Press, 1993.

Monger, G. *The End of Isolation: British Foreign Policy, 1900–1907.* London: Thomas Nelson and Sons, 1963.

Morgan Young, A. *Japan under Taisho Tenno, 1912–1926.* London: Allen and Unwin, 1928.

Morikawa, H. *Zaibatsu: The Rise and Fall of Family Enterprise Groups in Japan.* Tokyo: Tokyo University Press, 1992.

Morishima, M. "Economy and Culture: Aspects of the Modernisation of Japan." *International Social Science Journal* 40, no. 118 (1988): 459–68.

———. *Why Has Japan Succeeded? Western Technology and the Japanese Ethos.* Cambridge: Cambridge University Press, 1982.

Morita, A., E. M. Reingold, and M. Shimomura. *Made in Japan: Akio Morita and Sony.* New York: E. P. Dutton, 1986.

Morley, J. W. *The Japanese Thrust into Siberia, 1918.* New York: Columbia University Press, 1954.

Morris-Suzuki, T. *The Technological Transformation of Japan.* Melbourne: Cambridge University Press, 1994.

Motono, I. "The Alliance Must Be Made to Last." *New East* 1, no. 1 (1917): 20–22.

Murakami, H. *Japan: The Years of Trial, 1919–52.* Tokyo: Japan Culture Institute, 1982.

Muramatsu, T. *Westerners in the Modernization of Japan.* Tokyo: Hitachi, 1995.

Murashima, S. "The Opening of the Twentieth Century and the Anglo-Japanese Alliance, 1895–1923." In *The History of Anglo-Japanese Relations,* vol. 1: *The Political-Diplomatic Dimension, 1600–1930,* edited by I. Nish and Y. Kibata, pp. 159–96. London: Macmillan, 2000.

Murphy, K. C. "Neither Out Far Nor In Deep: The American Merchant Experience in Japan, 1859–1899." Ph.D. diss., University of Michigan, 1994.

Murphy, R. Taggart. *The Weight of the Yen: How Denial Imperils America's Future and Ruins an Alliance.* New York: W. W. Norton, 1996.

Myers, R. H. "Japanese Imperialism in Manchuria: The South Manchurian Railway Company, 1906–1933." In *The Japanese Informal Empire in China, 1895–1937,* edited by P. Duus, R. H. Myers, and M. R. Peattie, pp. 101–32. Princeton, NJ: Princeton University Press, 1989.

Nagura, B. "Nihon Seikōsho no kopporetto gabanansu to Nichi-ei kankei" (The corporate governance of Nihon Seikōsho and Anglo-Japanese relations). In *Nichi-ei kōryūshi, 1600–2000* (The history of Anglo-Japanese relations, 1600–2000), vol. 4, edited by J. Hunter and S. Sugiyama, pp. 215–48. Tokyo: Tokyo University Press, 2001.

Nakagane, K. "Manchukuo and Economic Development." In *The Japanese Informal Empire in China, 1895–1937,* edited by P. Duus, R. H. Myers, and M. R. Peattie, pp. 133–57. Princeton, NJ: Princeton University Press, 1989.

Nakamura, N. "The Formation of a Railway Transportation System in Japan's Railway Industry." *Japanese Yearbook on Business History* 16 (1999): 31–62.

———. "Meiji-Era Industrialization and Provincial Vitality: The Significance of the First Enterprise Boom of the 1880s." *Social Science Japan Journal* 3, no. 1 (2000): 187–205.

Nakamura, T. *Economic Growth in Prewar Japan.* New Haven, CT: Yale University Press, 1983.

————, ed. *Matsukata zaisei to shokusan-kogyō seisaku* (Matsukata's fiscal policy and the increase production and promote industry campaign). Tokyo: United Nations University Press, 1983.

————. *Senzenki Nihon keizai seichō no bunseki* (Analysis of prewar Japanese economic growth). Tokyo: Iwanami Shoten, 1971.

Nakatani, I. "The Economic Role of Financial Corporate Grouping." In *Banking in Japan*, vol. 2: *Japanese Banking in the High-Growth Era, 1952–1973*, edited by W. M. Tsutsui, pp. 251–84. London: Routledge, 1999.

Nihon Sekiyu. *Nihon sekiyushi* (The history of oil in Japan). Tokyo: Nihon Sekiyu, 1958.

Nippon Denki. *Nippon denki kabushiki gaisha nanajūnenshi* (The seventy-year history of NEC). Tokyo: NEC, 1972.

Nish, I. *Alliance in Decline: A Study in Anglo-Japanese Relations, 1908–23*. London: Athlone Press, 1972.

————. *The Anglo-Japanese Alliance*. London: Athlone Press, 1966.

————. "British Foreign Secretaries and Japan, 1892–1905." In *Shadow and Substance in British Foreign Policy, 1895–1939*, edited by B. J. C. McKercher and D. J. Moss, pp. 57–76. Edmonton: Alberta University Press, 1984.

————. "Echoes of Alliance, 1920–30." In *The History of Anglo-Japanese Relations*, vol. 1: *The Political-Diplomatic Dimension, 1600–1930*, edited by I. Nish and Y. Kibata, pp. 255–78. London: Macmillan, 2000.

————. *Japanese Foreign Policy, 1869–1942*. London: Routledge and Kegan Paul, 1977.

————. *The Story of Japan*. London: Faber and Faber, 1968.

Nishikawa, S., and O. Saito. "The Economic History of the Restoration Period." In *Meiji Ishin: Restoration and Revolution*, edited by M. Nagai and M. Urrita, pp. 175–91. Tokyo: United Nations University Press, 1985.

Nomura, J. *Nihon kinyū shihon hattatsushi* (A developmental history of Japanese financial capital). Tokyo: Kyōseisho, 1931.

Norman, E. H. *Japan's Emergence as a Modern State*. New York: IPR, 1940.

O'Brien, P. P. "Britain and the End of the Anglo-Japanese Alliance." In *The Anglo–Japanese Alliance, 1902–1922*, edited by P. P. O'Brien, pp. 267–84. London: RoutledgeCurzon, 2004.

Ogawa, G. *Conscription System in Japan*. New York: Oxford University Press, 1922.

————. *Expenditures of the Russo-Japanese War*. New York: Oxford University Press, 1923.

Ohkawa, K. *The Growth Rate of the Japanese Economy since 1878*. Tokyo: Kinokuniya, 1957.

Ohkawa, K., and H. Rosovsky. "Capital Formation in Japan." In *The Cambridge Economic History of Europe*, vol. 7, part 2, edited by P. Mathias and M. M. Postan, pp. 134–65. Cambridge: Cambridge University Press, 1978.

————. "A Century of Economic Growth." In *The State and Economic Enterprise in Japan*, edited by W. W. Lockwood, pp. 47–92. Princeton, NJ: Princeton University Press, 1965.

Ōkurashō henshū. *Meiji Taishō zaiseishi* (Meiji Taishō financial history). Vol. 12. Tokyo: Zaisei Keizai Gakkai, 1937.

Ono, G. *Expenditures of the Sino-Japanese War*. New York: Oxford University Press, 1922.

————. *War and Armament Expenditures of Japan*. New York: Oxford University Press, 1922.

Otani, M. *Tabako Ō Murai Kichibei* (Murai the Tobacco King). Tokyo: Sekai Bunko, 1964.

Ouchi, H., and T. Tsuchiya, eds. *Meiji zenki zaisei keizai shiryō shūsei* (A collection of early Meiji financial and economic historical sources). Vols. 10 and 12. Tokyo: Meiji Bunken Shiryō Kankōkai, 1963.

Overlach, T. W. *Foreign Financial Control in China*. Reprint. New York: Arno Press, 1976.

Ozaki, R. S. "Japanese Views on Foreign Capital." *Asian Survey* 11, no. 11 (November 1971): 1071–83.

Packer, F. "The Role of Long-Term Credit Banks within the Main Bank System." In *The Japanese Main Bank System: Its Relevance for Developing and Transforming Economies*, edited by M. Aoki and H. Patrick, pp. 142–87. Oxford: Oxford University Press, 1994.

Paprzycki, R., and K. Fukao. *Foreign Direct Investment in Japan: Multinationals' Role in Growth and Globalization*. Cambridge: Cambridge University Press, 2008.

Patrick, H. T. "Japan, 1868–1914." In *Banking in the Early Stages of Industrialization*, edited by R. Cameron, pp. 239–89. New York: Oxford University Press, 1967.

Peattie, M. R. "Japanese Treaty Port Settlements in China, 1895–1937." In *The Japanese Informal Empire in China, 1895–1937*, edited by P. Duus, R. H. Myers, and M. R. Peattie, pp. 166–209. Princeton, NJ: Princeton University Press, 1989.

Platt, D. C. M. *Britain's Investment Overseas on the Eve of the First World War: The Use and Abuse of Numbers*. London: Macmillan, 1986.

————. *Finance, Trade, and Politics in British Foreign Policy, 1815–1914*. Oxford: Clarendon Press, 1968.

Pollard, S. *Britain's Prime and Britain's Decline: The British Economy, 1870–1914*. London: Edward Arnold, 1989.

Pope, A. "The Imperial Matrix: Britain and the Australia-India Gold Trade, 1898–1919." Ph.D. diss., Curtin University, 1993.

Pressnell, L. S., ed. "Gold Reserves, Banking Reserves, and the Baring Crisis of 1890." In *Essays in Money and Banking in Honour of R. S. Sayers*, edited by C. R. Whittlesey, and J. S. G. Wilson, pp. 167–228. Oxford: Clarendon Press, 1968.

———. *Money and Banking in Japan*. New York: St. Martin's Press, 1973.

Ranis, G. "The Financing of Japanese Economic Development." In *The Industrialization of Japan*, edited by W. J. Macpherson, pp. 342–57. Oxford: Blackwell, 1994.

Reader, W. J. *Imperial Chemical Industries: A History*, vol. 1: *The Forerunners, 1870–1926*. Oxford: Oxford University Press, 1970.

Remer, C. F. "International Trade between Gold and Silver Countries." In *Selected Essays in Chinese Economic Development*, edited by R. H. Myers, pp. 597–632. New York: Garland, 1980.

Reti, S. P. *Silver and Gold: The Political Economy of International Monetary Conference, 1867–1892*. Westport, CT: Greenwood Press, 1998.

Robbins, K. *The Eclipse of a Great Power: Modern Britain, 1870–1992*. 2nd ed. London: Longman, 1983.

Roberts, J. G. *Mitsui: Three Centuries of Japanese Business*. New York: Weatherhill, 1973.

Roberts, R. "The Bank of England and the City." In *The Bank of England: Money, Power and Influence 1694–1994*, edited by R. Roberts and D. Kynaston, pp. 152–84. Oxford: Clarendon Press, 1995.

Robertson, R. *Globalization: Social Theory and Global Culture*. London: Sage, 1992.

Robey, R. *The Monetary Problem: Gold and Silver*. New York: Columbia University Press, 1936.

Rose, E. L., and K. Ito. "M&As in the Japanese Banking Industry: The More Things Change?" In *Japanese Firms in Transition: Responding to the Globalization Challenge*, edited by T. Roehl and A. Bird, pp. 139–57. Amsterdam: Elsevier, 2005.

Rosovsky, H. "What Are the Lessons of Japanese Economic History?" In *The Industrialization of Japan*, edited by W. J. Macpherson, pp. 229–53. Oxford: Blackwell, 1994.

Russell, F. A. A. *History of the Gold Standard*. Sydney: Simmons, 1932.

Rymes, T. *On Concepts of Capital and Technical Change*. Cambridge: Cambridge University Press, 1971.

Saito, S. "The Industrial Bank of Japan during the Inter-war Period." In *Finance in the Age of the Corporate Economy*, edited by P. L. Cottrell, A. Teichova, and T. Yuzawa, pp. 118–28. Aldershot, UK: Ashcroft, 1997.

Sakudo, Y. "From Ancient Coins to the High Yen: The Story of Japanese Money." In *The Electric Geisha*, edited by A. Ueda and M. Eguchi, pp. 147–53. Tokyo: Kodansha, 1994.

———. *Nihon zaibatsu keieishi: Sumitomo zaibatsu* (Japanese management history: Sumitomo zaibatsu). Tokyo: Nihon Keizai Shinbun, 1982.

Sarasas, P. *Money and Banking in Japan*. London: Heath Crawton, 1940.

Saw, R. *The Bank of England, 1694–1944*. London: George G. Harrap, 1944.

Sayers, R. S., ed. *Banking in Western Europe*. Oxford: Oxford University Press, 1962.

———. *The Bank of England, 1891–1944*. Vol. 1. Cambridge: Cambridge University Press, 1976.

———. *The Bank of England Operations, 1890–1914*. London: P. S. King and Son, 1936.

———. *Central Banking after Bagehot*. Oxford: Clarendon Press, 1957.

Scalapino, R. A. *Democracy and the Party Movement in Prewar Japan: The Failure of the First Attempt*. Berkeley: University of California Press, 1953.

Scammell, W. M. "The Working of the Gold Standard." In *The Gold Standard in Theory and History*, edited by B. Eichengreen, pp. 103–19. New York: Methuen, 1985.

Schaede, U. *Choose and Focus: Japanese Business Strategies for the 21st Century*. Ithaca, NY: Cornell University Press, 2008.

Schaede, U., and W. W. Grimes. "Introduction: The Emergence of Permeable Insulation." In *Japan's Managed Globalization: Adapting to the Twenty-First Century*, edited by U. Schaede and W. W. Grimes, pp. 1–8. New York: M. E. Sharpe, 2003.

Schalow, T. R. "The Role of the Financial Panic of 1927 and Failure of the 15th Bank in the Economic Decline of the Japanese Aristocracy." Ph.D. diss., University of Michigan, 1989.

Schiltz, M. "An 'Ideal Bank of Issue': The Banque Nationale de Belgique as a Model for the Bank of Japan." *Financial History Review* 13, no. 2 (2006): 179–96.

———. *The Money Doctors from Japan: Finance, Imperialism, and the Building of the Yen Bloc, 1895–1937*. Cambridge, MA: Harvard University Asia Center, 2012.

Schumpeter, E. B. *The Industrialization of Japan and Manchukuo, 1930–40*. In *Japanese Economic History, 1930–1960*, vol. 8, edited by J. Hunter. London: Routledge, 2000.

Schumpeter, J. *The Theory of Economic Development*. Oxford: Oxford University Press, 1934.

Sendo, M. *Nihon kaigun kayakushi* (A history of Japanese naval explosives). Tokyo: Nihon Kōgyō Gakkai, 1967.

Shaw, W. A. *The History of Currency, 1252–1896*. Reprint. New York: Augustus M. Kelly, 1967.

Shibusawa, E. "The Development of Banking in Japan." In *Fifty Years of New Japan*, 2nd ed., vol. 1, edited by S. Okuma, pp. 486–532. New York: Kraus, 1970.

Shimokawa, K. *The Japanese Automobile Industry: A Business History*. London: Athlone Press, 1994.

Shinjo, H. *History of the Yen*. Tokyo: Kinokuniya, 1962.

Shinohara, M. "Economic Development and Foreign Trade in Pre-war Japan." In *The Economic Development of China and Japan*, edited by C. D. Cowan, pp. 220–48. London: Allen and Unwin, 1964.

Shinomiya, M. *Nihon no jidōsha sangyō: Kigyōsha katsudō to kyōsōryoku, 1918–70* (Japanese automobile production: Corporate activities and competitiveness, 1918–1970). Tokyo: Nihon Keizai Shinbun, 1998.

Smethurst, R. J. *From Foot Soldier to Finance Minister: Takahashi Korekiyo, Japan's Keynes*. Cambridge, MA: Harvard University Asia Center, 2007.

Smith, T. C. *Political Change and Industrial Development in Japan*. Oxford: Oxford University Press, 1955.

———. "Pre-Modern Economic Growth: Japan and the West." *Past and Present* 60 (1973): 127–60.

Spalding, W. F. *Eastern Exchange Currency and Finance*. 2nd ed. London: Pitman and Sons, 1918.

———. *A Key to Money and Banking*. London: Blackie and Sons, 1938.

———. *The London Money Market*. 3rd ed. London: Pitman and Sons, 1924.

Stearns, P. N. "Britain and the Spread of the Industrial Revolution." In *Britain Pre-eminent: Studies of British World Influence in the Nineteenth Century*, edited by C. J. Bartlett, pp. 7–30. London: Macmillan, 1969.

Steeds, D. "Anglo-Japanese Relations, 1902–23: A Marriage of Convenience." In *The History of Anglo-Japanese Relations*, vol. 1: *The Political-Diplomatic Dimension, 1600–1930*, edited by I. Nish and Y. Kibata, pp. 197–223. London: Macmillan, 2000.

Stern, S. *The United States in International Banking*. New York: Columbia University Press, 1951.

Storry, R. *A History of Modern Japan*. Harmondsworth, UK: Penguin, 1960.

Suzuki, T. *Japanese Government Loan Issues on the London Capital Market, 1870–1913*. London: Athlone, 1994.

———. "Senkanki Rondon kinyūshijō niokeru Nihonseifu no gaisai hakkō" (Japanese government loan issues on London's financial market between the wars). In *Nichi-ei kōryūshi* (Anglo-Japanese Relations, 1600–2000), vol. 4, edited by Y. Kibata, I. Nish, C. Hosoya, and T. Tanaka, pp. 162–68. Tokyo: Tokyo University Press, 2001.

Takahashi, Kamekichi. *The Rise and Development of Japan's Modern Economy*. Tokyo: Jiji, 1969.

Takahashi, K. *Takahashi Korekiyo jiden* (Autobiography). Tokyo: Chikura, 1936.

Takahashi, M. *Modern Japanese Economy since 1868*. 2nd ed. Tokyo: Kokusai Bunka Shinkōkai, 1968.

Takekoshi, Y. *Economic Aspects of the History of the Civilisation of Japan*. Vol. 3. London: Allen and Unwin, 1967.

Tamaki, N. *Japanese Banking: A History, 1859–1959*. Cambridge: Cambridge University Press, 1995.

Tatewaki, K. *Zainichi gaikoku ginkōshi* (A history of foreign banks in Japan). Tokyo: Nihon Keizai Hyōronsha, 1987.

Taussig, F. W. *The Silver Situation in the United States*. Reprint. New York: Greenwood, 1969.

Teranishi, J. "Financial Sector Reform after the War." In *Banking in Japan*, vol. 1: *The Evolution of Japanese Banking, 1868–1952*, edited by W. M. Tsutsui, pp. 137–58. London: Routledge, 1999.

———. "Japan: Development and Structural Change of the Financial System." In *Banking in Japan*, vol. 2: *Japanese Banking in the High-Growth Era, 1952–1973*, edited by W. M. Tsutsui, pp. 88–144. London: Routledge, 1999.

Terauchi, M. "The Alliance Is the Will of Heaven." *New East* 1, no. 1 (1917): 18.

Thomas-Emeagwali, G. "Technology Transfer: Explaining the Japanese Success Story." *Journal of Contemporary Asia* 21, no. 4 (1991): 504–12.

Tipton, F. B., Jr. "Government Policy and Economic Development in Germany and Japan: A Skeptical Reevaluation." *Journal of Economic History* 41, no. 1 (1981): 139–50.

Toby, R. P. *State and Diplomacy in Early Modern Japan*. Stanford, CA: Stanford University Press, 1991.

Tokugawa, I. "A Reminiscence of London." *New East* 1, no. 1 (1917): 28–29.

Toshiba. *Tōshiba kabushiki gaisha gojūnenshi* (The fifty-year history of Toshiba). Tokyo: Toshiba, 1940.

Toshiba sōgō kikakubu shashi. *Tōshiba kabushiki gaisha hachijūnenshi* (The eighty-year history of Toshiba). Tokyo: Toshiba, 1963.

Totman, C. *The Collapse of the Tokugawa Bakufu, 1862–1868*. Honolulu: University of Hawai'i Press, 1980.

———. *Early Modern Japan*. Berkeley: University of California Press, 1993.

Triffin, R. "The Myths and Realities of the So-Called Gold Standard." In *The Gold Standard in Theory and History*, edited by B. Eichengreen, pp. 120–40. New York: Methuen, 1985.

Truptil, R. J. *British Banks and the London Money Market*. London: Jonathan Cape, 1936.

Tweedale, G. *Steel City: Entrepreneurship, Strategy, and Technology in Sheffield, 1743–1993*. Oxford: Clarendon Press, 1995.

Umemura, M., and T. Nakamura. *Matsukata zaisei to shokusan kōgyō seisaku* (Industrial promotion policy and Matsukata finance). Tokyo: UNU Press, 1983.

Utagawa, M., and S. Nakamura, eds. *Materiaru: Nihon keieishi Edoki kara genzai made* (Material: Japanese management history from the Edo period to the present). Tokyo: Yuikaku, 1999.

Utley, F. *Japan's Feet of Clay*. London: Faber and Faber, 1936.

Uyeda, T. *The Small Industries of Japan: Their Growth and Development*. Japanese Economic History, 1930–1960, vol. 10, edited by J. Hunter. London: Routledge, 2000.

Van-Helton, J. J. "Empire and High Finance: South Africa and the International Gold Standard, 1890–1914." *Journal of African History* 23 (1982): 529–48.

Wadsworth, J. E. "Banking Ratios Past and Present." In *Essays in Money and Banking in Honour of R. S. Sayers*, edited by C. R. Whittlesey and J. S. G. Wilson, pp. 229–51. Oxford: Clarendon Press, 1968.

Wakatsuki, R. *Meiji/Taishō/Shōwa sekaihishi: Kofuiori kaikoroku* (Memoirs of secret world history). Tokyo: Kodansha, 1983.

Warner, F. *Anglo-Japanese Financial Relations: A Golden Tide*. Oxford: Basil Blackwell, 1991.

Whale, P. D. "The Working of the Prewar Gold Standard." In *The Gold Standard in Theory and History*, edited by B. Eichengreen, pp. 49–62. New York: Methuen, 1985.

Williams, D. "The Evolution of the Sterling System." In *Essays in Money and Banking in Honour of R. S. Sayers*, edited by C. R. Whittlesey, and J. S. G. Wilson, pp. 266–97. Oxford: Clarendon Press, 1968.

Withers, H. *War and Lombard Street*. London: John Murray, 1918.

Wray, W. D. "Japan's Big Three Service Enterprises in China, 1896–1936." In *The Japanese Informal Empire in China, 1895–1937*, edited by P. Duus, R. H. Myers, and M. R. Peattie, pp. 31–64. Princeton, NJ: Princeton University Press, 1989.

Yamaguchi, K. *Sakoku to kaikoku* (Sakoku and the opening of Japan). Tokyo: Iwanami, 1993.

Yamamoto, Y. *Ryō kara en he* (From ryō to the yen). Tokyo: Minerva, 1994.

Yamamura, K. "Japan, 1868–1930: A Revised View." In *The Industrialization of Japan*, edited by W. J. Macpherson, pp. 400–430. Oxford: Blackwell, 1994.

Yamasaki, K. *Honpō kaheiseido kaiseiron* (Treatise on the reform of the monetary system in Japan). Tokyo: Nihon Hyōronsha, 1932.

Yamauchi, M. *Nichi-ei kankei keieishi* (Anglo-Japanese management history). Hiroshima: Keisui, 2010.

Yamazaki, H. "The Yokohama Specie Bank during the Period of the Restored Gold Standard in Japan (January 1930–December 1931)." In *Finance and Financiers in European History, 1880–1960*, edited by Y. Cassis, pp. 371–403. Cambridge: Cambridge University Press, 1992.

Yamazawa, I., and Y. Yamamoto. "Trade and Balance of Payments." In *Patterns of Japanese Economic Development: A Quantitative Appraisal*, edited by K. Ohkawa and M. Shinohara, pp. 134–56. New Haven, CT: Yale University Press, 1979.

Yanaga, C. *Japan since Perry*. Hamden: Archon, 1966.

Yokohama Specie Bank. *Yokohama shōken ginkōshi* (A history of the Yokohama Specie Bank). Tokyo: Nishida, 1976.

Yonekawa, S. "Recent Writing on Japanese Economic and Social History." *The Economic History Review*, second series, 38 (1985): 107–23.

Yoon, B. N. "Domain and Bakufu in Tokugawa Japan: The Copper Trade and Development of Akita Domain Mines." Ph.D. diss., University of Michigan, 1995.

Yoshihara, K. *Japanese Economic Development*. Tokyo: Oxford University Press, 1979.

Yoshino, T. *En no rekishi* (History of the Yen). Tokyo: Shiseidō, 1955.

———. *Nihon ginkō seido kaikakushi* (Reformational history of the Bank of Japan system). Tokyo: Tokyo University Press, 1962.

Yoshitomi, M., and E. M. Graham, eds. *Foreign Direct Investment in Japan*. Cheltenham, UK: Edward Elgar, 1996.

Young, G. K. *Merchant Banking: Practice and Prospects*. London: Weidenfeld and Nicolson, 1966.

Young, L. *Japan's Total Empire: Manchuria and the Culture of Wartime Imperialism*. Berkeley: University of California Press, 1998.

Yukio, C. "Exposing the Incompetence of the Bourgeoisie: The Financial Panic of 1927." In *Banking in Japan*, vol. 1: *The Evolution of Japanese Banking, 1868–1952*, edited by W. M. Tsutsui, pp. 109–17. London: Routledge, 1999.

Zeigler, P. *The Sixth Great Power: A History of One of the Greatest of All Banking Families, the House of Barings, 1762–1929*. New York: Alfred A. Knopf, 1988.

Index

Harvard East Asian Monographs
(titles now in print)

117. Andrew Gordon, *The Evolution of Labor Relations in Japan: Heavy Industry, 1853–1955*
119. Christine Guth Kanda, *Shinzō: Hachiman Imagery and Its Development*
121. Chang-tai Hung, *Going to the People: Chinese Intellectual and Folk Literature, 1918–1937*
123. Richard von Glahn, *The Country of Streams and Grottoes: Expansion, Settlement, and the Civilizing of the Sichuan Frontier in Song Times*
124. Steven D. Carter, *The Road to Komatsubara: A Classical Reading of the Renga Hyakuin*
126. Bob Tadashi Wakabayashi, *Anti-Foreignism and Western Learning in Early-Modern Japan: The "New Theses" of 1825*
127. Atsuko Hirai, *Individualism and Socialism: The Life and Thought of Kawai Eijirō (1891–1944)*
129. R. Kent Guy, *The Emperor's Four Treasuries: Scholars and the State in the Late Chien-lung Era*
130. Peter C. Perdue, *Exhausting the Earth: State and Peasant in Hunan, 1500–1850*
131. Susan Chan Egan, *A Latterday Confucian: Reminiscences of William Hung (1893–1980)*
132. James T. C. Liu, *China Turning Inward: Intellectual-Political Changes in the Early Twelfth Century*
134. Kate Wildman Nakai, *Shogunal Politics: Arai Hakuseki and the Premises of Tokugawa Rule*
137. Susan Downing Videen, *Tales of Heichū*
138. Heinz Morioka and Miyoko Sasaki, *Rakugo: The Popular Narrative Art of Japan*
139. Joshua A. Fogel, *Nakae Ushikichi in China: The Mourning of Spirit*
140. Alexander Barton Woodside, *Vietnam and the Chinese Model: A Comparative Study of Vietnamese and Chinese Government in the First Half of the Nineteenth Century*
141. George Elison, *Deus Destroyed: The Image of Christianity in Early Modern Japan*
144. Marie Anchordoguy, *Computers, Inc.: Japan's Challenge to IBM*
146. Mary Elizabeth Berry, *Hideyoshi*
147. Laura E. Hein, *Fueling Growth: The Energy Revolution and Economic Policy in Postwar Japan*
148. Wen-hsin Yeh, *The Alienated Academy: Culture and Politics in Republican China, 1919–1937*
149. Dru C. Gladney, *Muslim Chinese: Ethnic Nationalism in the People's Republic*
150. Merle Goldman and Paul A. Cohen, eds., *Ideas Across Cultures: Essays on Chinese Thought in Honor of Benjamin L Schwartz*
151. James M. Polachek, *The Inner Opium War*
152. Gail Lee Bernstein, *Japanese Marxist: A Portrait of Kawakami Hajime, 1879–1946*
154. Mark Mason, *American Multinationals and Japan: The Political Economy of Japanese Capital Controls, 1899–1980*
155. Richard J. Smith, John K. Fairbank, and Katherine F. Bruner, *Robert Hart and China's Early Modernization: His Journals, 1863–1866*
157. William Wayne Farris, *Heavenly Warriors: The Evolution of Japan's Military, 500–1300*

Harvard East Asian Monographs